Awakening Hope

Book Two of the Peter Chronicles

AL MINER and LAMA SING

CoCreations Publishing

Awakening Hope: Book Two of the Peter Chronicles
Copyright ©1990 by Al Miner

Cover art and book design by Susan M. Miner

ISBN -13   978-0-9828786-0-6

1. Lama Sing 2. Psychics 3. Trance Channels 4. Life After Death
5. The Peter Project
I. Miner, Al II. Lama Sing III. Title

Library of Congress Control Number: 2010911195

Printed in the United States of America

For books and products, or to write Al Miner,
visit our website: **www.lamasing.net**

Contents

As we commence with this new work, dear friends, we would add our humble gratitude and joy to those of the Channel's for the opportunity to be with you once again in this manner, and to share the awakening consciousness in one soul who has come to be called Peter.

Lama Sing

Peter's journey beyond death is an exception. His spirit agreed to explore the afterlife to extraordinary depth that we might better understand, along with him, the wonder of life beyond. His service not only gifted us but also Peter himself, for the brilliance of his spirit grew magnificently.

Al Miner

CHAPTER 1
Leaving Peter Behind
FEBRUARY 1, 1991

You will recall the ceremony that occurred with Zachary, Paul, and Peter in the Great Hall concluding with a time of joyous sharing, a time of conscious reconnection for Peter with his family during their Christmas celebration and with his dear friend Abe who was celebrating Hanukkah. Peter heard and felt their prayers for him, and saw them moving towards him as beautiful luminous spheres of light.

After experiencing the warmth and love as these spheres reached him, he asked Zachary and Paul to join with him in sending prayers back to his family and friends. The emotion of experiencing the prayers grew to such intensity that Peter found a sense of wellbeing he had not recalled ever having known before, and a sense of knowing that all of these loved ones will one day be together again.

In the present, Wilbur, David, Zachary, Paul, and Peter are gathered once again on the small knoll in Peter's garden. It is a gathering that has not been called for any particular purpose, but, as Peter has come to realize through his past interactions with this group, there is rarely an event or an occurrence that does not produce some treasured insight, some valuable experience, and some significant joys.

The group is speaking casually, occasionally making light-hearted jest with one another, like a simple get-together on Earth. Zachary is, of course, providing considerable lightheartedness, as is his manner.

"Zachary," Peter asks after in a break in the conversation, "how often do you travel to other realms?" Before he can respond, Peter continues, "I remember when I first arrived here in the Garden that each time I would go within myself or take a *spiritual rest*, as we've come to call it, just prior to that, you'd leave. Remember? Now why was that, Zack? Precisely where did you go? What did you do there? And who did you do it with?"

There is a long pause, as Zachary, reclined upon the lush expanse of emerald green, fidgets with a few blades of grass. He suddenly looks up. "Haven't I always said it? Peter can ask more questions than anyone I've ever met. One question at a time would do, don't you think, Pete?"

Chuckling, the group then becomes more attentive, one sitting up, another straightening a bit of clothing, and all shift the focus to Peter.

Peter tilts his head. "You and I both know, Zack, that if I don't slip in all my questions at once, before I can get in follow-up questions to you, we're off on some other experience, or you've detoured me so much that I can't remember what it was I was going to ask in the first place."

Again, a murmur of laughter passes through the group, creating little ripples of light and sound that has now become so familiar to Peter.

Zachary, not taken aback for an instant by Peter's retort, continues on smoothly, "Well, you see, Pete, I was a very busy fellow during those times. I had a lot of chores. They could have been handled by most anyone else, but I was *chosen*. And a person has to bear his or her own responsibility in a group, right?" Without waiting for a response, he continues on, winking as he does, "So, I had to go off to deal with lots of other, well, activities. Some of them had to do with exploration. Others had to do with, I guess you'd call it, support. Others were like learning experiences. Understand?"

Again, there is a pause.

Peter looks at Zachary and, seated somewhat on his haunches, shifts his weight from one side to the other (largely out of habit, for he obviously has no discomfort here). "As always, Zack, your answers are direct and complete. Still, not exactly what I'm looking for, in this instance. I'm asking you now to look into my mind and heart, and answer my questions. Unless of course that violates some confidence."

As though he had been struck a blow of some sort, Zachary sits bolt upright. "Good heavens, Pete, you know I have no secrets from you or any of this group," making a broad sweeping gesture with his arm. "Furthermore, even if I did, do you think I would mention it? Pique your interest and then withhold it? Goodness, that wouldn't be polite, much less the way one friend would treat another." With that, he slowly lowers himself back down with his elbow upon the grass, and begins to fidget with the blades again, obscuring his face from the others, save for Paul.

Peter is caught a bit off guard. "Gosh, Zack, I didn't mean it that way. What I'm trying to say to you is, I'd really like to know more about who we are, where we are, and what we are to do. Or should I presume that we can lay around here on this wonderful little hillside for the rest of eternity, doing essentially whatever suits us?"

Paul now interjects, smiling, "Well actually, Peter, we can do just that if we choose."

Zachary makes no response and continues to fidget with the blades of grass.

David turns away to shield his humor at these goings-on.

Wilbur is seated diagonally from Zachary, looking a bit serious about it all, turning from one to the other, smiling, but obviously more intent on what's being discussed than any of the others save for Peter.

Zachary, still looking down, is the one who speaks next. "Well, Pete, what would you think of doing something just like that? I mean, you, had been chosen to do certain works, you will recall. And because of your work, we have regained our group, and joyfully so, I might add," glancing up at Wilbur, who, seeing the warmth of Zachary's smile, relaxes. "So then, Pete, what would you do? What would you choose to do if you could choose anything at all?" With the last word, he rolls himself a bit to look Peter square in the eye.

"Now wait a minute, Zack. All this started with me asking you a simple question … okay, several questions. Now all of a sudden, as usual, you've tossed the ball into my court."

"I threw nothing at you." Zachary chuckles as he replies, obviously knowing this was not a literal comment by Peter. "I'm only attempting to point something out to you, Pete." He rises again to a seated position, crosses his legs and leans on his elbows to look directly at Peter.

"Okay, hold on a moment here, Zack. I don't think I'm going to let you get the upper hand this time, though I must admit, in the past, there have been some really outstanding experiences as the result. But this time, if you would … Where did you go when you left Paul and me? How's that? One question: Where?"

"No problem. I can handle one question. One question at a time is never a problem for me. Don't you agree, Paul?"

Paul, amused at this bantering back and forth between his two dear friends, nods and looks down with a wide smile.

There is silence.

Peter then looks at Zachary. "Well? Answer my question, then, Zack. Where did you go?"

In one graceful, fluid motion, Zachary rises to his feet, looks down, and straightens his cloak, brushing it here and there, which causes sparks, snaps, and crackles as he does so. "You want to know Pete? Let's go, then. I'll show you where I went."

Looking up at his friend who is standing over him, Peter smiles. "I knew it! I knew you'd do this, Zack. I ask you a simple question, and this is always what happens."

Smiling down, Zachary extends Peter a hand, "Well then, Pete, if you knew, why'd you ask?"

Peter grasps Zachary's hand and rises to his feet. "Touché, Zack. I must admit, I'm ready for an adventure. I want to learn some more. Is that acceptable to the rest of you?"

Paul also rises now, assisted by the other hand of Zachary. "Always a pleasure."

Wilbur, looking a bit more uncertain now, glances from David to Peter, from Paul to Zachary, receiving a warm smile from all of them. But turning back to David, he asks softly, "Are we needed, David?"

David rises and walks up to Wilbur, placing an arm on his shoulder. "Why don't you go with your friends and I'll go back to the Crystal Workers' Realm, as Peter calls it, and see to things. As we've indicated to you before, Wilbur, and discovered in our experiences together, there is always sufficient response to any need, in any realm, for any purpose. So go and have your adventure, and I'll see you upon its conclusion." He turns to look directly at Zachary.

Zachary looks squarely at David, recognizes the intent, and nods. He then looks to Wilbur and extends his hand. "Wilbur, it's time for you to have a holiday. And let me tell you from past experiences, a holiday with friend Peter here is an outing one shan't quickly forget."

All laugh at this as David turns and walks down the knoll and off into the white misty cloud, waving, bidding them a good adventure.

All now turn to look at Zachary, who simply motions with his hand for them to follow.

A bit apprehensive, yet excited, Peter extends an arm to Wilbur and another to Paul, and off they go like schoolchildren down the pathway, to the left of the Great Hall.

As they do, Zachary raises his hand and twirls it in the air, creating the jingle-jangle sound we hear that has come to be a sort of hallmark of his.

Paul and Peter laugh, joined by Wilbur, and they all break into song as they follow behind Zachary.

In past, the movement from Peter's Garden involved moving into a white cloud-like mist from which they emerged into such as the Crystal Workers Realm. Here, there is the appearance of moving along a pathway of greenery, with lovely manicured landscaping to the right and left, which seems to be increasing in its density and in its height until the path is almost enveloped by the lushness of this brilliant multi-hued, green growth.

Peter is looking to the left and right, and up at the greenery, which seems be almost reaching out, radiating the essence of its own being. "Well, it appears that we are being enveloped by something."

Zachary follows quickly, "Yes, indeed. The envelopment is a part of the journey."

"What is happening here?" asks Wilbur. "What are these plants doing? Are they going to close off the path? How will we proceed?"

Zachary, still at the lead position of the group, chuckling a bit, responds over his shoulder, "If it gets too thick, don't worry. I'll make a pathway through it for us. But I don't think that will happen."

Peter is still looking all about. "This is really something! I can almost feel the life-force of these plants, you know? It's like I am actually a part of these plants or vice-versa. Do you feel that Wilbur?"

Wilbur, obviously a bit more nervous about these outings than Peter for the present, answers quietly, "Yes. I ... I certainly can. Pleasant, but a bit unnerving."

Paul is silent, but smiling broadly, as he brings up the rear, having fallen in behind Peter and Wilbur.

After a time, Zachary raises his right hand and swirls it in the air, making the jingling sound again.

In that moment, still moving, they find themselves in

what appears to be an opening, which becomes broader as they continue on. Then, the canopy of greenery over them parts, and the vegetation returns to a more normal size.

Zachary stops and turns to face the group, who almost run into him. Smiling broadly, he states to Wilbur and Peter, "Take a look back there, fellas, and tell me what you see."

They slowly turn to look, and to their amazement, they see a solid wall of greenery, rising to great height and with no opening whatsoever.

"Neat trick, eh wot, Pete?" Laughing loudly, Zachary turns to begin moving again.

Wilbur and Peter awkwardly attempt to follow while still looking behind.

Paul, chuckling, has stepped over to the side a bit in order for his colleagues to have a better view of what Zachary was showing them.

Zachary continues on for a short time and begins to walk up what appears to be a slight incline. As he does, a broad expanse of stairs comes into view.

Peter perceives these and notes that like the greenery, they, too, are meticulously crafted and appear to be of marble or alabaster, or something of that sort. They are broad and rise up a considerable height, surrounded by the lush greenery to the right and left.

Suddenly, Peter and Wilbur see that they are all on a large, very ornate, circular patio-like area. On its periphery are many benches, some fountains, lovely arbors with seating arrangements within them, and little rivulets of water over which stone walkways have been placed.

Peter, to his surprise, sees that there are small groups of people here and there about this beautiful patio-like area.

Wilbur whispers in amazement, "Gosh, this is beautiful, just breathtaking … so radiant, and energizing. Exactly the type of energy one would want to use with crystals." Stepping away from the group, obviously captivated by what he is experiencing, he bends to look at a small rivulet of water. It is too small to be a stream, he thinks. Perhaps it is just a channeled passageway for some spring to flow, as it might be hidden underground on this rise in the land. As he studies the water and looks about, he is watched by Peter, Paul, and Zachary, who compassionately await his attention once again.

Peter is nudged by Zachary to move over by Wilbur.

Recognizing that Zachary wishes him to accompany Wilbur, Peter dutifully does so.

He stands looking down at the water, as Wilbur is crouched looking into it and the works around it. "Marvelously done isn't it? It's a source of continual wonder for me to see such fine workmanship."

As though he hadn't heard those comments, Wilbur, still looking down at the water, raises his hand, calling as he does, "Peter, come here if you would, please. Look at this water!"

Peter bends and they crouch side by side, Wilbur pointing at the water. "Look how the light moves within it. Doesn't it seem to you that this is more than water? I mean, that it looks like the water is a flow of something besides water. Does that make any sense to you, Peter? Or to any of you?" He turns to look at Paul and Zachary, who are now standing behind the two.

"It makes a good deal of sense to me, Wilbur," answers Paul, "and I am certain that Zachary would be willing to answer any of your questions about this realm. And also," now directing his comments to Zachary, smiling, "why you came here, Zachary, as well as why you left us alone in those former times in the Garden, as Peter was inquiring."

Zachary gives Paul a wink and then takes the lead. "Right, my friends. What do you say we gather over here under this lovely arbor? There are some nice seats here, and a few other things I would like to show you."

Taking Wilbur and Peter each by an arm and, and with no effort whatsoever, raising them to an upright position,

Zachary turns and enters an arboretum, which is covered with lattice, upon which beautiful plants are growing, some with brilliant flowers.

In a state of wonder, Wilbur and Peter follow Zachary into the chamber-like area and, once again, feel the essence that they encountered on their journey to this place. Motioned to seat themselves by Zachary, they find themselves on benches in a circular pattern. In the center is a round, pedestal-like table, with nothing on it.

As they sit there, Wilbur and Peter look about, and there comes a period of awkward silence.

Zachary has his hands clasped upon one knee and, in his fashion, is semi-reclined upon one of the benches. Paul is off to one side.

In the silence, Peter notes several openings or entries into and out of this small garden area within the larger patio and, as he looks towards one of them, he can see several entities heading towards them. A bit surprised, and perhaps even a little apprehensive, he reaches over to touch Wilbur and realizes that he, too, has seen their approach.

Wilbur turns to Zachary. "There are some others coming, Zachary."

Without looking in the direction the entities are coming from, Zachery smiles and nods, "Yes, I know."

Peter turns quickly. "You are expecting them?"

"Yes, I am, Pete."

Peter, receiving no further comment, asks further, "Could you tell us who they are and why they are coming?"

"I can, but why not let them speak for themselves?" With that, Zachary rises and bows towards the opening.

Peter and Wilbur turn to see that the entities have entered and are now in the arboretum with them.

Peter studies the first entity, who appears to be perhaps a bit older than some of the entities he has seen. To that one's right are two others, both of whom appear to be female. One, he immediately recognizes as having been with him in the Garden earlier, and who has come to be called "the Keeper" of his book. The one to her right he knows as her companion. When he turns to speak to Wilbur, he can see that Wilbur is showing signs of recognition as well.

Without invitation, the male entity steps forward, smiles, bows, and speaks in a voice Peter would not have equated as belonging to this entity. "Welcome. Welcome, my friends. I am pleased, Zachary, that you brought your friends with you." Turning to Peter and Wilbur, "I presume you know my friends here?" gesturing to the females.

Peter, a bit at a loss for words, nods awkwardly, a little too vigorously. With his head still bobbing up and down, he turns to look at Wilbur, who is smiling and nodding as well. This surprises Peter, for he had no idea that Wilbur might know these two female entities. And it surprises him even more that he seems to know the male entity.

At that moment the male entity steps forward and extends a hand to Peter, and Peter raises his hand in return. As he does, looking the entity in the eyes, he suddenly remembers he had seen the entity and met him during the ceremony in the Great Hall.

"Oh f-forgive me, I-I had forgotten our earlier meeting."

"Not at all, Peter, you've had a busy time of it here since your arrival, and that is to be expected. You are to be complimented at the rapidity with which you have adapted and, perhaps to some extent, *endured* the unique but delightful teaching methods of our friend, Zachary, here." He extends a gesture, and warmly looks at Zachary.

Zachary smiles and looks down.

"Please, please," the entity continues, "do be seated. We wish you to feel welcome and comfortable here, and we wish to serve you as best we can, so please be at ease. You are among friends, and your desires are ours as well."

Staring at the female entity who is called the Keeper of

his book, Peter speaks. "My, It is good to see you again … both of you … I mean all of you, of course. I had so many other questions I had wanted to ask you, and did so hope I would have an opportunity again. And, well, here you are, and it's just great to see you again, both of you … and you, sir, as well."

Zachary chuckles. "I think what Peter is trying to say is, 'Welcome, to all of you.' Let me add here that Peter has accomplished a great deal since we were last together. Paul and I," turning to look at Paul, who nods, "are very proud of him and indeed honored to be with him in whatever works or activities he would choose. And as you know, Benjamin," looking at the male entity, "we spoke in the Great Hall with the Entity of Wisdom; and we have been, in a manner of speaking, given a *commission*."

The man now identified by name as Benjamin nods, smiles, and states with emphasis, "Yes, Zachary, I am aware of that. I think the choice has been an excellent decision, and obviously from the outward emanation, you shall do well in your commission," looking from one to the other and then back to Wilbur, who shrugs and looks, along with Peter, at Paul and then at Zachary.

It is Wilbur who speaks, much to the relief of Peter who feels a bit on the spot. "Would it be possible for you explain what you mean by *commission*?"

"Well," Benjamin begins, "that's just a term we have come to use to identify a chosen path of experience, or work (as it might be called in the Earth realm). Though it's not really work. It's more in the nature of helping. It's joyful helping, wouldn't you say so, Zachary?"

"Oh I would indeed, Benjamin. Wouldn't you Paul?"

Smiling, and looking at Peter and Wilbur with a warmth unquestionably reassuring, Paul states softly, "It is all of that, and more. I feel, Peter and Wilbur, it is an opportunity of blessing. We are all honored and very excited and joyful whenever we receive a commission. It is an opportunity (to answer your unspoken question, Peter) to answer what you might think of as a call for help, an answer to a prayer, a response to a need. Does this make sense?"

Nodding rather vigorously again, Peter and Wilbur look back and forth at one another and then back at Paul, obviously hoping he will continue.

After some silence, Wilbur asks, "Is that rather like our work in the Crystal Workers Realm? Where we are attempting to assist those who are in service in the Earth realm?"

Paul smiles. "Somewhat, Wilbur, but not precisely. In this case, there will be no one acting as, what is called, a *channel of blessings* between the entity in need and us." Pausing for a time, obviously waiting for the thought-form to gain some footing within the consciousness of Wilbur and Peter, Paul continues. "You see, there are many entities in many realms who are at various stages of consciousness. Some of them are trapped, in a manner of speaking, in a realm of their own creation, largely structured and built by habit and by expectations, and also, in many respects, by fear. Our commission, in this case, is to assist someone who is known to be rapidly approaching a point of receptivity." Paul pauses again.

"Receptivity?"

"Yes Peter. It is a point at which an entity has arrived at a realization that makes for an opening in their consciousness. It is rather like when you were saturated with a certain event or condition while in the Earth, and you suddenly decided that you would definitely change the structure that was permitting the condition to exist. At that point you were very *open,* in our terms, and in accordance with what we have shared with you called Universal Law, assistance can be given by such as us that can be very helpful to that entity. Do you understand this?"

After a pause to absorb this, Peter and Wilbur look at one

another, nodding, and then at the group, each of which is now studying Peter and Wilbur.

"Well then," states Benjamin, "perhaps it would be best, and perhaps most expeditious, if we were to simply get on with it. Is that acceptable to all of you?"

Zachary shifts on his perch. "Quite so, Benjamin. Get on with it. That's the ticket. You know me, always ready to get going, get doing. Too much talk and no action, well, that just doesn't build anything. The best way to learn is in doing," turning to look directly at Peter and then Wilbur, who both begin to chuckle.

Soon the entire group is laughing, color and light radiating from them and seeming to echo back to them from the enveloping greenery and color.

Peter, reeling from the percussion of the energy, looks at Wilbur who is smiling from ear to ear, and they laugh all the louder.

Looking at them all, Peter sees Benjamin and the female entities differently. Benjamin, who appeared older than Peter has come to expect in the realms he has visited so far, now looks totally changed. It is as though the laughter eradicated the outward signs of age and in their place is a radiant face, seemingly illuminated from within, with eyes of a crystalline blue that sparkle almost musically in accordance with this event. The females are shining wondrously and, as they do, Peter, being almost directly across from the Keeper of his records, marvels at the impact, the effect that is coming to him from her.

She notes Peter's reaction, and smiles all the more, nodding, slightly embarrassing him.

Peter doesn't know what to do but to nod back.

In a few moments, Benjamin rises and steps to the circular table in the center of the arboretum, and Peter's Keeper of record rises and steps forward as well.

Turning to look at Peter, Benjamin stretches out his hand,

"Peter? Wilbur? Will you come here to the table please?"

Peter and Wilbur are standing awkwardly at the table. Benjamin is to Peter's right, directly across from Peter is the Keeper of his record, and directly across from Wilbur is the Keeper's friend and colleague, who Peter notices is smiling broadly at Wilbur. He notices, too, that Wilbur is somewhat disarmed, just as Peter had been, but is smiling back, looking from time to time at Benjamin and then at Peter.

As they all realize the awkwardness of the situation, it is Benjamin who laughs. "Please do relax, everyone. Peter, you'll understand more of this very quickly, but for now, just understand that there is good reason for all that has transpired and all that you are experiencing. Wilbur, you know some of these things from your experiences in the Crystal Workers' Realm. While Peter can't remember his earlier experiences fully at this point, I am certain he will soon enough, and then you'll both feel a bit more at home, relaxed."

Peter, somewhat surprised again to hear the suggestion of something he had forgotten, now has his interest very much piqued.

Benjamin looks carefully at Peter, then at Wilbur, and then turns back to Peter. "Peter, it is good for you to know more of yourself, but it is good for you to know it when it is most appropriate for you. It is not that we or some force of God is blocking it. It is that your own higher self is ordering much of these events and experiences so that you will be firm in the foundational restructuring of your consciousness, and thereby achieve the highest and best result.

"The Keeper of your record has come forward in this meeting today because the commission that you are about to embark upon requires an inordinate amount of, what we shall call for sake of reference, balance or polarity. While we have every confidence in you, Peter, we do not wish you to be in any sense vulnerable. This applies equally so to you Wilbur. Forgive me if I am directing my comments primarily to Peter, but I know you understand that it is he who has been given the commission directly, and therefore it is appropriate."

"Benjamin, sir, I am not a bit troubled by this, or by your protocol. I am frankly relieved by it. Better Peter than I, to receive such a commission." With which they all laugh again.

It is Benjamin's carefully measured words that silence the laughter. "Peter, the entity that you have come to know as the Keeper of your record does not need a name, per se, any more than you do. But for the purposes of the current level of your consciousness or progression you are familiar with such things as names, physical forms, three-dimensional consciousness or perspective, the sensations of the five physical senses as are associated with your just-previous Earth incarnation, and all that sort of thing. So, therefore, out of deference to those as perspectives and reference points for you, it is perhaps well for you to be able to call your companion, or the prime polarity source for you in this forth-coming work, Elizabeth.

"Wilbur, we know that you need less of this than Peter at present. But for continuity here, it is perhaps well for you also, and all of us, to be able to call Elizabeth's companion by a name, and so we have chosen one given to her in a previous incarnation … Rebecca.

Peter and Wilbur are obviously both excited and relieved to have names with which to address their companions.

The gathering around the table now extend hands to one another, and Peter marvels at the incredible warmth, the feeling of compassion and understanding, the gentleness, and the unique and marvelously brilliant feeling that he receives flowing to him from his new colleague, Elizabeth.

Rebecca is doing the same with Wilbur. As Peter views them, he can see a luminosity that races back and forth, apparently through their enjoined hands across the table. It seems to circulate within each, and then surround them in a sort of radiance, more or less unifying them. Peter can't help but wonder if the same thing occurred during his handclasp with Elizabeth.

Benjamin speaks to the back of Peter's head, "Yes it did, Peter."

Snapping his head about to look squarely into Benjamin's eyes, which are dancing with humor, compassion, and love, Peter stammers a bit, "Uh … Oh … I keep forgetting how it works here. But I couldn't help but wonder, you know. What I see is what I use to compare, and by comparison I gain understanding. As Zachary says, when I am given an experience, I learn a lot more than if I'm just told something. You know, sort of like in the Earth, doing something instead of just reading about it gives one a lasting impression of what is being learned. Whereas just reading it and not doing it, leaves one rather empty. Wouldn't you say?"

A burst of laughter comes from Zachary and then Paul, as Zachary looks over at Ben. "See? I told you, the man's a veritable fountain of questions, one after the other. This fellow has more words than anyone I've ever seen. A veritable delight. Always a stimulation. Don't know another person who can speak as voluminously and with such rapid fire as Peter, unless of course it might be me."

All again rise into good cheer, until Benjamin brings them into unity, stifling his own loving humor. "I should like Zachary and Paul to join us here, please, and as we all gather around this table, let us consider what is before us. It is a simple table, but note that it is circular."

As Peter listens and looks down at the table, he notes that the tabletop begins to more or less shimmer and to move as though he were looking into a cloud.

Benjamin gestures at the table with a nod and then looks at Peter and Wilbur. "In the circle is the symbol of eternity, the One God, the completeness of us all."

Peter's mind is racing with the vision before him. Glancing quickly at Wilbur, he notes that Wilbur sees it too.

"As we share in this circular pattern of life," continues Benjamin, "I would remind you all, no matter where you are, that just as this circle has no beginning and no end, so are we all one. Peter, Wilbur, Paul, Zachary, Rebecca, Elizabeth, wherever you shall be, at whatever labors might be before you, know that each of us, all of us, are with you; and as well, the spirit of God as the source of our existence, our life, our wisdom, our love and our grace. In any times of need, call and we shall be with you. Do remember this."

As he completes this remark, Benjamin looks everyone in their eyes and calls their names individually. He pauses for a time, continuing to look warmly into the eyes of each and notes the return of warmth by a smile, a nod, and, of course, from Zachary, a wink.

Finally, resting his eyes upon Peter's, he speaks. "I am aware that you have many questions, Peter, and perhaps just as many doubts. In order than we might attend to those, and thereby proceed on to the works before us defined in your commission, I felt it well for us to gather here very informally to discuss whatever you feel is important to you at this point."

There is a pause, after which, Peter, a bit awkward at the pause and the expectation of comment from him, glances from Zachary's face and then to Paul's, and then to Wilbur and back to Benjamin. "Well, sir, you are correct in that I do have many questions. And I guess, as much as I hate to admit it, I have some doubts, as well. I understand in principle much of what has transpired recently, but in terms of specifics, I have no idea what we are about to do."

"Would you care to verbalize some of those questions or doubts, Peter, for the benefit of all of us? Perhaps we can then, collectively, assist you in understanding better what is before us."

Receiving nods from several, and warm smiles from everyone, including Benjamin, Peter pauses, takes what seems like a deep breath, sparkling a bit as he does. "Well, it's the commission. I don't fully understand what we are to do. I mean, I understand the description you gave me," looking at Benjamin, and then over to Zachary, and finally at Paul, "but a few more details and some clearer idea of what I or we are to do would be helpful. And another thing that I don't understand at all yet is this business of what you call *polarity*. The only thing I can bring to mind is a magnet, its plus or minus at each end, and stuff like that. I don't understand how that could possibly relate to two people ... or whatever we are."

A rippling note of humor passes through the group, much more audibly apparent from Zachary, as might be expected, who now is looking down to hide portions of his face so that he can't be seen completely.

"Well, I guess it sounds silly to you in some respects," offers Peter with a bit of embarrassment, "but it seems very serious to me. I mean, you all obviously have placed great importance in this commission, and certainly in the Great Hall there was no question in my mind that it was important, and is. So, I wouldn't want to mess it up or do the wrong thing. Do you understand, sir?" turning to Benjamin. "I mean, have I expressed myself adequately?"

"Indeed you have, Peter. It's not so much a question of what you are to *do*, you see, as much as what you are capable of *being*. Before you struggle with that too much, let me answer for you what I mean by *being*. In the Earth plane, you had various devices that performed functions for you and enabled you to, in turn, accomplish something. The best example I can give as a parallel is the electric lighting apparatus. It is, in its expression in the Earth, capable of being a source of illumination. Therefore, when you reach for its controlling switch and turn it on, it illuminates the area for you, as long as it is functioning properly and has been constructed in a manner that it can do its intended work. Is this a correct?"

"Yes sir, it is indeed. That's exactly how we see such things in the Earth. Very frustrating when you turn a light on in a dark room and the bulb is burnt out."

"Precisely so, Peter. And so it is that we want you to be prepared to be a light to others who are in need. We wouldn't want you to be like that light and have a burnt-out bulb when the time comes where light is needed. That's what I mean by *being* rather than *doing*. A light doesn't do *for* you; it provides a way for you to do for yourself. You, then, can think of yourself as a light going into darkness, prepared to illuminate when the call is given to you for light."

Pausing and searching Peter's expression for indications of questions or doubt, Benjamin is obviously pleased that it is apparent that Peter has absorbed much of the intent of his illustration.

"I see, and how is it that Elizabeth is involved in this work with us? Regarding the question of her polarity, or our polarity, would you use that in the example you have given? Perhaps it will help me gain even more understanding."

"Very well, and it is wise of you to ask for the answer to involve the example given. If you remember to follow such patterns, you'll have good understanding in the future."

Obviously pleased with himself, though he doesn't fully understand his wisdom, Peter smiles slightly and looks down at the table.

"Referring to the lamp analogy, then, you are familiar with electrical current, we know, and you are familiar with the term polarity in that respect, are you not?"

"Well, yes, I guess I am, basically."

"Very good. Then you know that, without a ground, the electrical current cannot complete its circuit, and will not function in order to illuminate the bulb, in the case of the incandescent bulb, that is, and perhaps others as well. So, therefore, the parallel here is simply defined as positive and negative energy polarity. Thus, you and Elizabeth complete a circuit of sorts, and as such, enable the potential of illumination by being as sufficient or as great as need be. Is this clear?"

"It is clear in principle, sir. But how do I try that? I mean, do we each have, uh, 55 volts, or uh, you know, something like that, to make the right current? What's the mechanism, if it can be put in terms that I am familiar with."

"Think of it this way, Peter. You could consider that you both are complete, and that would be accurate. In other words, both of you possess both positive and negative polarity. There is no question of this, for you are complete and self-sufficient, in and of yourselves. However, to use your earlier term, the *hook* ... "

This causes Peter to start, for now he knows, in Benjamin's use of this expression, that Benjamin heard his comments earlier in the Garden as well. Turning to look at the group, particularly Zachary, he is met with a barrage of laughter, which, of course, illuminates and echoes throughout the greenery surrounding them, and a period of luminosity transforms the group, as they are absorbed in this joy.

As they calm themselves, Benjamin continues, "As I was saying, the hook is that you are so familiar with certain aspects of this, and have so identified with those aspects, that you haven't regained, fully, the potential to utilize your completeness, and that's where Elizabeth comes in. Elizabeth has dwelled in realms beyond the Earth for a considerable measure of Earth-time. She has regained much of her balance, and what she has not regained is complimented by your presence and made complete.

"For sake of illustration, you could think of her as the grounding mechanism for the current which is within you. In other words, you might think of yourself as positive, and she negative, and together you complete a circuit; but this time it's not electrical in nature, though there is some parallel. It is eternal, it is spiritual. Does that help?"

Peter, looking from Benjamin and then to Elizabeth, studies her for a moment, which invokes a smile from her. "What does that have to do with her appearing to me as a female?" And, as he turns back to Benjamin, "For that matter, what does it have to do with me looking like a male? In other words, what I am saying is, *are* we male and female? Is she a woman and I a man, just like in the Earth plane? How does all of that work here? I have yet to see a child, so therefore I would conclude that there are no marriages, and no resulting births, and … "

Peter is interrupted by uproarious laughter pouring from Zachary and then from Paul, who finally have to turn themselves from the others as Zachary literally hoots and howls, throwing brilliant beams of light, color, and sound as he does.

This laughter is echoed by the others, though much more contained, While Wilbur is laughing, he is fidgeting a bit, looking down, obviously not fully understanding either. And Rebecca and Elizabeth can be heard laughing, but only barely, for Zachary's laughter is overshadowing them all.

Finally, Zachary catches himself and turns to Peter. "Pete, you have out-done yourself. I declare, that is the funniest thing I've heard in centuries! So good to have you back. We've missed you my friend. Do continue. I can't wait for the next one."

At this, Peter himself has to laugh, nowhere near the magnitude that Zachary's laughter had been, but to the extent that it seems to give permission to the others.

As they revel in the light and color that is reflected back to them, Peter turns to Benjamin. "Well, you said to ask whatever was in my mind! And Zack, here," with an off-handed cast of his right hand toward Zachary, "has warned you all that I have lots of questions. So? What are the answers, please?"

Benjamin straightens himself. "Well, if you give it much thought, Peter, you'll know the answer. I'm certain as I speak to you, that you do, so I consider your questions to be more in the nature of inviting us to answer to fill in the gaps. Would that be a correct assessment?"

"Uh, well, that sounds good enough for now. If you'll carry on, sir, I'll inquire afterwards." He smiles at Zachary, who obviously is struggling to contain himself, since sparks and rivulets of light are radiating from him.

"It's this way, Peter. You are at a juncture of sorts, where we are about to offer you some experiences, which will, as Zachary so often puts it, 'teach you by doing,' provide you the experience that will be self-illuminating and thereby answer your questions.

"But before we offer you this, let me see if I can help you in this way. You are not yet fully awakened, Peter. And before you jump to question me on that, just believe me, for you'll see it shortly for yourself, and understand. From your present perspective, there is much about you, in terms of your consciousness, your awareness, and your level of acceptance that rightfully prevents you from having full, unlimited consciousness before you are ready. It would be like over-loading the circuit of the illuminating device, the lamp. Too much current coming in the wire would explode the bulb, an over-load, or trip the circuit. See?

"No, what you call marriage and child-bearing do not occur here. There is no need, for that process truly serves an entirely different purpose. You'll understand this later, when you get to that point. But for now, to answer your question, that's not a procedure here.

"Now you might think a bit sadly about the loss of the joy of having children or having children around. Don't dwell on that either, for you're going to see the child in others and this will not only equal the joy you experienced in the Earth with having children but will surpass it immeasurably. There again, Peter, you will understand this better when you encounter that situation where it can be exemplified to you."

"Well, I did not expect that you would answer this question of male-female in much of a different manner. Though I had to ask, you know. But carrying that just a bit further, then, if I understand you correctly, Elizabeth and I, and I guess for that matter, Wilbur and Rebecca over there …" (Wilbur becomes much more alert, evidenced by a bit of sparkling around his cloak), "are to afford one another a certain measure of balance or polarity, and this balance will enable us to do the commission better. Is that a good summary?"

Nodding an affirmation, Benjamin remains silent, waiting for Peter to continue.

"Well then, how's it all to happen? Is our group going to go somewhere, you know, like we did when we went to Wilbur's realm, Zachary?" turning to look at him. "And then, it will progress from there? Or how's it going to work?"

Having been acknowledged by the look from Peter, Zachary responds, "Well, Pete, I guess that's my cue once again to say, how about an outing? How about an experience? This is getting to be, if you'll forgive me, Benjamin, a bit too boring for me. You know me, always ready for adventure."

Smiling and nodding at the same time, Benjamin states, "He's right. That was his cue and we all knew it. Very well," turning to look at Wilbur, "Wilbur, how are you doing? Would you like to take this journey with us?"

Looking from one to the other around the table, and then, for a prolonged period of time at Rebecca, he turns to look back at Benjamin, "Sir, I am certainly willing and heartily prepared to accompany and assist wherever I am needed. This, I hope, goes without saying." He pauses to look again into the eyes of all the others, and turns back to Benjamin, "But if I am not needed, if there is no good purpose to be served by my adventuring with Zachary here and the others, I believe I could contribute much to fellow workers in the Crystal Realm, if I were to be given some time to study these surroundings … the detail, the interaction, the mechanisms, and particularly the process that has enabled the flow of water out there," to which he turns to point at the small stream passing across the surface of the patio. "And I believe that Rebecca could assist me, ably, in understanding how we might use such techniques in the Crystal Workers' Realm." Pausing a moment to study Benjamin's face and then the others, "But of course, sir, if I am needed or can make a contribution, I would certainly opt first for that choice."

There is a pause, a period of time where Benjamin studies Wilbur and Rebecca carefully.

Wilbur fidgets, obviously unnerved by the concentrated attention.

Without speaking further to them, Benjamin turns swiftly to Peter. "Would that be acceptable to you, Peter?"

Peter is caught unawares by this sudden authority given to him. "Well, uh, I have no idea. I guess it would be just fine. It's Zachary's adventure." He turns to look at Zachary, inviting him to assist him.

"It's quite all right with me, Pete. Wilbur can maintain contact with us at all times, at any rate, and we with him. So if either of us is in need, of course we'll know it. Just like Benjamin told us as we sat about the table, remember?" He then points to the table.

Smiling, the others nod and look at the table in unison and then back at Benjamin.

"Very well. Wilbur, Rebecca, our best is with you. Have as much leisure and latitude here as suits you to satiate your quest for awareness, for knowledge, Wilbur. And Rebecca, you may inquire of any of the others here for assistance."

Rebecca smiles at Benjamin and then at Wilbur, taking his arm and leading him from the table as he waves and smiles at the others.

Immediately, Benjamin looks at Zachary, "Ready?"

"Always."

With a murmur of humor, Peter observes, "That's true, I believe. He is always at the ready, sir."

Benjamin stands, motioning for the others to stand, and

walks out the opening of the inner arbor, through which he had earlier entered. When he is just outside the opening, he stops and turns to Peter, "Now Peter, I would like you to come stand here at my side." Peter steps forward to be at the right of Benjamin. "And you, Elizabeth, to be on the other side of Peter there. Paul and Zachary, you have your choice. You may either lead or follow."

Paul turns to look Zachary and, immediately knowing Zachary's thought, turns back to Benjamin, "Well, sir, Zachary needn't even speak. I know that we shall lead, if that's permitted."

"Indeed so, Paul. You and Zachary lead. That will give me a good opportunity to answer Peter's questions as we proceed, the first of which I already perceive in him."

Still amazed at this mindreading ability, Peter answers, "Yes sir, I was wondering, where we're going. Is there a name for where we are going? And how shall we get there. And is this something anyone can do? And … I guess I'll stop there or Zachary will be teasing me again."

Smiling broadly, they all study Peter as Benjamin speaks, for they know what he is about to say and what is about to transpire.

"Try to listen with more than your consciousness, Peter, as I say these things to you. It will make it easier for you, and we'll progress much more rapidly. And you'll re-gain much of your earlier ability and consciousness as a result."

These comments truly get Peter's attention, for there is nothing he wishes more than to regain this mysterious lost consciousness or memory, and to know more about it, and himself, and where he is and what is happening.

Benjamin notes that Peter has understood the meaning behind his words. "Very good." He looks at where Zachary and Paul are standing, approximately some three or four meters in front of the others, and turns back to look at Peter. "What we are about to do here is leave Peter behind."

Peter, as can be expected, is nearly overwhelmed, to the extent that he cannot fully understand what is being said. "Sir, you are leaving me behind?"

"No, we are not leaving *you* behind. We are leaving the identity *Peter* behind." Without saying any more, he turns to Zachary and Paul and simply nods.

They both turn from their position of facing the others and appear to step forward, and in an instant are enveloped by something indistinguishable. In their place, where they had been previously standing, are now two luminous spheres, floating, pulsing, and moving as though they are rotating.

Only after a few moments does Peter begin to recognize them both by the similarity to their cloaks, as he had come to know these in their earlier travels.

Benjamin turns back to study Peter's face. "There! You see? Now we have left Zachary behind and Paul behind, haven't we?"

Peter is flustered. "Well, uh, I think I can grasp conceptually what it is you are attempting to tell me. In other words, now I see two … whatever that is over there."

Zachary's laughter can be heard emanating from the one, startling Peter dramatically, sparkling his cloak and causing static all around him.

A soft touch of warmth passes all through him, and immediately the errant static energy around his cloak stops, and he turns to recognize that Elizabeth has touched him. He turns to look at Benjamin.

Benjamin states simply, "Polarity. That's what I meant. She is your polarity and you are hers. Think about that and hold it. Keep that thought. Teamwork is perhaps how Zachary would define it for you." He turns to look at the two hovering spheres of luminosity. "Right, Zachary?"

"Right, Ben. Teamwork. That's the ticket. Always work in a team. Harmony, that's the way to go. Individuality is good only to a point. Right, Pete?"

Utterly flustered at the prospect of speaking to a sphere of light, Peter struggles to respond, "Yes, uh, that's right, teamwork is good. Uh, is that *really* you in there, Zack?"

Laughter is heard as Zachary responds, "Hold on a second, Pete. Watch the sphere on your right. Carefully now, watch it closely. Here I come!" There is a sort of whisping sound and Zachary appears, in form, in the place of the sphere of light. "See, Pete? Me, all the time. Great trick, huh? Too bad we can't do this one in the Earth plane! What a ticket this would make in some side-show!" Then he raises his hand and wiggles his fingers as though to say good-bye, steps backward, and transforms into the sphere of light once again, this time annotated by flashes of little red ripples obviously indicating his humor.

Peter's excitement is palpable. "I've seen it, and I know it's true, but I can hardly believe it. It's incredible." Turning to Benjamin, "Are you saying that I can do that? I mean, is that what you meant by *leaving Peter behind*?"

"Yes."

"Well, can I do it now? What's it feel like? How do you move? How do you talk? How do you see? I don't see any eyes. I see nothing but that light … or whatever it is.'

Benjamin turns half way towards Zachary, "You were right, Zack, there are lots of questions in this one, aren't there?"

Benjamin then reaches out to grasp one of Peter's arms. "Here, Pete, come forward. Let's move up to those floating spheres of light," and he pulls Peter forward, Elizabeth following equidistant from him on the opposite side of Peter, until they are right face-to-face with these spheres of luminosity. They are so close that Peter stiffens visibly.

"Wait a minute. Wait a minute! What do I do? Please! I don't want to hurt them. Tell me what's going on here, Benjamin, so I know what to do, or else my cloak will start all that funny stuff again."

"There's nothing to fear, Peter. There is no way you can injure them or hurt them or violate them. Just do whatever you feel."

Feeling extremely awkward, Peter cannot think of anything to do, so he extends his hand, as though he is intending to shake Zachary's hand.

This is a most humorous situation, and it creates joyful laughter.

Zachary extends a little pillar of light to connect in what you might call a handshake.

Peter is bewildered. There is an immediate reaction on his part, for as much as he tries to grasp this thrust of light extending from the sphere that is Zachary, he cannot. There is naught to grasp.

Then as Peter observes the sphere, he perceives that it transforms its color. It shifts. The patterns move in different directions, and he begins to feel something in his hand, very subtly, very gently, almost as though it is merely a suggestion of something there. The more he observes, looking from his hand to the sphere of light which is Zachary, the more dense, the more strongly definable become the colored patterns. After several moments, he can feel a hand in his, and looking from his hand and up, he finds himself looking into Zachary's eyes once again, with Zachary smiling as he does.

"Your mouth is open, Pete, close it. It's not polite, you know. Interesting isn't it? You can do the same, Pete, want to try it?" Without hesitating, Zachery steps forward and swings Peter into the spot he held just the moment before.

Still holding Peter's hand, "Now, Pete, close your eyes, and don't protest! It's a waste of time. Remember? Close your eyes and go within yourself until you find the place of peace, of quiet."

Obediently, taking a last look at Zachary and Benjamin off to the side, and Elizabeth on the other, and seeing Paul smiling at him, Peter closes his eyes. He feels a swirling, pulsing motion, as though he is being drawn deep within himself, irresistibly, into something that he would only call, from his Earth reference, an incredible vacuum, a void. And yet, in this sense of darkness there is luminosity! There is a sense of permanence, of eternal nature, a sense of well-being.

He begins to feel aglow. He feels within himself that he has been enveloped in a golden sphere of faith, of comfort, of support, of sustenance. He feels incredibly well and joyful. He feels, above all else, complete.

Pausing in this sphere of space, Peter can hear Zachary's voice as though he were standing beside him. "Excellent, Pete. Now, open your eyes and look. But remember, you haven't any eyes so you'll have to think of opening your consciousness in the place of your eyes."

Puzzled, Peter simply follows Zachary's advice. He thinks of opening his eyes and perceiving.

"Good, Pete, you've got the idea. Now, think of me. You remember how I look. Think of me."

Obediently, Peter musters a memory from within himself and sees Zachary. Instantly, he actually *sees* Zachary and Zachary is there. He knows this because to the right and left of Zachary are Elizabeth and Benjamin. And behind them is the patio, the arbor they were just in. He can see the table inside the opening, and he feels himself instantly before it. As he does, he catches himself and thinks, *No, I need to focus on Zachary*, and swoosh, he is back in front of Zachary.

"Well, had a little outing, did we?" Laughing, Zachary turns to Benjamin and Elizabeth. "See? Didn't I tell you? Nothing can hold him back. A quick learner too."

They all smile broadly, avoiding laughter for fear of unsettling Peter.

Still perceiving in accordance with Zachary's instructions, Peter asks, "Hey Zack, can you see me?"

"Sure, I can see you. Say, Elizabeth, can you see him?

Elizabeth responds softly, "Yes, I see him well."

"Hey Ben," asks Zachary over his shoulder, "do you see him too? I mean, Elizabeth and I aren't imagining this, are we? Can you see him?"

"To be sure, Zachary. He looks fit and well."

Peter pauses for a moment. "Well, Zack, what do I look like?"

"Look into my eyes, Pete, and see your own reflection." Zachary moves up very close to Peter.

Peter is startled to see two spheres of light. One, he recognizes as Paul, and the other … He asks, "Zack, is this *me?* I mean, that light next to Paul … That's me, right?"

"Right-o, Pete. Doing better all the time. Sharp as a tack. Okay, let's take the next step. Are you ready?"

"Yes, I think so."

"I want you to open your perception totally. By totally, I mean, you remember you don't have physical eyes now, right?"

"Yes, I know that, Zack. I don't know how I'm seeing you, but I'm seeing you clearer than ever before. I've never seen this clearly before."

"And how are you hearing me? Do you have any ears?"

"Well I presume not. I can't feel any. For that matter, I don't seem to have anything. I'm just here. I'm just, uh … What *am* I, after all, Zack?"

"We'll talk about that later, Pete. Just wanted you to acknowledge that you have no physical appendages or sensory organs, yet you can perceive, true? I mean you hear me, you're speaking to me. I hear you, and you can see me, true?"

"Yes, on each point."

"Well then, I want you to now reach out and touch me."

"With what Zack? I'm just some sort of luminous egg it seems, with no hands or arms."

Laughing, the trio quickly calm themselves, as Zachary explains, "Not an egg at all. You are simply in your truer form. And before you ask what I mean by your tru-*er* form,

it's that there are other forms beyond this. But don't dwell on that. For now, sufficient at hand is the task before you." Smugly rocking on his feet for a moment for having made such a wise comment, Zachary then continues, "Reach out and touch me, Pete. Remember, you go within, and first you create and then you act. Create and act. Think of the desired result and implement it."

There is a pause as Peter attempts to remember this teaching from the past. "Okay, Zachary, I'm going to give it a try here, but I don't know how to, uh, you know, formulate this inside myself. Before, with my other form, I would think of my hand going out to touch you, or something like that. But I don't know how to make this, whatever it is, go out and touch you."

"Limitations, Pete. The old Pete ... Got to get rid of all that, and break free into the new. Old habits are tough to break, but you can do it. Just think of touching me. Just think of doing it, okay?"

"All right, Zack, here I go," and a ray of light begins to extend from Peter to Zachary, pauses a moment to touch Zachary's left shoulder, and immediately withdraws. "I did it! Well, I *think* I did it. Did you feel me touch you?"

"Sure did, along with fireworks and visual display. Great act. You needn't use the light, though. You can just do it. But it's your option to do as you wish. Do it again."

"Okay, here I come." This time there is only a hint of luminosity as Peter turns to touch Zachary.

"Much better, Pete. Now, once more. This time, I would like you to think of yourself as having already touched me. Now you know what you feel. You already touched me. It's done. So, you need to take no action but to define and assimilate the perception."

There is another pause as Peter reflects on this, and then makes several attempts. "I believe I've got it. What I did was, I remembered how you felt the first time and I visualized that, and instantaneously I could feel you."

"Okay. Good, Pete. Now do this with Benjamin. You haven't touched him, but I want you to touch him, just like you did in the last example. In other words, *don't* touch him. I want you to think of having touched him, and then actualize that. Make it real within yourself."

"But how … "

"Never mind how. Just do it, that's all. Have the faith to do it, Pete. You can."

There is a period of time wherein Peter is obviously struggling, for Benjamin represents to him an authority figure. So, the idea of reaching out to touch him in the first place seems to be improper, and in the second place, because he's not that familiar with Benjamin, this feels to be an invasion.

Benjamin discerns this concern. "I give you permission to touch me, Peter. In fact, I welcome it," smiling at the light, which is Peter.

Somewhat relieved, Peter strains, attempting to grasp the concept Zachary has told him.

"No, Pete, too hard. You'll blow a circuit. Remember? Easy does it. Go within and just be, and then reach out and *know* that you have touched Benjamin. Then assess that and tell me your perception."

After a few moments, Peter asks, "I believe I've done it, right, Benjamin? I touched you?"

"Indeed so, Peter, right here on the forehead. Missed my shoulder a bit, but that's all right. It was a good hit."

Peter is laughing now, the stress relieved. "Sorry about that. I *thought* I hit your head. I guess my aim wasn't too good."

"Practice, Pete," he hears from Zachary. "*Practice makes perfect.* You know that old Earthly saying. Okay, Benjamin, we're ready."

"Wait a minute! I'm existing in a non-physical state. I can't find my self. I'm not sure what I am, and you say we're *ready*? Ready for what?"

"Come back here, Pete," at which Zachary extends his hand, grasping something inside of Peter.

Peter can feel a pulling sensation in the midst of his being and, in an instant, he finds himself *Peter* again, the Peter he's always known.

"Have a good trip?"

"Quite an experience, Zack! Wonderful, but weird. Really weird. I couldn't tell where I was, who I was, what I was, or anything. Yet it didn't bother me too much, I felt so good. And it seemed like I was aware of anything I wanted to be aware of. Did you see me go over to that table? I was there in an instant! All I had to do was think of it and I was there. I could see that table every bit as clear as when I was seated in front of it with my elbows on top of it. In fact, I could see it better, like I could look into the depths of the thing. And ...."

"Whoa, whoa! Hold your horses, Pete," and they all chuckle. "One thing at a time. Remember your circuits. We have some more work to do, and Benjamin here has got lots of responsibilities, remember? We can't be keeping him. That wouldn't be proper."

"Oh, r-right," stammers Peter, embarrassed. "I do apologize. It's just, well, you know, my nature."

"And a delightful one, Peter, I must say. But Zachary is correct. Not that I have limited time to give you, for truly I can give you whatever your needs are. But we have a commission. Remember? So in preparation for the commission, we would like to show you more, so you will fully comprehend the nature of who and what you are, by doing. And so we have arranged that we take a journey, all of us, by going into these altered forms of expression and traveling together. As we do, you will learn much by experiencing, as your dear friend Zachary always tells you. Is that acceptable to you?"

Peter pauses only a moment to look at his companions, including Paul, who has now come into his familiar form, as well. "Why not. This is terrific. Remember when we were on the hill in the garden and I said I wanted some experiences? This is what I had in mind, something like this." He smiles at Elizabeth, and receives from her a warm smile and a nod.

Benjamin then steps forward. "Very well, if you will follow, then," and he becomes a wondrously radiant luminous sphere, sparkling in alternating gold and blue-white color, and then becomes simply a pure luminous sphere of light.

Next, Paul advances and repeats the same process.

Then from Peter's other side, Elizabeth steps forward and, likewise, becomes a luminous sphere.

Finally, Zachary places a hand upon Peter's shoulder and looks him in the eye, "Well, it's you and me, Pete. Let's have at it." With that he grasps Peter's hand and they both step forward, becoming luminous spheres.

Peter feels the sensation of movement and can hear Zachary speaking to him. "Pete? Hey, Pete, are you with us?"

"Oh, sorry, Zack. Where are you?"

"Well, look about. Just look about, and you'll see for yourself where everyone is."

There is a ripple of laughter and Peter remembers Zachary's earlier instructions, repeats them, and instantly perceives a vast openness in which he can see the spheres of light, which are, as he interprets, Benjamin, Paul off a bit, Zachary to his side, and Elizabeth on the other. "This is simply glorious, Zachary! And we're moving, aren't we?'

Zachery chuckles. "Indeed so, Pete. And, if I might add, at a rapid clip too, eh wot?"

Paul speaks softly from in front of them. "This is a good opportunity for you, Peter. I would remind you of your journey through the colors, as there are some parallels here that could be useful to you in understanding and creating a definition within yourself of how this sort of movement takes place. If you'll look about, you'll be able to perceive indicators of demarcation points."

"If you will reach out and touch Elizabeth," suggests Benjamin, "you'll be able to perceive what Paul is telling you more clearly."

"Okay. Uh, reach out and touch Elizabeth. Yes sir, I'll do that … Elizabeth?"

"Yes?"

"Do you mind?"

"Not at all, Peter." Elizabeth laughs softly.

Peter again recalls Zachary's instructions. This time, they are astonishingly clear in his consciousness, and he is able to enact them instantly without any effort. As he does, he feels an impact at the end of the extension of his consciousness, and at the moment of the impact there is a swooshing sound as Peter feels himself enveloped with a remarkably fluid sense of warmth. It reminds him of being in the Earth plane, when a ripple of energy would pass through him in a moment here or there in various experiences.

At this thought, suddenly he realizes that his awareness now is totally different. Whereas before he had perceived only a vast space, seemingly devoid of much of anything but depth and breadth, Peter can now see other spheres of light. Some are moving this way and others that. He can hear sounds, wonderful sounds, soft and gently flowing, occasionally rising here and falling there. He feels a sensation of incredible well-being, and a sense of completeness, of closeness, of oneness with all of existence. "This is marvelous, Benjamin, sir. So marvelous."

"Good. Hold that thought, keep it. It's important to you. And now we shall move, if it's acceptable to the rest of you, to the place of our commission. Ready everyone?" To which he receives an affirmative response, albeit weakly from Peter, who is still holding to Elizabeth.

There is an audible and tangible perception of passing through something, like a pop or a whoosh.

(To describe this to you further, our group is passing through a level of demarcation that defines a realm of consciousness, likened unto a veil, as the Channel describes it. Yet it is not. It is simply the outer fringe of the extent of consciousness of this particular level.)

In a moment, there is another whoosh, pop, the experience accompanied by colors, sounds, and lights, all continually changing, and they pass through yet another level of consciousness.

Finally, our group finds itself at a level that, to Peter, is very similar to the Earth. He looks around and, with a start, sees people, real people, walking about, speaking, engaging in various activities. Clinging all the more tightly to Elizabeth, he asks in an almost whisper, "Where are we? What is this? Is this Earth?"

He recognizes Benjamin's voice and sees the sphere of light move in front of him, and he can, in his consciousness, perceive that the sphere is, indeed, Benjamin. "No, Peter. This is the realm of our commission, or, perhaps more appropriately, *your* commission, but this is not the Earth. It is a realm beyond it. In this realm are those entities, or *people*, who exist here because of their own choice, or their own limitation, albeit self-imposed.

"At some point in time, one of them will reach a point wherein they are willing to release the past, their old expectations, habits, and desires. And that one will call out. Your commission, along with Elizabeth, is to answer that call. For your reference, I will identify the entity to you. It is that one over there by that post, leaning back looking down. The one with the blue shirt, the black trousers, and the white shoes and with the hole in the front top. Sufficiently described for you to perceive?"

"Yes, Benjamin, I can perceive him. My goodness, he looks out of sorts. What in the world is wrong with him?"

Benjamin laughs softly. "It's not what is in the *world* that's wrong with him, though it's true that things in the previous life in the Earth, just past, have put him here. It's what's within *him* that's wrong, and he's been working with that for longer than you can imagine. But now, we believe he's about ready to leave here, and you can help.

"So now, I leave you. Paul, Zachary, care for them. Elizabeth, Peter, great joy and blessings in your work." Without a moment for Peter to protest, the sphere of light that is Benjamin goes into itself, and is gone.

So, dear friends, we will conclude here, perhaps much to the Channel's chagrin.

But there must always come beginnings and endings, must there not?

CHAPTER 2

A Bridge of Love
MARCH 27, 1991

We find our group still, in essence, hovering before the entity leaning against the post, just where we left them. We have not followed along with the course of your time as it moves but, rather, have sustained a connective consciousness to this experience. Therefore, little has transpired here in terms of what you consider to be time. Only what you would perhaps call brief moments. See?

Peter is in a state of some wonder, observing the entity who is to be the target of his commission. Looking at his friends, his colleagues, he sees them in what he considers to be their altered form, albeit identified earlier by Zachary as the truer one.

Elizabeth speaks softly, "Peter, are you doing well? Do you feel balanced and in harmony with yourself?"

He pauses momentarily. "Yes, indeed, Elizabeth. Actually, I feel remarkably well, far better than I can recall ever feeling. It's like I have no sense of any limitation, no feeling of any Earth-like needs or pressures, if you know what I mean by that."

Elizabeth nods, in the sense that Peter can intuit her response, rather than visibly seeing in the physical sense.

Peter next hears Zachary's voice resonate within him, as though he were speaking in the outward sense, "Well, Pete, so here we are. Do you have any questions or any information that you need regarding the work before us?"

"I am certain you know the answer to that before I even speak, Zack. Of course I have questions, perhaps several dozen of them. But the main one is, what happens next?"

Zachary responds in a tone uniquely soft for Zachary. "Peter, what happens next largely depends on you. One of the great gifts that you possess, unique within our group, is that you can remember what it feels like to be in the Earth plane. You can remember the sensations of emotion, you can recall the aspects of feelings that are directly associated with the physical form. Now, good friend, I suggest that you go within yourself to discern what you feel to be most appropriate in this moment. Right, Paul?"

Paul, who has been quite silent is heard communicating these words, "Zachary is correct, Peter. I agree with him, that what you have to offer is multi-faceted in that you have a vivid memory of the Earth will all its limitations and feelings, which should prove to be invaluable in helping our commission attain his freedom from this place of limitation. Of course, it is his choice. To add just a bit to Zachary's comments, I suggest that when you seek within yourself, you try to reach out and touch the entity just in the same manner as in the exercise Zachary had you perform with himself and Benjamin earlier. Do you recall it?"

"Yes, I remember, particularly so with Benjamin. That did give me a bit of a start, if you know what I mean." Peter can sense, more than hear or see, the affirmation from his colleagues and the associated warmth and compassion of their true understanding and love for him.

After a pause, Paul continues, "Note that our commission does not truly have physical form, but is only imaging himself in that to which he is accustomed. Then, as you reach out to him, do it with some caution so you don't disrupt him, but yet to the extent that you can *know* him, know about him, and understand where he is in his thinking and in the other aspects of his being that are more oriented to the Earth. Is that sufficiently clear to you, Peter?"

"I believe so, Paul, and I thank you. It appears I'll have to do it before I can truly answer your question. So, if you think it's appropriate, I'll do so now."

"Right-o, Pete, have a go at it," responds Zachary, back to his more light-hearted nature.

Peter pauses. He remembers that he is sustaining his connection, his contact, with Elizabeth, like grasping her arm or the folds of her spiritual cloak. In that moment, he receives an affirmation from her that this is fine and that it may indeed be continued. With that reassurance, he turns his attention inward.

Both he and Elizabeth shift outwardly in their coloration and in their luminosity, and seem to merge into one greater sphere of light. In that moment, it can be perceived with higher sight that a silvery shaft of light moves slowly, almost cautiously, out from their combined sphere of light and ever so carefully touches the entity upon the shoulder.

The entity gives no indication of being aware of this, but does shift his weight slightly and looks off to the side, as though anticipating someone coming.

Within several moments, the light withdraws itself from the entity and back into the greater sphere of light that is Elizabeth and Peter. After several moments, the sphere of light visibly divides, and now, in its former position, are once again the two spheres identified as Peter and Elizabeth.

"Wow! I had nearly forgotten many of those feelings. Quite an experience to have myself reminded of them and of the joy that has taken their former position within my mind or heart. It seems as though the entity has a sort of hodge-podge of emotions stirring within him, and the main one that I could report to you," directing his comment to Paul and Zachary, "is sadness, a sense of a longing, as though he's trying to re-member something that is meaningful within him. I get the feeling from him that he's had so many experiences that have been sort of redundant, over and over again, the same thing, like listening to a record on Earth that is stuck in a certain groove and keeps going over the same melody again and again and again. Also, there is a very strong feeling of loneliness, which I don't, frankly, understand completely since quite a number of other entities are here. Well that's about it. That's pretty much what I felt from him. Is that what you were looking for, or what I should have sought?"

It is Paul who speaks first. "That was excellent, Peter. We could tell he was, what we call, nearly ready, but we couldn't discern completely in the way that you can. Oh, we can reach into Universal Consciousness and draw out whatever understanding is necessary to deal with any situation present, but for someone to be equipped, as you are, to be capable of being in his presence as an aid to him … Well, that is just a wonderful opportunity for us all. And we thank you for being present."

Zachary speaks next. "Well done, Pete. I think you should feel quite proud of yourself, not too much, but a little." Peter can feel Zachary's familiar laughter resonating within him. "What do you feel you should do at this point, Pete? We're taking our direction from you now. You are more or less the resident expert in this situation."

There is a long pause. "I'm not sure how you mean that, Zack, whether you are joking or serious. I suspect you are mostly serious. Right?"

"Completely serious, Pete, though one needs to keep a good sense of humor, don't you think?"

"Suits me, Zachary. Then, let me see … If someone in the Earth were lonely and longing for something that was difficult to define or couldn't be remembered, I guess I'd try to become a friend, try to strike up a conversation to cheer them up and help them identify what would make them happy, if they are, in fact, unhappy, as this fellow seems to be."

"Well, then, Pete, is that what you're going to do?"

"Wait a minute, Zack! What are you saying? That I am supposed to do that? I mean, it doesn't appear that he can even see us. After all, we're only a few yards in front of him, and he's not given any indication of our presence, nor has anyone here, for that matter," as he notes the presence of a number of other entities scattered about within their present locale, and others moving to and fro actually right between them and the entity leaning against the post.

"Well, how else would you like to go about it? Do you see another solution? Is there another path you think might be an improvement on that?"

"Well, don't you have some gimmick you can use here, Zack? I mean, like the butterfly or Wilbur's hat? You know, like making the music and all those things. Haven't you got one of those that would apply here?"

"Oh, sure. We have lots of things like that. But one needs to be mindful of whom one is serving. And there is Universal Law to be considered here, which comes from God and is the essence of all existence. In order for one to be in the most, I'll call it, pure state, Universal Law is a mandate. It's not that it's forced upon us, but just that it's recognized as the way to live, to experience and to be. If I were to use any of those gimmicks, as you call them, I would cause a ruckus here in this realm. Probably disturb several of those guys over there around the corner. And that woman walking down the way would probably have quite a start, don't you think?"

Peter acknowledges the references given by Zachary. "Well, yes, I suppose so. But wait a minute now. You're talking about what Law again? Universal Law, did you say?"

"Right, Pete. It's simply that each entity, each realm, each consciousness, has their own unique right to their own choice. Another way of stating it is, each entity has the right to be an individual. And where two or more gather and believe or subscribe to the same concept of existence that, in essence, forms a realm of existence in which they all interact.

That's what our friend over there is doing, and that's what this realm is. If I use my gimmicks, I'll disturb that, and I would have disturbed the *fabric of existence*, which is Universal Law. I'd have to quickly make a great effort to mend that fabric, for I'd be responsible for that action. See?"

"I think so. I think I see, Zack. So, what you're saying is, the ball's in my court. Right?"

"Yep. It's your commission, and we're along because you wanted us to be, and because we're your friends. And whatever you are about to do, we want to share it with you, very much."

There is a long pause, and Elizabeth can be heard next, "Peter, why don't we try it? I'll go with you, if you'd like. We an alter our form, our expression, back to something similar to what you were that Benjamin called the *Peter that was left behind*, which would be more familiar to this one. And then move into his realm of existence. Does that suit you?"

Reflecting inwardly a moment, visibly sparkling around the edges of the sphere of his existence, Peter responds equally softly to Elizabeth, "That is extraordinarily kind of you, Elizabeth, and I would certainly welcome your presence and participation in any effort here. Then, Paul and Zachary, you're going to stand on the sidelines?"

"To an extent, Pete."

"Yes," answers Paul, "but we'll be right here all the time. You'll be able to see us, but our commission won't. Nor will anyone else, until or unless they're ready."

"Well, okay. Elizabeth, I guess since you've suggested it, you know the procedure. Am I correct?"

"Yes, I am quite familiar with it, Peter, and it's very simple. If you will allow me, I will draw you forth into the form appropriate for this realm."

Pausing and waiting for an affirmation from Peter, she hears, "Well, yes, of course, Elizabeth. But, I hate to see you go first. This doesn't look like a very hospitable realm. I would go first, rather than you first, if I knew how to. But I don't. So, thanks."

Peter can hear muffled laughter floating to him from Zachary and even Paul.

Then, as Peter carefully perceives Elizabeth, he sees her seem to smoothly flow outward, and sees her orb of light dim somewhat. As it does, an undulating ribbon of light moves outward from it. Simultaneously, he can feel a tugging in the area that he would consider to have been his solar plexus. At the end of the ribbon, Peter can see a shimmering, growing and intensifying, until instantly Peter can perceive Elizabeth. She's slightly different than he had remembered her. Not as bright or luminous, but every bit Elizabeth.

He feels himself being strangely drawn. He can see Elizabeth's eyes as though they are light reaching to him, pulling him, and he feels himself moving, rather like floating or wobbling about on a current of air.

Suddenly, there is another whoosh, and in that instant he can see his hand. He wiggles his fingers, and he moves about a bit, for once again he has become *Peter*.

"Goodness, that was really interesting, Elizabeth."

She nods and smiles, studying him. "Do you feel okay, Peter?"

"Quite well, thank you. I'd like an explanation on how you did that at some point, when we have the opportunity."

"I'd be glad to explain it to you when we've completed our commission."

Shifting his focus at that moment to the entity leaning against the post, Peter is curious to note that the entity has still paid them no mind whatsoever, but continues to look down at his feet as he disturbs a few stones or pebbles on the ground, moving them this way and that. He has his hands in his pockets and is leaned back, head down, bowed over somewhat, just biding his time.

Peter takes stock of the realm in which they are now expressed. He sees it as being profoundly less luminous than that of the Garden. It even seems different than the Earth, as he remembers it. It lacks the brilliance of greens and the luster of blue. He notes that it seems to be not daylight and not night, but a strange sort of in-between, a dull, gray-black color that requires a bit of illumination to truly see. Things seem misted over, just as one would appear who is standing in the shadows along a street.

In that moment, Peter realizes that it *is* a street, and that the post the entity is leaning against is a lamppost. Behind him are the steps leading up to many different buildings, some of brick, some of stone, one after another. *Tenements*, he thinks.

In that moment, he hears Elizabeth. *Tenements?*

Yes. Tenements are like apartment buildings, or flats. Big cities have them. Frequently, where an area is short on space, they are built with common walls, one on top of the other, so that it looks like many houses stacked on top of one another. Just like that over there. He points to the structure just behind the entity.

Others are wandering to and fro, and as Peter looks at them he notes that, curiously, they lack light. They seem to possess no real inner radiance. He sees some that momentarily spark a bit of this or that color, but for the most part they are without luminosity. Also, there is a sense of density in the realm, which Peter can remember from the Earth as being associated with frustration, limitation, habit, forgotten goals, lost dreams, and visions that have dimmed. This realm, Peter reminds himself, is very much like a slum in which many find their lives beginning and ending, the summation of the experience for many seemingly meaningless, without purpose, either detrimental or contributive to any beyond the family circle.

Elizabeth is observing, noting all of Peter's thoughts as though he were speaking to her.

Understand what I'm thinking, Elizabeth?

Yes, very clearly. Thank you. It was a valuable experience. It has been quite a number of Earth years since I have been in a physical body in the Earth, and I appreciate this little update, if I might call it that. So, what shall we do, Peter? We have forms now, and if we wish, we can make ourselves known to the gentleman. What do you think?

Peter looks from Elizabeth over to the man leaning against the post. *Well, following my intuition, as Zachary and Paul encouraged me, I'd say we might just sort of wander over there and see if we can strike up a conversation.*

Very well, Peter. This time you lead and I'll follow.

Smiling at one another, Peter reaches out to grasp Elizabeth's hand, which she warmly accepts.

Having moved near the man, Peter experiences a moment of fluster, not knowing how to begin, since it has been a while since he has considered people with such a plight.

Suddenly, the man looks up and stares Peter directly in the eye. As he does, Peter feels a sensation of cold pass through him, chilling him, moving throughout his being, growing and growing.

In the next split second, Peter feels warmth converging on him, flowing from his hand that is clasped by Elizabeth. The warmth passes through his body as though forcing the cold out of him. He turns to nod a thanks to her, and she smiles gently.

"Hello, there," Peter begins awkwardly and more or less automatically.

The man looks at them, from one to the other, then back to Peter, and says simply, "Hi," and looks back down. Continuing to push a couple of pebbles about on the ground next to his foot, he asks, "Where are you going?"

"Going?"

He looks back up at Peter. "Yes, going. You're walking down the sidewalk, aren't you? Where are you going?"

"Oh, uh …" Peter is obviously taken aback. "Well, we're just, uh," turning to look at Elizabeth, "taking a walk, a stroll, you know, that's all."

"Well, you'd better watch yourselves walking around here. Not a very nice neighborhood, you know."

"Oh, well, I thank you for that, but Elizabeth and I are capable of caring for ourselves."

"Yeah? Well, I've known lots of people who've said that, and they aren't around here any more. Know what I mean?"

Peter is flustered at the directness and deliberateness of the man. "Oh, uh, yes."

"It's a shame, you know. This used to be a nice neighborhood. My father used to tell me how every evening on the weekends everyone would get together, and they'd sing and play instruments and dance. Some would sing folk songs from their homeland, and others would bring food and drinks. It was one big family. And then everybody got to fighting among themselves, wanting control or wanting someone else's money. And now … Well, look what it's gotten us. And I've been here for so long, I can't remember coming, and I don't guess I'll ever leave." With that, the man looks down.

Peter is shaken, visibly and audibly. "Well, uh …"

In the next moment, he can hear within himself Paul's soothing voice. *Rely upon what you feel, Peter. Rely upon what is within you. Remember, you came here in a form that is unlimited. You are still unlimited. Draw upon that. Look behind you.*

Peter turns to see a luminous ribbon of light undulating back to where his spherical light still remains. Adjacent to it is Elizabeth's sphere with a similar ribbon of light, reaching from it to the Elizabeth that is standing beside him.

Peter responds silently, *Very well, I'll try my best.*

That's all you can do, Pete. He hears from Zachary.

"Well, uh, listen … My name is Peter and, as I mentioned, this is Elizabeth. What's your name?"

He answers without looking up, "Name's Todd. At least, that's what everyone calls me. And that suits me fine."

"I knew a guy named Todd once. I liked him very much. He always had something interesting to say about everything and, in a way, you remind me of him."

"I do? That's something. No one's ever said anything like that about me that I can recall."

"You mentioned that you've been here a long time. Why is it that you stay here?"

Todd shrugs his shoulders, his hands in his pockets. "Where else is there to go? I mean, once you're here, you're here, and that's it."

Peter can feel a sense of warmth coming to him from Elizabeth, and he begins to realize that he is not actually in physical form, and that neither is Todd. Pondering this and feeling the sense of understanding coming from Elizabeth, Peter realizes that there is a key point here and blurts it out. "Todd, how long have you been dead?"

Todd visibly stiffens. His hands jerk from his pockets and he glares at Peter. "What do you mean by that?"

"Well, uh …" Peter is flustered again, concerned that he may have said something he shouldn't have, that maybe Todd doesn't even know he's dead.

Don't waver, Peter. Have confidence and faith, Peter can hear from Paul.

And from Zachary, *Yes, indeed, Pete. Believe that you're being guided, that the guidance is true and it won't fail you.*

"You do know you're … uh … dead, don't you, Todd?"

Todd is no longer leaning against the post and is studying Peter very intently. "I know I'm not, well, in the same form that I was before, and I know that I went through something that felt like death. But that was so long ago, and nothing changed much. I'm not even sure whether I'm dead or alive. Worse than that, I feel like I might have gone to the wrong place, if that makes any sense. It all just seems like more of the same old stuff. I remember the preacher who used to stand on the corner every Sunday and read and preach to us. I remember that as a kid. And he never talked about anything like this. I remember hearing about the hellfire, brimstone, smoke, and all that, but other things he talked about, too. Glorious riches. You know, fruit and honey and all that junk. But I'll tell you, either one of those, no kidding, either one, would be better than this! This isn't nice. It sure isn't happy. This is non-existence! What'd you say your name was? Pete?"

"That's right," carefully guarding himself not to over-react. "It's Pete and Elizabeth."

"Well, Pete, you must not be from around here." Then, looking over at Elizabeth, "Neither of you. I don't remember seeing you before, although you sorta seem familiar. Maybe I just remember you from … Well, Lord knows where."

"Lord?" asks Peter.

"Yeah, you know, God, Lord, heavenly Father, and all that. He's the only one that probably knows the answer to any of this."

"You mean you believe in God, then?"

"Well of course I do, but I don't know why. After I got here, I sure lost a lot of my faith, I'll tell you! The only thing, I guess, that lingers with me is the memory of my mother, who was always encouraging us kids to have faith, no matter what. She was something, that woman. Never will forget her kindness, her love. I can still feel all that whenever I think of her. You know what I mean?"

"Yes, I do, Todd, and those are good thoughts to keep, I'd think. Wouldn't you think so, Elizabeth?"

Elizabeth smiles very warmly, looking at Todd directly, and her smile seems to have a very visible effect upon him. "Yes, I would think those are very good thoughts to hold," she states softly, "particularly when one is in need or feels a sense of loneliness. In those instances, the feelings for one's mother and for God seem almost synonymous, don't they?"

Todd is visibly moved by the warmth he feels from Elizabeth. For the first time since Peter and Elizabeth have been with him, his face softens and a hint of radiance comes from his eyes. "Gosh, that is nice to hear! I mean, it's been so long since I've heard anyone say something so nice, Elizabeth. I hope you two will stay here and we can get together and talk some more. I don't really have any friends left here. I don't think like they do any more. They're out having fun, as they call it. But it's a strange thing with these gangs when they have their fights and all that, I saw this one fellow get shot and a few minutes later get up, dust himself off, and walk away, as though he'd never been shot at all. But, well, we're already dead, so, I guess you can't die twice, can you?" and Todd laughs a bit.

It's the first laughter Elizabeth and Peter have heard from him. They join in the laughter with him, hoping to encourage him to lighten up even more and to open himself.

Todd's eyes do become brighter. "Say! Tell me about where you two are from. I mean, you're dead, too, right?"

Smiling very broadly, Peter looks over at Elizabeth "Well, I don't know about that, Todd. I don't feel dead. In fact, I feel more alive now than I've ever felt. And look at Elizabeth, here. Did you ever see anyone in physical body look as radiant and as lovely, as warm and as loving as she does here?"

Elizabeth looks down, obviously taken aback by Peter's compliments, but Todd echoes them, "Oh, yes, she's all that! You, too, Peter. You two must be from somewhere else. Could you tell me about it? I mean, I'm really getting tired of this place. It's become such a heavy thing for me, I feel like I might never leave here. And then there are those guys. They're always trying to drag me into their way of thinking, their fights for power. What are they getting out of it anyway? It's like being on a merry-go-round. You keep reaching for the brass ring, but the guy in front of you always gets to it first or it's always just an inch from your grasp."

There is a pause in the conversation. Todd shifts his weight, leans back against the post again and looks down. "Well, I don't suppose you can help. I guess my lot here is what I've earned or something. You know, like this is my penance or … What do they call that, those Eastern folks down the block? Karma, or something like that. Just a word for *you've sown the seeds, now you've got to reap the harvest*. Well, gosh, it sure is a long harvest," and his foot goes back to toying with the pebbles.

"Listen, Todd, from what I understand, no one needs to remain in any state that doesn't make them joyful."

Todd stops and immediately looks up at Peter. "Are you serious? Are you telling me that I don't have to stay here if I don't want to?"

"Well, yes, Todd. That's what I'm saying to you."

"No offense, Pete, but give me a break, will you? Anyone can see that I don't want to be here. I haven't wanted to be here for so long, I can't remember when it started. And I'm still here. So what are you saying?" again looking down and moving the pebbles with his foot.

Elizabeth glances at Peter and receives a nod. "Well, Todd, I believe what Peter is trying to say to you is that it's what's inside of you that determines whether or not you stay here or go somewhere else. Is that what you meant, Peter?"

"Yes. Todd. I was in a physical body not that long ago. I can't remember when it was, maybe an Earth year or so ago, something like that but it doesn't matter. The bottom line is, I've met a lot of new friends. They're wonderful. And they've shown me things that … Well, I wouldn't have believed them, but I experienced them and now I know them to be true. You can see Elizabeth and me, right?"

Glancing up, Todd nods and looks back down.

"Well, if you see us, it's because we've come here to be with you. But this isn't where we live, and it doesn't have to be where you live, either."

Looking up again, Todd straightens himself, shifting his weight, "Look, Pete … Excuse me for calling you that, but Peter just doesn't fit around this neighborhood, if you know what I mean. Anyway, as I said, I haven't wanted to be here for years, but I am. Right now I'd rather be almost anywhere else than here. But I'm still here."

"Well, that's why Elizabeth and I have come, Todd. That's why we're here. We came to help you get out of this place."

"Really? And how do you plan on doing that?" looking squarely into Peter's eyes.

"To be honest, I've never done anything like this before, and the answer to your question is, I'm not really all that sure."

This causes them all to begin to laugh, and soon, the three of them are laughing so loudly that a number of others scattered up and down the street have turned to look at them.

Noticing this, Todd calms down enough to whisper to Peter and Elizabeth, "We're not used to hearing laughter around here. About the only time you hear it is when some-one's done something to someone else and they're gloating. But laughter like what's just happened with us, the kind that just bubbles over … that's not a common thing here. So we'd better watch ourselves."

"Watch ourselves for what?"

"Well, you know. These aren't the nicest people. I just wouldn't want anything to happen to you. Know what I mean?"

"I understand what you mean, but what could happen? I mean, how can you threaten someone who's already dead? That's pretty funny, don't you think?"

But instead of laughing, Todd looks him in the eye again and answers seriously, "You know, that's really true. I hadn't thought about it that way. Threats that I'm used to around here don't have much meaning, I guess. Like the fellow I mentioned in the gang shootout … got shot, fell down, died, and got up and walked away. I guess a threat doesn't mean very much."

"No, it certainly doesn't," agrees Elizabeth. "And I'd like to share something with you both, from a perspective that you might perceive as feminine. What's missing, Todd, with regard to your question as to how to go about leaving here, has to do with something your mother probably told you about, and that is that you have to have a goal … some sort of ray of light in your life. She probably said something to you like, 'Have something to work towards. Believe in it, and it will come true. If you believe in it and work towards it, it will happen.' Please excuse me for interrupting, but I felt that important."

"So, Todd," Peter continues, "are you ready to get out of this place?"

"Are you joking? Like I said, I've been ready for such a long time."

"Well, I have some friends who can help."

"Friends?" Todd glances over Peter's shoulder and behind Elizabeth. "Where are they?"

"Well, they're here, but you can't see them."

"You're kidding me, right?" Todd chuckles.

"Nope. In fact, Elizabeth and I were here for some time before you saw us."

"Really? Wow! You know, a couple of times, over the time that I've been here, it seemed like I saw several people appear and disappear. You know? I thought it was just my eyes, or maybe something I ate," giving them a wink. "But whatever they were doing or whoever they were, they didn't stay very long."

"Well, Todd, we're here and I'm going to ask for some help for you. But first, I have to know that you really want it."

"I'll take any help I can get to get out of here. Just tell me what it'll cost me."

Peter smiles. "As far as I know, it won't cost you a thing."

"Come on! They don't want anything for helping me out of here?"

"Nope. In fact, they seem to enjoy helping others."

"Well, that would be a big change. Nobody helps anybody around here, unless they're helping themselves, if you know what I mean."

"I think I understand, Todd, but if you are willing, we'll help. Are you?"

"Well, if it's not going to cost me, and I won't owe anybody anything, what have I got to lose, except this place. And that I'd gladly lose!"

"Okay then, we'll have to work through this together, because, like I said, I'm not real familiar with this."

Todd turns to Peter with a puzzled look, "Boy, you are an odd one! You're telling me you came from somewhere else better than this, just to help me? And that you're willing to work to get me out of here but don't know how?"

"Yep, that's true."

"Why? What's in it for you? Nobody does anything around here unless there's something in it for them. It sounds fishy to me. I'll go along with you until I figure out what your angle is because I really want out of here."

"Sure, Todd. That's fine, because I know you won't find any angle, that what I'm doing is what I'm saying, nothing more and nothing less."

"Somehow, I believe you, Pete. And I certainly see in you, Elizabeth, something wonderful that I haven't seen for … Lord knows how long. Let's do it, then."

"A man after my own heart."

A few awkward moments pass, as they stand looking at one another.

"Well?" asks Todd. "What do I do, Pete?"

"Close your eyes."

"No funny business!"

"No funny business," laughs Peter. "Remember, what could I do to you? You're already dead."

"Oh, that's right! Okay, I'm closing my eyes."

"What do you see?"

"Darkness."

"Is that all?"

"Yep, that's it. Just black as black can be. Nothing else."

Peter glances anxiously at Elizabeth, "Gracious, what'll we do next, Elizabeth?"

"I know about this, so I can help with this part." She turns to Todd and states softly, "Todd, think about a very happy time for you."

Todd thinks for only a moment. "Mom, Dad, my brother, Sundays. Sunday dinner after church, the family all together, happy, laughing. That was before all the other stuff happened and my brother was killed in the street fight and my dad got sick and Mother eventually did, too."

"Well, focus on them in the happy part."

"Okay. I'd like to do that. Haven't done it for a while."

As Todd remembers, Peter sees little emanations of light coming from him, and then he can detect the movement of the two spheres of light representing Paul and Zachary as they position themselves behind Todd.

Elizabeth steps forward now and gently touches Todd's shoulder. "Todd?"

"Yes, Elizabeth?"

"Think about the very happiest time you can remember, a time when you were joyful inside. When was that?"

Suddenly, Peter can see it. He *remembers* it along with Todd. It was Todd's mother's birthday. He was about six or seven years old, and he had made his mother a gift. He had made it himself and written words on it in his own hand, and was about to present it to his mother as a gift. "I remember giving my mother a gift,"

Peter is suddenly warmed by his insight and realization. Encouraged by this, he steps forward to be at Elizabeth's side as she continues to question and guide Todd.

"What about that made you feel good, Todd?" she continues.

"It was just so nice to give her something. You know? I guess she had given so much to me and to our family, to everyone. She was such a good person. I guess it was the idea of giving something back. When I gave it to her, I felt like she truly knew how much I loved her."

In that moment it is as though a floodgate has been thrown open. Energies, lights of all colors, vibrations and sounds, pour forth from this one called Todd.

Peter perceives Paul and Zachary swiftly envelop the group, the lamppost, and this little area of this realm in a sort of very large bubble of light, as the emotional energy continues to pour from Todd. His body begins to shake, and he sobs and cries out, all of which continues in varying forms for a considerable measure of Earth time.

Finally, Todd's memories come to a place of rest.

Softly, Peter speaks. "How do you feel in this moment?"

Equally softly, Todd answers, "I feel as though I have unburdened myself somehow. I guess this had been bundled up inside of me. There's no way to share this kind of thought or emotion in this place, and I guess I forced myself to become calloused, and buried these feelings deep inside myself. I feel very good now, Peter. And even though I know that once I open my eyes I'll be back here and things will be as they were, I want to thank you and Elizabeth very much for these few minutes of this joy. It does feel so good."

"Wouldn't you like to continue this feeling?" asks Elizabeth.

"Yes, Todd. Why not continue on with how you feeling right now?"

"Do you really mean that, Peter? Elizabeth? Could I really do that?"

"Yes, you can," Peter answers. "I'm sure of it." Hearing an encouragement from Zachary and Paul, "In fact, if you would like, we'll leave here once and for all, right now."

Todd can resist no longer. In that moment, his eyes burst open and he flings himself upon Peter. "Whatever you want, I'll do it. I want to love and be loved again. I want to share. I want there to be happiness. I don't want to fight anymore. I want to see my mom and dad. And I want to be good, like they were … good people and loving God. That's what I want."

Swoosh! There is a very audible sound. Zachary is visible. And now Paul is visible.

Todd turns, and, seeing Paul, instantly yells out to him, "Mikey! Is it you?"

"Yes, Todd. It's me."

There is a moment here that we are incapable of describing to you. We ask your forgiveness. It is in the recognition between two souls who have shared a bond, a bridge of consciousness and love; and who have now crossed that bridge once again and opened the pathway of love and compassion, that it might flow unobstructed from one to the other. The essence unleashed in the entity Todd is beyond description. It is the spontaneity of joy and hope and fellowship.

Peter and Elizabeth stand in wonder at what is transpiring. Zachary is actively moving around them all.

Suddenly another light appears, which Peter perceives to be Benjamin, and Paul holds Todd at arms length, "Let's leave this place, Todd. Let's go to a place of joy. Come. This is my friend Benjamin. He's come to help you, as well. And this is my friend Zachary, and of course, you already know my dear friends Peter and Elizabeth."

Benjamin repeats, "Yes, let us leave," and he turns, and as a sphere of consciousness, they begin to slowly move.

Todd is shaken a bit at first, and Peter remembers his own experience passing through the colors as Todd is now doing. In that moment, Peter begins to perceive the colors again, first this one, then that, more intense here, less intense there. As the colors have more and more energy or density, Peter and Elizabeth move back, off to the side, and he observes Paul and Todd moving exactly as he and Paul had moved not that long before. Leading them is a brilliant light he knows to be Benjamin. At his side yet is Elizabeth, and on his other side now is Zachary.

As he looks upon himself, he realizes he has returned to that sphere of light in which he arrived, as have Zachary and Elizabeth. "Goodness, what an experience that was. That was our commission?"

"Right-o, Pete. That was it."

"We succeeded, then?"

"Top of the mark, Pete. Couldn't have done better if you had been an old-timer at it. In fact, I've never seen anyone do a better job than you and Elizabeth did for Todd. You can feel joyful at having completed your commission with perfection. You've done well. I'm certain that in the Hall of Wisdom this will be repeated to you many times over. But now, it's time for us to move to where we might re-balance and have a bit of a rest to allow our consciousness to digest this experience, and to arrive at a state of even higher balance.

"You see, each experience that you have moves you just a bit. If you'd look back at your experiences, as you remember them, each one lifted you up a notch or two, in a manner of speaking, higher in your level of spiritual acceptance. So, when we enter into a state of spiritual rest, as we've come to call it light-heartedly, we have really moved into a state of existence that we call prayer, or oneness with God. And not to get too *heavy* for you at the moment (in your Earthly vernacular) but to be explicit, all of this that you have performed here in this work has been through something that we identify as grace. That grace comes from God, and that grace is within you, and Elizabeth, and me, Todd, Paul, Benjamin, and all the rest. But what you and Elizabeth did here in this work was to help Todd find it again. See? A nice tidy job. Paul and Benjamin will carry on from there. See?"

Zachary moves to the forefront of the trio. Elizabeth and Peter move side-by-side, and Peter extends a *hand of consciousness*, so to say, to her, which she joyfully accepts.

Zachary then states softly, "Here we go, folks. Hang on."

They begin to move, and Peter once again perceives the incredible depth and breadth of wherever it is they are, and he feels the succession of passage, through what he can best define as strata, or little areas of altered energy. These are felt and sensed by him as a subtle pop, as though he is popping through some sort of membrane-like substance, which somehow he knows has the effect of preservation. Almost instantaneously, they find themselves before the patio area, and back in the forms known as Zachary, Elizabeth, and Peter.

What you have experienced here has been the freeing of a soul from a realm of consciousness of his own choice. The soul accepted that opportunity, and this has been a successful commission.

Until we meet next, know that our prayers are ever with thee, just as we would ask that your prayers would now be with Todd and Paul and Benjamin.

CHAPTER 3

Multiple Expressions
MAY 12, 1991

As we return to the point at which we previously departed, resuming the commentary as we observe the activities, it should be noted that, to some extent, we are turning backward to do this, for much has progressed here in the movement of Earth time as you measure it.

Zachary is seated before the table in what has come to be known as the inner arbor of the patio area. Outside of the arbor, Wilbur and Rebecca are moving to rejoin the group, which has only recently returned from its appointed commission.

Across from Zachary at the table Peter and Elizabeth are seated. Peter is intently asking her about several of the aspects of their commission, namely, how she moved into Todd's realm and was able to draw him in as well.

"It's not so much that I actually did anything, Peter, but that I simply made it understandable for you to express yourself in a form of your choice. As I went first, this made the image acceptable to you and, therefore, your subsequent movement to join me in that expression or form was thereafter merely one of acceptance. Is that clear to you?"

"I can grasp it. It's fascinating. How many times I sat in my office figuring, calculating, trying to reach certain goals. And then you come along and simply state you're going to do thus and such, and in a moment's passage not only did you do what you said you were going to do, which seemed at the time to me to be incredible, but somehow or other, you enabled me to accomplish it, as well."

"Not much different than your butterfly, Peter. Remember? Same principle, just a different work or goal," offers Zachary softly.

Peter turns to Zachary. "Well, I understand that, but what's missing in my mind are the mechanics of the activity. For example," he turns to cast a glance around the lovely little arbor in which they are positioned, "take that bench over there by the bushes. Suppose I say to you that I want to be a bench. Okay, I know that's absurd, but in some respects, were I to try to explain to someone what we just did, it would sound just as absurd.

"What I'm driving at here is, what are the limitations of this sort of thing? If I wanted to be a bench, which I don't, of course, but if I did, is that possible, too? You know, what's the difference between the extremes? A sphere of light or a stone bench are both objects. I understand that the light is, well, I'm not sure what to call it here … living, as opposed to the bench being what we would think of in the Earth as an inanimate object. Do you get my drift?"

Elizabeth is looking down, nodding and smiling, and Zachary has leaned over, propped his head on his hand with his elbow resting on the table. "Pete, who could miss, with a graphic depiction like that one? We've got the picture all right. Now, *would* you like to become that bench over there?"

"Wait a minute, Zack. Don't play around here. I might get stuck in the thing."

All laugh loudly at this, and at that moment Wilbur and Rebecca stroll into the arbor. They are greeted warmly, seat themselves at the table, and after a discussion about the commission and such, they return to the topic.

Zachary explains, "Wilbur, Rebecca, we were talking about extremes of expression. Peter had quite an experience with expressing himself in a non-physical form."

Peter glances at Wilbur and Rebecca to see if they understand, and is a bit surprised to see them both nodding and smiling. Unable to contain himself, Peter asks, "You're nodding. Does that mean you know what we did? I mean, do you understand what Zachary's talking about here?"

Rebecca and Wilbur exchange a smile with each other, and Wilbur turns back to Peter. "Yes, Peter, we were afforded the opportunity of observing some portions of the commission. Benjamin returned here and enabled us to link up and see, sort of like we do often in the Crystal Workers' Realm. So we were with you to an extent, certainly in spirit, and in the perspective of knowing what transpired."

"Incredible! It's one thing to have someone in the Hall of Wisdom tell me about something I did that was observed by that one somehow, but golly, Wilbur, Rebecca, I think of you as friends."

Peter receives a warm nod, indicating from both of them that they consider themselves the same, and continues on, "Well, I think you know what I'm trying to say here. There are so many things that escape me. I know how they can be done to a degree, for you have all helped me to see this."

"Excuse me a moment, Peter, if I might," Wilbur interjects. "It is you, as well, who has afforded me a great deal of insight and growth recently, in the event that you forgot."

Somewhat flustered to be reminded, Peter straightens himself. "Uh, well, yes, uh …" and glances over at Zachary.

Zachary has turned away from the group trying to contain his humor and, as his eyes catch Peter's, he gives Peter his traditional wink, which makes Peter more comfortable and balanced.

"Uh, thanks, Wilbur. I appreciate and respect your comments, but remember, I never made any statements implying that I was any more knowledgeable. I only shared some of my own experiences."

"Well, that's all it's about, Pete," offers Zachary, "shared experiences."

"Explain yourself, please, Zack."

"Okay. If you gain an insight, an understanding, it's like having a little bit of light in a pot. If you take some of that light out of that pot and you give it to another, then that light doubles. And if they in turn give some to another, and those to another, and those to still others, and so forth, where do you suppose that light of experience that you gained will end up? Why, you could illuminate a whole realm with just that one good intent. Get my meaning?"

"I think so. But let me come back to the issue here, for this is one point I seem to keep stumbling over. We were talking about the bench."

"The offer still stands. If you'd like to become that bench over there, I'll show you how," with a note of humor in his voice.

"You keep telling me that, Zack, and I keep saying I don't want to be a bench. I was only using it as an analogy."

Straightening himself and placing his hands and arms on the table, Zachary looks directly across at Peter, eye-to-eye. "I'm doing the same. I'm returning your analogy with an offer that is completely valid. It may seem humorous to you, and I admit to being a little tickled at your reaction to it, but that's the example that I'm trying to point out to you here. Why would you think it impossible or unlikely, if you'll forgive me a rather humorous possibility, that you could become trapped and forevermore a bench?"

After a bit of laughter from the entire group, Peter continues, "Okay, Zack. I am beginning to get the impression here that you are helping me make some significant discovery, and I admit to being humored at all this. So, let's spare everyone your usual procedure of leading me and, if you could, please just give me the discovery."

All eyes turn to Zachary. "Okay, Pete. Here it is. I'll lay it right out on the table. This table. Look here. See this table we are seated around?" He pauses and looks up at Peter as he puts his hand on the table in the center.

"Yes, I see the table."

"Well, how do you suppose this table exists here? Do you suppose someone manufactured it in St. Louis, and then some sort of celestial trucking company delivered it here?"

The humor echoes inside the arbor, and many entities outside the arbor turn to smile, as though they too are sharing in the joy of this little discovery adventure of Peter's.

Peter himself is swept up by the humor and laughs the loudest of all. "That's a good one, Zack. I guess I hadn't thought of the details too much. How, in fact, did this table get here, barring the possibility of a St. Louis manufacturing company and celestial trucking lines?"

"Excellent question. Thought you'd never ask."

The others are containing themselves.

"Peter, I told you, and the others told you as well, and you've been shown, that all things that exist anywhere, whether in the Earth, here, or any of the other realms …Todd's, the Crystal Workers', the Garden, they all exist because of the agreement between the souls there. So, if we follow that thought down to a finite point, if what I'm telling you is true, then we are all agreeing that this table exists and therefore it does."

"Okay, go slowly from this point on, Zack. If we all agree, then it exists. Suppose for a moment I disagreed and I didn't like the table. What then?"

"Well, that's a rather tricky question to answer. Let's say for a moment our group creates a sort of mini-realm within a realm, and that we consider this arbor here to be a realm within this greater realm. Agreed?"

They all silently nod, as they look from one to the other.

"Okay, now, just for a moment, think of ourselves being isolated, perhaps encapsulated in a large sphere of light. Remember the sphere of light I kept around the group in Todd's realm?"

"Yes, I do! I was impressed at that, and I'd like to know how you did that."

They all chuckle as Zachary nods and glances at each of them, as though to say, *Questions, questions!* "Okay, but one thing at a time. Maybe this will help you. We have our mini-realm, which is the arbor here. All of us in this realm have to agree in order for existence to manifest itself. Is that acceptable to you all?"

They all nod in approval.

"Now, then, Pete, you were saying that you didn't like the design of this table. It was too clumsily made and didn't please you entirely. Was that correct?"

"Uh, okay … as an example. But I don't actually feel that way."

"Well, you have to do better than that, Pete. You have to *not agree*."

"Okay. Not agree. Let's see, now…" There's a pause, and then, "How do I *not agree*?"

"Think of something perhaps better than this table. I don't know. It's you that doesn't like the thing. We all liked it fine until you brought it up."

This humors the group tremendously, and the outpouring of laughter is melodious, completely accompanied by color, sound, and light.

"Okay, I get what you're driving at. I would rather this table be hexagonal, and I think I would like it much more if it were a swirling mixture of beautiful blues and whites and …"

Before Peter can finish his statement, to his amazement, the table vibrates a split-second and it is as he described it. "Wow! That's incredible! How'd you do that?"

Holding his hands up so as to not touch the table, Zachary feigns amazement. "I was about to ask you. Nice trick. How'd you do that?"

"Seriously, Zack. How did that happen?"

Shifting himself and bringing his arms back down to rest, Zachary glances quickly up at Peter, "Don't mind if I rest on it, do you?"

Smiling broadly, Peter shakes his head without speaking.

"Good. So, in our little mini-realm, we all agree and, therefore, existence is in accordance with our agreement. When you said you didn't like the table as it was, that was a negative. When you stated that you had something you liked better, that was a positive. Then, all it required was agreement by our group, which you silently had, and the improvement is here as you see it," rubbing his hands over the table.

Wilbur is somewhat amazed, though not completely. "If I might interrupt here, that was the fastest response I've ever seen. I mean, in the Crystal Workers' Realm, we've done things like this, not just like this, mind you, but similar. But I've never seen it accomplished so quickly." He glances from Zachary back over to Peter, obviously somewhat awed by this demonstration.

"Now, wait a minute, Wilbur. Don't assign too much of this accomplishment to me. You were sitting right there the whole time. You know what transpired. I was only baited by Zachary over there," giving Zachary an exaggerated wink, imitating him and smiling broadly.

Zachary shakes his head. "Not really, Pete. You actually did the whole thing. All we did was make the way passable for you. We identified the mechanism and convinced you that it was possible, and then you created. And the creation, I must admit, is lovely. Therefore, because it is accepted by all of us here, it will remain. And it will be, no doubt, a source of admiration for others who will come. See?"

"Okay, then, let's move away from finite objects for a moment," Peter continues, "let's talk again about the experience in Todd's realm. When Elizabeth moved into a form from the sphere of light, I noticed a sort of ribbon of light that connected the sphere that was previously her to the expression or physical-like form that became her, if you follow my rather confusing dissertation."

Zachary gently nods for Peter to continue.

"Well, shortly after that, I found myself drawn to her side. There I was in a form like hers, sort of physical-like. And when I looked back, I had the same ribbony shaft of light connecting me to the sphere of light that *I* was previously. Now, here's the question …"

"Oh, good," teases Zack, "thought you'd never get to it."

All smile, and Peter continues, "So there we were, Elizabeth and I, standing (in essence) in Todd's realm. And sort of hovering in mid-air a few yards away from us were Elizabeth and I as the forms of light. Now, that's two of us, to my mind. In other words, I was Peter in Todd's realm *and* Peter as the sphere of light in Todd's realm."

"That's true. Go on."

"I have nothing more to *go on* with. What I'm asking is, how can that be? Do I have the potential, do all of us have the potential, to express ourselves in multiple forms?"

There is a long pause, as Wilbur looks at Zachary and Rebecca and then across the table to Peter and Elizabeth. "If I might interject, Peter, it might be good for you to visit our Crystal Workers' Realm some time and actually participate in some of our works. We do things somewhat similar to this, and I think you'd find them revealing and, I hope, inspiring, as you see some of the very wonderful works done by many of the dedicated souls working there."

Peter looks over at Wilbur. "I would like to do that, Wilbur. I have always wondered exactly what it was you did there. I can't quite grasp the concept of crystal-working, or whatever it is, and I would, at some point, appreciate being able to observe this to grasp the concept to a greater degree."

"Is that something you want to do now, Pete?" asks Zachary, looking at Peter, serious and inquiring.

"Well, uh … I don't know. I hadn't really given it any

thought, Zachary. I do if it's appropriate, and if it suits the work before us. By the way, what do we do now? Will there be more commissions? Where is Todd? And what about Paul and Benjamin? And ..."

Interrupting, Zachary laughs, "There he goes again. Question after question. Incredible, isn't he? A delight. Let me pause you for a moment here, Pete, and address your first question. Yes, you can express yourself (as you called it) in multiple forms. And beyond that, you can express yourself in multiple forms in multiple realms. How's that one?"

Peter stares at Zachary, becoming very serious. "Express myself in multiple forms in multiple realms? You mean I could be expressed in Todd's realm and here at the same time?"

"Quite so, Pete. In fact, that's precisely what you did just a while back, during the commission."

"Wait a minute. I don't understand this at all. I was expressed as a sphere of light and also at the same time as Peter in Todd's realm. Are you saying that I was also here?"

"That's it. That's what I'm saying. Remarkable, isn't it?" smiling broadly and winking deliberately back at Peter.

"I've got to chew on that one for quite a while, Zachary. Maybe it would be a good idea to accept Wilbur's offer to go back to the Crystal Workers' Realm after all. Sounds like that would be a good break from what my mind is groping with."

"Good, idea. In fact, it should provide you with additional insight to the digestive problem your mind is having at this point. But to be utterly explicit, it's not your mind that's digesting it. It's your consciousness. In order to have a *mind* you'd have to have a head to put it in. Right? And remember what you told Todd? You are not in a physical body. What you have is the semblance of one. Oh, it's every bit as real. In fact, in some regards, it's probably moreso. You have, within that total consciousness, an agreement that consciousness may be, for each of us, at varying degrees or levels of awakened-ness (if that's a word) or awareness (if that's a better one). Understand?" Zachary leans over on his elbow again to peer directly at Peter.

"I can grasp it. I don't have a problem grasping ideas and concepts. In fact, I was always fairly adept at that in the Earth."

"We know."

"I don't say that in any form of bragging. It just was something that came naturally to me."

"We know that, too."

"What I'm trying to say here is …"

"You're saying it quite well, Peter. Don't justify or try to defend it. All of us here, with the exception, perhaps, of Wilbur, who doesn't know you quite as well as the rest of us, know those qualities about you. I suspect that Wilbur knows this pretty well about you, too, don't you, Wilbur?"

"Oh, yes, I can see that quality in Peter very clearly, and I do admire him for it."

Again somewhat embarrassed and awkward at the focus upon him, Peter returns to his series of comments. "Let me see if I can get a handle on this business of expressing myself in multiple forms in multiple realms. For example, I didn't know that when I was expressed here in this," and he sweeps his hand to demonstrate where he's pointing, "arbor place, that I was here at the same time I was in Todd's realm."

There is a pause as Zachary studies Peter. "How do you know you didn't know?"

"Well, now, that's absurd, Zack, if you'll forgive me. If I knew, I would know. And I don't know, so therefore I didn't know. Or was it that I didn't knew or know?"

They all burst into laughter.

"Look here, Pete, knowing is something that is very, very dependent upon having a need to know. In other words, if you were to use some of your wondrous curiosity and had the need to know what was transpiring here while you were in

Todd's realm, you could have known in the twinkling of an eye, as they say. But you were focused intensely in Todd's realm, and therefore you lost sight of the fact that you were also expressed here. For that matter, Pete, even as we speak, you are still expressed in the Garden."

"You're kidding!"

"No, I'm not kidding. I'm completely serious."

There is silence as Peter's eyes search Zachary, trying to determine where this is all heading. And Zachary returns Peter's searching gaze with nothing but warmth, obviously hiding nothing and trying to reveal everything.

"Well, prove it."

"Goodness, Peter. You sound just like Todd." And they all start laughing again. "Okay, I'll prove it to you. Or perhaps better stated, I'll help you to prove it to yourself. Okay?"

"Agreed."

"Close your eyes for a moment and picture, in your consciousness, the Garden."

Peter closes his eyes, and the others close theirs, as well.

As the arbor begins to fade from Peter's consciousness, he searches his memory of the Garden. Instantly, the little knoll there, one of his favorite places, floods his consciousness. There is a little audible sound and a feeling of some movement, and Peter opens his eyes.

In utter amazement, his mouth drops open as he looks around.

Zachary is over to his left. Rebecca and Wilbur are straightening themselves, having assumed a seated position on the ground, and as he glances to his right, he looks into the eyes of Elizabeth, who has found a comfortable position seated to his right between him and Zachary.

Zachary, reclined in his traditional position, head resting upon one hand that is propped up on the elbow, smiles broadly. "See? You've been here all the time. Perhaps you were only dreaming, Peter. Perhaps the arbor is nothing but a dream. Perhaps the realm in which Todd existed is also nothing but a dream."

Still in amazement, Peter struggles to express himself. All the while, his cloak is popping and snapping. He can feel a rush of calm and warmth, and looks to see Elizabeth's hand resting on his shoulder. "Thank you, Elizabeth," he states softly. "I'm having a bit of a time with this, as you can see."

She simply smiles and nods to affirm she knows this, removing her hand as she does.

"Zachary, you are saying things to me that I am having a great deal of trouble processing in my… I'll call it, consciousness, since I am mindless."

They all laugh uproariously, and for some time, sounds cascade and bounce about, and colors twinkle and sparkle.

"Wow, talk about honesty, Pete! You take the cake. But you're not mindless in the sense of having no knowledge. You are simply mindless because minds are in physical bodies. Consciousness is unlimited. Get the meaning? And I didn't mean to bait you. You're not dreaming, in the sense of that word's meaning in the Earth. This is all very real. Todd's realm is real. The inner arbor is real. The Crystal Workers' Realm is real. And, in fact, yes, last but not least, the Earth is real. But reality depends on the participants. That's all I'm trying to tell you. Where you have a need or a desire, you create. Remember the butterfly?

"So, what I'm encouraging you to do is to reduce the tendency of thinking in limited terms. Now, if you like, we can close our eyes and go back to the inner arbor, and I can assure you that the same thing will happen as just transpired. A few moments after your eyes are closed and you open them, we'll be right back there, again. If you'd like, we can do the same thing to almost anywhere, providing we would be in accordance with Universal Law as we did that."

In wonder, Peter studies Zachary for a while. Then, "Not to change the subject, Zack, but that Universal Law you talk about … I need to know more about that, too."

"Indeed you do, and indeed you shall, Peter. But we have an invitation before us, and it doesn't seem polite to simply ignore it. What do you think?"

Peter remembers then that Wilbur's invitation is still standing, and Wilbur is beaming at the opportunity of returning to his beloved Crystal Workers' Realm. "Well, Wilbur, if it wouldn't be an imposition, I …"

"Oh, not at all, Pete!" Wilbur blurts out, "I have so many things I'd like to share with my colleagues there. Rebecca and I learned so much during your commission and in observing the stream of light in that other realm. I talked to many of the entities there and they showed me so much of their consciousness and how to use it. I would feel it a blessing if I could share this knowledge with my colleagues. Perhaps they could do better works as the result. So, if …"

Zachary interrupts gently, smiling, "Wilbur, you've been hanging around Peter too long. You're beginning to sound like him. One question at a time, please."

All smile at Wilbur, who now knows what it is like to be singled out, and he looks down, a bit embarrassed.

Peter comes to his rescue, feeling a sense of camaraderie since he had just experienced the same spotlight of attention. "Don't worry, Wilbur. Zachary doesn't mean anything by it. It's just his way," looking over and winking at Zachary.

"Goodness, Peter," Zachery responds. "I think you're beginning to sound like Paul and me now. Hmm, I'll have to study that. Anyway, Wilbur, we'd be delighted to accompany you, wouldn't we, Pete? Elizabeth, Rebecca, is that acceptable?"

They both smile warmly and nod, and Peter answers, "Yes, let's go. I'm always ready for an adventure."

The four of them stand and begin to move down the path and to Wilbur's realm in the method that has become traditional, but turning to check on Zachary, they see that he hasn't moved.

He calls out to them, "We won't learn anything that way. If you would, come back here, and we'll go to Wilbur's realm taking the shortcut."

They look at one another and reassemble, awkwardly shifting about until they are standing in a circle.

Zachary continues, "Now, as you just did, Peter. Only this time, Wilbur, since it's a realm uniquely special to you, would you create that image for us?"

Wilbur nods, "I would be most honored."

Following Zachary's lead, they all place their arms upon one another's shoulder, linking themselves in a circle.

Peter studies Wilbur's face, and looks around the group, noting that each has closed their eyes except for Zachary who is looking directly at Peter, eyes wide open.

Inside of his consciousness, Peter hears Zachary saying, *Eyes open, eyes closed, it makes no difference. Your choice. Shall we keep them open, then, and see what happens?*

Startled by this inner communication, Peter thinks within his consciousness, *Yes, let's do. That sounds interesting. Won't it bother the others?*

Nope, not in the least. Has nothing to do with the procedure, except that it helps one learn these things. Once they're learned, it's not needed any more. Actually, clinging to them is a limitation. Use your tools as long as they're productive, but when you find a better way or a more productive method, why not replace the old with the new? Understand that?

Yes, surprisingly, I do. What happens next?

Well, let's stop communicating and just observe.

Right, Zack.

Again, Peter looks about from member to member of the group. Zachary is casually looking at him, and then he looks over to Wilbur, so Peter's eyes follow Zachary's. As he watches Wilbur, he notes that from what seems to be the top of Wilbur's form, a light begins to grow. As it does, Peter can perceive in it, as though he is looking into some sort of TV screen, the image of the Crystal Workers' Realm. This rather spherical blob of light, as Peter thinks of it, continues to grow and eventually surrounds them, and the image of the Crystal Workers' Realm becomes all-encompassing.

In an instant, there is that subtle audible sound again of the pop, and Peter realizes that they are standing before the great structure of the Crystal Workers' Realm.

There, at the entrance of the structure, Peter sees the radiant, smiling face of David.

He notes that the others are removing their arms from his shoulders, and he does the same. Wilbur waves excitedly at David and moves swiftly off the little rise just outside the door to greet David.

Peter can hear David inquire of Wilbur, as he places his hands on Wilbur's shoulders and looks him in the eyes, "Did you have a good adventure, a good outing, with our friends?"

"Yes, indeed, David! The things I've learned, the things I saw! The work that Peter and Elizabeth and Zachary and Paul and Benjamin did with their commission was beautiful to behold. And I have some information I believe will be very helpful to my co-workers here. And Peter," turning to gesture to Peter, "would like to learn more about our work here. Would this be permissible?"

Zachary is chuckling to himself, almost as though muttering, *Just like Pete. Getting to be exactly like him. Incredible. Words and words, questions and questions. Wonderful.*

Peter smiles at Zachary, having perceived that observation. Elizabeth and Rebecca are also smiling, and Peter realizes that they, too, have been conscious of these loving inner thoughts.

All now move down to the entry, each greeting David. He inquires in depth of Peter about the commission, congratulates Peter and Elizabeth on a job well done, and invites them all to enter into the Crystal Workers' Hall.

As they enter, Peter notices that the realm seems to be considerably brighter than he remembered it. Looking around, he notes with interest that there appear to be many more very large and very beautiful crystals gathered around what is definable here as the north wall. The crystal workers themselves are generally aligned along the south wall, with some towards the west end, while the group has entered through what could be thought of as the east entry.

At this point, Peter sees a familiar face at the opposite end of the Hall, and waving to him is Paul. Peter cannot contain himself. He rushes through the group to grasp Paul, giving him what looks similar to a bear hug, and Paul is smiling broadly and laughing.

As the group moves over to join them, Peter is asking, "How are you? And where is Todd? Is he doing well?"

Paul, quite accustomed to Peter's continual flow of questions, smiles with incredible warmth, and Peter notices that Paul seems different somehow. So much so that he comments, "Paul, you look different. You look more radiant, much more vibrant, than I remember you. And it hasn't been that long, has it?"

Paul shakes his head gently. "No, it has not been a great deal of time. And perhaps I am lighter and brighter, but then so are you, as are Elizabeth, Rebecca, Wilbur, Zachary, David, Benjamin, and the entirety of the Crystal Workers Realm, as are other realms. Pausing, Paul waits for Peter to speak, knowing from past experience that he will in very short order.

"Well, why is that? I mean, what is the reason for that, if you can explain it to me?"

"I would be pleased to explain it to you since the reason is largely due to the success of your commission."

Peter demonstrates his shock, and his cloak sparkles and snaps, as he is taken aback greatly by the implication that that work could have an impact of such a magnitude. It is only after Zachary and Elizabeth have assumed positions to his right and left that Peter's cloak begins to rebalance itself and shift to what is now simply a very luminous state.

"Are you saying to me, Paul, that because of that commission, all of these people, all of us, that we've all somehow or other become brighter?"

Incredible love and warmth flows from Paul's eyes, as he softly answers, "That is precisely what I am saying, and it is, in fact, a truth."

Peter cannot contain himself, even with the presence of Zachary, whose power is well known, and with Elizabeth, whose depth of love and compassion is unexcelled in the presence of this Hall. They are barely able to keep Peter expressed in this finite form. He begins to shift and flow, looking more in this moment as a great sphere of light, the colors upon the outer periphery swirling in brilliant patches, as though each color is moving about the sphere striving to orient itself, striving to blend with the other colors. The activity is so electrifying that the Hall is illuminated, and all therein pause in their works to watch this activity.

Slowly, very slowly, Peter begins to resume his balance. Zachary and Elizabeth have turned to face him full on. Elizabeth, Zachary, Paul, and David each assume a cardinal position around Peter. The color around him flows and begins to subside, blending into oneness, taking on the radiance of a golden-white orb, the beauty of which is beyond description. Within it now Peter can be seen clearly, transforming, slowly changing, becoming less of Peter and more of the light.

The situation reaches a point of some stability where no change appears to be taking place, and Peter seems to be suspended within this great sphere of golden-white light.

Now, behind Paul a movement is growing and shaping, which captures Peter's attention. A beautiful shaft of light has focused itself off behind Paul, and there is the expression of the entity from the Hall of Wisdom who had so awed Peter!

The entity comes forward in his form, and as he does, Paul turns to greet him.

Then Paul steps back and the entity comes forward from behind Elizabeth and shifts his position to be directly in front of Peter.

With no visible effort, the entity, who stands in wondrous raiment of incredible silvery blue and white light, reaches what looks like a hand into Peter's orb of light and touches him. There is a perceptible sound, and the light of the entity from the Hall of Wisdom moves into and around Peter.

As it does, Peter's cloak changes, and now beautifully bears many of the same colors as the wondrous entity from the Hall of Wisdom.

The entity smiles at Peter and, without a word, turns to Paul, speaking softly, "Well done."

Turning to Peter again, he smiles and nods, and then moves back to the spot where the light was focused. The light reappears and the entity is gone.

Peter stands in a form recognizable as Peter, expressed as Peter, but different. His cloak is beautiful, like flowing music swirling around him, incredibly clear and rid of errant colors. There is a beautiful luminous sheen to it of blue-white, very similar to the entity from the Great Hall.

Peter remains motionless, unable to speak, stunned.

The incredible beauty of the event that has transpired has touched everyone in the room.

Peter begins to hear, very softly at first and difficult for him to believe, what he perceives as applause. He looks to see that all of the crystal workers are now standing and that they are, indeed, applauding.

Then, each one, one here and then another over there, activates their respective crystals, which Peter knows are placed across the room along the north wall. They begin to vibrate, as their individual tonal qualities are called to life, each in symphony with the next and then the others. The energy cascades down along the wall, until every single crystal is radiating light and color and emanating resplendent musical chords.

Each of the workers leaves their position and comes to gather around Peter, Paul, and Zachary, Elizabeth, Rebecca, David, and Wilbur.

Peter does not understand what is transpiring, but he knows he is different. He can feel it. And he sees differently. As he looks at each of these entities whose hands outstretch to him in a gesture of congratulation, of love, warmth, and respect, he feels himself reciprocating. As he does, he knows that he has the right to return it. Something has been given to him that he cannot comprehend. Yet he knows it, and knows it to be good. The wondrous entity from the Great Hall of Wisdom has given him a blessing, a gift so wondrous that it has illuminated not only him but all who perceive him.

Still glowing brilliantly, and with the passage of some time, Peter turns back to Zachary and Paul, who have quietly come to his side, as has Elizabeth to his other side and who is now also strangely glowing in a manner he detects is similar to his own glow.

Wilbur and Rebecca too have changed. Wilbur smiles and motions that he is going to join his colleagues. Peter simply nods, knowing that Wilbur has much to convey to them, that there is significance in his sharing that information, and that their work might be enhanced, as well.

Peter turns in another direction and becomes aware of David. As their eyes meet, David bows gently to Peter, and Peter feels something from David that he never knew before. He understands that David now sees him, Peter, as accomplished. And he, himself, knows intuitively that he has, for reasons not yet fully known to him, advanced.

He feels a nudge, a touch, on each side of him, and sees the smaller group, Zachary, Rebecca, David and Elizabeth, urging him gently towards the entry of the Crystal Workers' Hall. The other entities are now busily about other activities here in the Great Hall. Peter allows himself to be more or less led towards the entry.

As they pass by the vast array of crystals aligned along the north wall, each reflects back to the group a collage of color, sound, and light, as though they themselves are an energy activating the crystals.

To move beyond the Crystal Workers' Realm, it is Zachary who creates an image this time, and all being in agreement, they move into the familiar Realm of Laughter, whereupon they come together, join arms, and form a group of joy and laughter.

Zachary speaks, bringing great relief to Peter as he does. "Quite a day's work, Pete! We need to lighten up this group just a bit. Let me tell you this funny story," and he embarks on a tale that inspires Peter to laugh. As the others join in, the laughter echoes all throughout this existence, and our group becomes one great sphere of laughter and good cheer as they spiral off into the distance, cascading light, color, sound, music, and so much more.

———————————

Much time is spent here, intended for the sole purpose of rebalancing and reorienting Peter.

Hereafter, the Peter we have known, the Peter with whom we have shared these experiences, will no longer be the same. Lest you feel in any wise a sense of loss or diminishment, or lest you feel that some great work will no longer be offered to you, do allay those thoughts. For what lies beyond is of more wonder, perhaps, than all of the experiences you have known to the present.

To further reveal the import of this most recent experience, what has been awakened within Peter is what we refer to as the Christ Consciousness. And the hand that touched Peter was that of the Master, the Christ. To the extent that you can grasp this, and to the extent that you can understand how this could be, then know that this opportunity is ever present for each of you, no matter where you might dwell or how you might be expressed.

What has predicated this? For what work has Peter received this blessing, this awakening? Some of you will consider that it is certainly his work with Todd. And perhaps that is so, to a degree. Others of you will argue that, no, it is Peter's willingness, his openness, the utter truth and honesty of his being. And to a degree, that is also true. But there is something much more than this that is yet to be seen and known. That shall be brought forth to you in times ahead, for we shall continue to participate with these of our friends in these realms.

For the present, know that it is our prayer that each of you shall find this same joy and a heart willing to contribute, as have Peter and his comrades, to an entity in need such as Todd.

CHAPTER 4
Formlessness
MAY 21, 1991

Preparatory to this work just ahead: If ever you have a moment of challenge or doubt, remember that in these same moments there will always be an equal opportunity for wondrous growth and illumination, illumination meaning, quite simply, the reawakening of an unlimited awareness within your own being. As the events transpire, we encourage you to hold a small portion of your thought attuned to what we have just stated.

Peter and colleagues have come to a point of rest, having paused in their movement through what you would consider to be time and space. In this state of restfulness, Peter's energies have become steadied. For the most part he is identifiable as the "Peter" of earlier times, except that he now has a beautiful light that radiates back to the observer, as though it is reflected from something within him.

An orb of light is visibly discernible around each present, and Peter's is very bright, equaled only by Elizabeth's. This is not to imply that she and Peter are spiritually elevated beyond the others. It is merely their current state of oscillation or energy or vibration. Present company includes David, who has joined the group.

Peter stirs and looks from one to the other receiving a warm reciprocation which is measurable from each. All eyes are now focused upon him, and while each is smiling, nonetheless, a note of some seriousness is clearly distinguishable from the earlier activities.

In a moment of awkwardness, due to the focus of the others on him, Peter attempts to break the concentration of attention on him with a bit of humor, albeit awkwardly. "Well, then, Zack, where's it go from here? I mean, what's next? It seems like each event I'm led into becomes more incredible than the previous. Sort of like building a series of steps, and when you reach the current step that seems to be it, yet right after that comes yet another step, and so it goes, on and on and on. Is that correct? Does it go on and on? Or have I reached what I could think of as the peak of the mountain? You know, sort of like the ultimate goal?"

Smiling broadly, obviously quelling an urge to remark about Peter's long, drawn-out question, Zachary responds with remarkable control, "It's the peak, Pete. The very top."

Now all eyes are focused on Zachary, and several of the group have lost their broad smile and are looking at him with a note of seriousness. Only after his typical exaggerated wink gives them the indication that there is more to come behind that statement do they relax.

"Really? You mean this is it?"

"Sure, Pete, that is, of course, unless you'd care to go further. You know what they say, climb one mountain and behind it is another, and behind that another and another. This could be called the pinnacle of a mountain, but there is, to be sure, a greater mountain ahead, or more appropriately, higher levels of consciousness."

After a pause, Peter asks, "Can you tell me about what lies ahead beyond this? Or do I stay in this state for a time? Or, well, how's it work from here?"

Zachary is smiling and still obviously holding back. "It's quite up to you at this point, Pete. You've earned a period of rest, or perhaps balance is more accurate. So it's truly up to you. You decide and let us know your choice."

The humor being contained within Zachary is now becoming evident. There are swirls of color and emotion that Peter can intuit, since he knows his friend very well now, indicative of something afoot. Something is definitely going on here.

With a visible radiance, David interjects, "Peter, if I might, it is as Zachary has explained. Much of what occurs from this point forward is utterly dependent upon you." Turning to Rebecca and Elizabeth, "Don't you agree?"

Looking from one to the other, they both nod, and Elizabeth speaks. "Peter, it's not that we are leaving you hanging, or in a situation which is intentionally without direction. It's rather that the situation is now one that you have earned. As the result of your works and your related growth, you can have a time of rest. And by rest, we are referring to a time of self-exploration, rebalancing, a time to become accustomed to your new consciousness."

The luminosity around Peter becomes excited just a bit, indicating that he has turned inward to reflect, and he pauses for a few moments. "As you all know, I am not given to long periods of idleness, and for some reason unknown to me, not consciously at least, I feel motivated to continue, to seek and to determine as much as I can about who and what I am. It comes back to me at times in great waves of, well, reality, I guess I could call it, that I'm, uh, dead. Yet, here I am. I haven't forgotten the life I left not that long ago and those who were in it with me, and those who have left that life as I have and gone on to other realms.

"So, if it's all the same to you all, I would just as soon have more experiences, if that's acceptable, and continue with whatever lies before me. And speaking of what lies before me, Zachary, how many levels are there, anyway? And how many times are you going to lead me through some event that each time I get some discovery or go through some trauma, and have some sort of … "

Laughter erupts from Zachary, as he has endured beyond his limit of controlling his humor. Widely noted for his good cheer and humor, he is rarely in a situation where he has not injected humor. "That's it. That's what I was looking for, the old Peter, still there in spite of all that light."

Joy burst forth from the entire group, spontaneously creating the familiar color, sound, and light, and off they go, spinning, until after a time they come to rest again.

Here, they converse at considerable in length, reviewing the events that have transpired to date, with Peter and Zachary having the usual exchanges of tit-for-tat type, and finally their conversation arrives at this point, where Elizabeth raises a possibility. "Peter, if you would like a new experience, I believe you are prepared for one that I have been looking forward to sharing with you." She turns to look at Zachary, David, and Rebecca. "Do you feel it appropriate?" All nod.

Zachary, leaning off to one side, is fidgeting with his cloak, typical of him just before something is about to transpire.

It is obvious that Peter has noted this, as little rivulets of golden light spew here and there from the outer periphery of his cloak, and the others smile and nod to one another warmly. Peter notes this, as well, and calms himself.

"She's right, Pete. This would be a truly good experience for you. I can vouch for it myself. Been there lots of times. Love it. And I know you will too."

"Where are you talking about, Zack?"

"Why, one of Elizabeth's favorite realms. Right, Elizabeth?"

"Yes, Zachary, it is a joyful experience that I believe you will find most stimulating, Peter." She looks around at the others, who simply nod and smile in agreement.

Peter looks around the group and then at Zachary, "Could you tell me something of this realm before we actually go there? For once, could you tell me what's ahead before I get into the middle of it?"

"Certainly, Pete. Whatever suits you. I've never intentionally held anything back from you, it's just that I wouldn't want to lead you or color your experience in any way. I've always thought it's best for you to draw your own conclusions. But if you think differently now, I'll be glad to discuss it with you, as I'm sure the others will." He returns to fidgeting with his cloak, brushing it, straightening it, adjusting it here and there.

Elizabeth, still smiling at Zachary, explains, "Peter, what we're talking about here is probably different than anything you could imagine at this point. You've known life in the Earth that, as you've said, you can still recall, and those are valuable memories. And you have experienced the Garden, the Green Realm or Patio Realm, Wilbur's Crystal Workers' Realm, Todd's realm, and others that you've been to but as yet haven't specifically identified."

She pauses, studying Peter, and as she does, he fixes his gaze upon her, visualizing as she speaks, as though she is projecting to him the memory of each of these experiences. "Yes, I remember and I see those vividly. Are you somehow or other showing them to me? Not to deviate here, but how do you do that?"

"Actually, Peter, I am not doing anything except providing the stimulus for you to experience what you have already experienced. Anything that you have done, any place you have been, lives on. Simply because you were in the Earth in linear time and have now left that physical body, doesn't mean that you have left the Earth."

"Whoa! Wait a minute. What do you mean, I haven't left the Earth?"

Zachary is chuckling in the background, and Elizabeth shifts her position a bit to glance over at him. She smiles, though not quite as warmly this time, as though she wishes he would field these questions from Peter.

Zachary does not respond, though he is obviously aware of this desire on her part.

David and Rebecca, delighted to simply observe, are also not making any effort to assist Elizabeth in any way.

The warmth of her smile returns as she realizes that they wish her to be the one to exchange with Peter. "What I'm saying to you, Peter, is quite simply that, wherever you have been, whatever you have done, a portion of you remains. You might think of it in this way: The memory of you is in the heart and mind of your family in the Earth."

There is a sudden rush of warmth. A brilliant flash of red and rosy pastels cascades over Peter as the memory of his family is obviously touching an emotional level within him. Instantly, he is aware of the images of his family, and some of his friends, including Abe.

"See what I mean?"

Peter shifts himself, obviously a bit uncomfortable. "Forgive me, Elizabeth, but no, I don't. What do you mean by 'See what I mean'?"

"Well, you have just revisited the Earth."

"What are you saying? I've been here the whole time."

Zachary glances up just as Elizabeth has turned to look at him, and he then turns to Peter, "What she's saying, Pete, is those little flashes of memory were actually flashes of visitations to the Earth."

Peter brightens. "No way. No way! They're just memories, that's all. I never left here. I had no sensation of movement. There wasn't any sense of the other experiences I had when we traveled from realm to realm, either. So, how can you say to me that I visited the Earth?"

Zachary looks down and smiles. "That's the way it is. Like it or not, that's the way it is."

"Oh-h, I get it. We've been down this street so many times before. You're going to prove it to me now, right?"

"If you say so, Pete."

Another gentle murmur of humor ripples through the group, though not so strongly shared by Peter this time. He is obviously a bit imbalanced. Yet, his cloak glows brilliantly.

Elizabeth speaks again, and her gentle words and gaze seem to have a soothing effect on him, as though some sort of healing light or balm is being poured over him as she speaks. "While you might consider Zachary's rather direct comments to be improbable, Peter, they are, in fact, true. The realm I would like to have you explore next, if we might call it a realm, I believe will exemplify this to you in a way that none of us here can offer you in thoughts or words." She turns to the others. "Do you agree?"

Receiving a nod from David and Rebecca, she turns lastly to Zachary, who straightens himself abruptly, feigning being caught off-guard. "Oh! Yes. Uh, well, of course, I do agree. But the key question here is, does Pete agree?"

"Agree to what?"

"To the existence of the realm that Elizabeth wishes to take you to."

"What difference does it make, if I agree or don't agree? I have a hunch you'll take me there anyway."

"Well, it's not quite that easy. It's a little different, this time? I can't just do this," and Zachary causes the jingle-jangle of bells, "and make this one happen for you. You have to be an active participant. You and Elizabeth are the primary ingredients in our next *adventure*, as you like to say." He smiles widely, but looks at Peter in a way that Peter has come to know means that the ball is in his court.

He calms and goes inward, reflects, and in accordance with Zachary's earlier training and Paul's vivid support, finds a confirmation. "Explain this to me. Suppose I do agree that whatever it is I have to agree to is okay with me. Then what do you mean by that agreement? It becomes real? Or that opens a door of some sort so we can enter in? Or what's the mechanism there? What difference does it make if I agree?"

"Remember what we talked about before? That your participation, your agreement, changed the table in the arbor, remember that? And we all joined with you in agreement? You improved on what was there after that, made it more beautiful and now that is a contribution of some significance to that realm. You will always be remembered for that."

"You're kidding. For that little thing?"

"Now, wait a minute. Who's ahead of whom here this time? You call creating or transforming one table into another a little thing? My, then you are doing well, aren't you?"

Rivulets of light, indicative of the humor, cascade about.

"Okay, Zachary, Elizabeth, you two have heightened my interest. My curiosity is at about Mach 10."

They all chuckle at that term, and Zachary comes back with, "Child's play, Mach 10. That's a turtle's pace here."

Peter shares the humor with the group, after making a mental note to ask Zachary about his comment regarding speed, and then there is silence as he looks about and finally speaks, "Well, what's next? Where do we go from here?"

"First, we have to have your agreement, just as we said."

"Okay, you have my agreement. Is that all there is to it?"

"Just about. Only a few more points we have to go over with you, if you don't mind. Elizabeth, would you care to discuss those with Pete?"

She nods a smile. "Peter, if you will, recall the experience of moving into the sphere of light. Can you recall it?"

There is an instant recall of the sphere, and Peter feels the essence of that experience. "Yes, I do. It was remarkable."

"Well, this is different in that, in the experience as the sphere of light, you were in a definable form. What we would like you to experience next has no form."

"No form?" Peter is incredulous. "What do you mean by *no form*? Nothing? How can something be nothing?" He looks over at Zachary. "I won't be able to see any of you or know that you are present?"

"Not at all. It's not like that. It's quite the opposite, in fact. You will have even greater awareness of our presence and that we are with you, and others, as well. Just not in the sense of a finite or defined form." Pausing to allow those thoughts to permeate Peter's consciousness, Zachary studies Peter carefully, as though visually and spiritually he is inspecting Peter's cloak.

Peter continues to focus his thoughts upon what is being given to him. "Well, could you give me more explanation, if that is possible, of existing without form? I can't even conceive of such a thing. Are you talking about being just thought? Or what?"

"You are on the right track, Peter," Elizabeth continues, "though it's actually beyond what you consider to be thought. It is in a realm of what we call consciousness because thought sort of typifies constraints, whereas consciousness can be unlimited. For example, in order for there to be a thought, there is usually a stimulus associated with the thought, like a need, a desire, a work, a goal, an experience of some sort. Consciousness, however, is without that sort of stimuli, although it can be present. Consciousness simply *is* and can experience in a multi-dimensional sense, unrestricted and unfettered without regard to the confines of a stimulating thought. For example, when you thought of the table, it was defined, and the thought-form had parameters. Those parameters were precipitated into the form, which became the table. Is this much clear?"

"I have a handle on that," glancing again at Zachary, who is obviously now thoroughly inspecting Peter, as though looking for anything that Peter is not comprehending.

"Well, when we move into this state, will we be able to return here, Elizabeth? I mean, is it possible we could, well, sort of get lost?"

"No, you can't get lost, in the sense that you would no longer exist. But you can become … How would you explain this to him, Zachary? Or David, or any of the rest of you?"

It is as though Zachary hasn't heard her words. He is now up and moving about Peter, carefully inspecting him, brushing him a little here and there.

Peter's curiosity is growing as to what Zachary is doing.

Surprisingly, it is Rebecca who speaks this time. "Peter, it is as though you can become one with all things. And by *things* I mean all finite expressions. It is like the wind in the Earth. While it blows through many lands, it becomes a part of each country, each state, each city, each neighborhood through which it passes, and it continues on."

"You mean we are going to become wind?"

The humor in this is predictable, of course, and after they collect themselves again, Rebecca continues. As she does, Peter studies her carefully and realizes in his consciousness that he has rarely recalled her speaking. He notes how wonderful it feels when she directs her words and thoughts towards him. They are similar to what he experiences when Elizabeth speaks and directs thoughts to him, yet different in that her uniqueness is as a flavor or essence that comes through to him like different-tasting pies.

(Our group is much amused as we observe that he has compared this mentally to cherry pie. We shall pause a moment here to collect ourselves. ...

Very well. We find that, as Peter thinks of the different types of pies, this is humorous indeed. We find it incongruous to the event here, typifying the rare, wonderful quality that is present in Peter, one that is so widely loved here and which endears him to all who know him.)

Rebecca speaks (fortunately, for our group as well as theirs), "Yes, Peter, what you are feeling now is right on the money, as you say in the Earth. You will retain the flavor that is Peter, just as you can remember a cherry pie because that flavor is unique to that pie."

Peter is momentarily astounded by Rebecca's astuteness, that she has peered within him and not only observed his thoughts but his memories and every single facet, every detail, of what he was reviewing in his consciousness.

Now noting over his shoulder that Zachary is behind him, fussing over him, unable to contain himself any longer, he turns to Zachary, half-joking and half-serious. "Zachary, whatever are you doing? Won't you please just come around here and join our group?"

"Oh, uh, sorry, Pete. Didn't mean to disrupt things, but I need to check you out before this trip. It's important. Can't have any holes here, no rough edges. One needs to be mindful for Whom one works, you know." Zachary coyly returns to his previous position, reclines, and props himself up on one elbow, straightening and dusting his robe. After a moment he glances up at Peter and explains softly, "Sorry, Peter, but it was a mandatory prerequisite to this trip. Okay?"

"Oh. Sure. It's just that I'm having a hard time grasping all this, and I guess the intensity with which I'm trying to understand puts me a little on edge."

"Oh, not at all. What you're experiencing is typical of entities in the Earth. You're on the edge of a new discovery, Pete, and one that will require you to release old limitations. They're like being bitten on the posterior by an English bulldog. Takes a week to get them to let go. Know what I mean?"

There is considerable laughter as Zachary projects the image, the visual thought-form, of what he means.

It eases Peter, as he can relate to this, recalling that he has had more than one canine grab his trouser leg and not wish to let go. "Okay. So what you're saying is, I'm stumbling over my own barriers, my own limitations?"

"That's it, Pete. You've nailed it right on the head."

Peter turns, much more relaxed now, to study each of the entities, and notes that Rebecca is glowing brilliantly. Obviously she has done well and somehow or other her contribution has added to her luminosity. "Now that's interesting. I can tell intuitively, or something, that Rebecca has made a significant contribution."

"Really? How do you tell that?" asks Zachary mirthfully.

"Well, look at her. She's glowing much differently now than before."

Zachary leans over exaggeratedly. "Goodness, you're absolutely right! She is aglow. Looks lovely on you, Rebecca. You should wear that color more often." Turning back and adjusting himself, Zachary glances up at Peter, feigning a hint of innocence.

"Well, I guess we'd best get at it then, Zachary, Elizabeth. So, how do we do it?"

"Oh, good. That's what I always like to hear. It seems to take you ever so long to reach that point." Zachery chuckles loudly. "Just kidding, Pete. As always, you're doing remarkably well. We're proud of you." He turns to Elizabeth.

She rises, in the sense that they have all been seated, from your perspective, though it is more like hovering. As she does, Peter, out of courtesy he learned in the Earth from his mother, rises as well. They all come closer together, and Elizabeth asks softly, "Do you remember in Todd's realm what that felt like?"

Peter pauses but a moment. "I sure do. It was a great feeling."

"Good. Can you recreate that thought?"

"I know I can. Just give me a moment." He turns inward and instantly there is the thought. When he reopens his perception, he sees the others as spheres of light. "Goodness, that was easy." Noting from each of them the individuality that they reflect to him, oddly, again like the uniqueness of a certain type of pie … a flavor, an aroma, an essence, a taste, a color. All of the physical senses seem to be combined into something far more vast, but they are references Peter uses to build understanding. "Is this it then, Elizabeth?"

Peter hears within himself, *This is the first step, Peter. Now I would like you to follow me just as you did in Todd's realm when I moved there first. Do you remember it?*

"Yes, I remember it."

Well, I would like you to move into that memory until I tell you to pause. Is that acceptable?

"Sure." Peter notes that Elizabeth reaches out to touch him in the same manner as she did before entering Todd's realm, contributing something to his essence like harmony, balance. Now he perceives that Rebecca is on his other side. He can tell because he remembers her uniqueness. To the forefront, as he might expect, is Zachary, and behind him, David (though there is no front or behind; these are given for your references only).

Move now, Peter, Elizabeth directs him, and he begins to remember, as though he is projecting himself from the sphere of light outward. It is easy. He flows and delights in the feeling of the undulation. It is an essence of being free, totally free, that he can fly, that he can be and do whatever is his wish. A few more moments pass and he hears a soft voice.

Pause here, Peter, please.

He searches about himself, trying to determine how it is that he goes about pausing.

At this thought, he can hear Zachary's gentle laughter, in front of him somewhere. *Right there, Pete. That's it. Just pause, and focus on my voice. Okay? Have you got it? Here, I'll give you something to focus on.*

Instantly, there is the jingle-jangle so familiar to Zachary at the start of his outings.

For the next few moments, Peter reflects. He realizes that he cannot perceive the spheres of light of any of them, himself or the others. He does sense a sort of curious luminosity, as though a living membrane-like circumference of light is around him, within which he is suspended somehow at the core, exactly at the epicenter of this tube or tunnel of light. In the next moment, he feels a flood of warmth flow over him, and something inside of him illuminates, just as when the Master touched him in the Crystal Workers' Realm.

Very good, Peter, he can hear from Elizabeth. *Now if you will, simply continue to hold that essence. Hold it as a thought for a moment, until you become one with it.*

To his amazement, he has absolutely no difficulty perceiving and holding this luminosity. In fact, he finds it wonderful, marvelous. So much so, that he begins to be drawn within it with remarkable speed and depth.

Okay, here we go, gang, he can hear Zachary say. *Let's stay together now.*

Even though he has heard these thoughts from Zachary, they are, in essence, meaningless to him. He is flooded with a sense of rapture, of joy, and can only barely discern that he seems to be moving at an incredible rate. Within this membrane of light, as he moves this way, it moves, as he moves that way, it moves that way as well. So that no matter what he does, he remains in the precise center of it. This continues for a time, until suddenly the membrane is no more, and the light that was its essence has now come to be all that Peter perceives.

In this brilliant light, he feels himself swirling, drifting, rolling, moving every which way. All the while, this wondrous radiance seems to be delving deeper and deeper into him, and he finds himself welcoming it. With the passage of considerable (what you'd call) time, he reaches a point that is immobile, static, stationary.

Softly, he hears or perceives or knows or feels Elizabeth's presence. *Are you well, Peter?*

Finding no means familiar to him of communication, he hears, as well as knows, his answer, *I'm incredible, Elizabeth. I ... I'm in a wondrous state. Yes, I am very well. Is everyone else with us?*

Instantly, there is, not words, not thought-forms, not images, but the realization of the essence of each individual in the group. He marvels at how unique Zachary feels to him. As he does, he asks, *Zachary, where are you?*

He feels and senses this response, *I am where you are, Peter. Precisely. Not to the left or to the right, but right where you are.*

How can that be, Zack?

Well, we are in a state that could be called formlessness. We are unlimited. So where you are, I am. And so is Elizabeth, and there is Rebecca and David, as well.

With the mention of their names, Peter can feel them, each one, as though they are all contained in one body. This creates an exuberance within him that is limitless. It is as though he is propelled by some force, unimaginable in its magnitude, through an array of experiences. He knows these, and he relates to them, but he cannot define them. There are no words, no images. There is nothing that he can draw upon from his memory with which to equate these experiences.

Softly at first, he begins to discern something. As it grows, he attempts to focus on it, and very slowly but continuously, Peter realizes that it seems like music. It grows, and is of incredible purity and brilliance. It seems to be everywhere at once, as though it is coming from within him and outside of him simultaneously. *Oh, my goodness, this is so beautiful,* is what forms in his consciousness.

Indeed so, he perceives from Zachary.

We thought you would like it, Peter. He can tell this is coming from Elizabeth.

And I personally am very pleased, since this is one of my favorite expressions, if not the favorite, he hears from David.

The sound continues to grow, and Peter communicates, *What is the source of that sound?*

You are, Pete, he hears from Zachary.

I am? I am the source of that beautiful sound?

Yep, that's you, Pete. That's what you sound like to the rest of us. Rather nice, don't you think?

The sound grows, and it flows here and there, as though it is resonating off of something and returning to him. Each time the sound resonates from some unperceived location, it returns to Peter blended with another sound. *Now, what's that, Zachary? Where there was one sound, I now hear two, as though two tonal qualities have come together in perfect harmony.*

That, Peter, is Elizabeth.

Oh, you're kidding me! That other sound is Elizabeth?

Well, in a manner of speaking, yes. It's Elizabeth.

Oh, my! That's beautiful.

Sure is, Pete. Carry on a bit and see what you find.

As though Peter is turning his awareness somehow, he hears, in what seems to be another direction, another echo or reverberation back toward him, adding yet another tonal quality, essence, or flavor, to the sound.

After a few moments, he hears softly, *Hi, Peter. It's me, David. How's that one?*

Is that your sound, David?

Yes, it is, in a manner of speaking.

What's this 'manner of speaking' that you and Zachary have both made reference to here?

Goodness, Pete, you certainly are astute ... even when you're formless.

Before he can get an answer, more sound comes to him, and Peter immediately recalls cherry pie. *Hello, Peter. Are you enjoying this?*

Oh, it's so lovely, Rebecca. It's a wondrous sensation, though I don't know how I'm sensing it. I have no concept of existence. I only know that I am, because ... well, I am.

There is reverberant warmth from many different directions, and Peter suddenly realizes that it is the equivalent of laughter when they were in other forms. Intuitively, he reaches within himself and generates a reciprocal warmth back to each of them, marveling at the resonance that it creates when it returns to him.

So it goes for a considerable time with Peter sending out one essence and finding it returning to him many times over. They all experiment and exchange back and forth until he hears Zachary say, *Peter, I'd like you to pause a moment here, and assess the work you've done.*

What do you mean, Zachary?"

Why, the beautiful music you've created.

I created music?

Sure thing, Pete. Just perceive. Just be conscious. Reach out and become one with this realm.

Peter finds, to his surprise, once again, that it is very easy for him to do so. As he does, he is awed by the wondrous flow of chords and melodies that seem to flow without interruption, one playing on the other, many, many different themes, all in perfect harmony with the other, turning, twisting, as though he can feel color, warmth, and depth. All of the associated physical senses and much more are stimulated to the highest level of pleasure and joy.

As he revels in the wonder of this collection of vibrational essence, he hears from Elizabeth, *Do you like it here, Peter?*

Oh, yes, Elizabeth. It's wonderful. It's absolutely wonderful. I haven't had a thought of anything finite the whole time we've been here, and I haven't missed it. I feel as though I am one with each of you somehow, and that you are one with me. Yet, I know that I exist as myself. It's incomprehensible, and yet here it is.

Peter, you have defined it well, perhaps better than any of us might. I would like you now to perform several exercises. Are you willing to do so?

With a moment's apprehension at the possibility of losing this experience, this most joyful state of existence, he responds, *Certainly. I have the utmost faith in you, Elizabeth and all of you. You are such wonderful friends. I cannot conceive what I might do without your presence.*

Well, Peter, those are good sentiments, and you will find them far more profound than you realize. But now, if you will, simply follow my vibration as I create it in greater magnitude for you. With that, a beautiful, pure tonal quality comes from a specific direction.

Peter focuses on it, and, as he does, he can feel it drawing him. He can perceive ever so slightly a sense of motion. Then, as swiftly as it began, it stops.

Elizabeth asks again, *Are you well, Peter?*

Indeed so. Never better, in fact. Is everyone still with us? He instantly perceives in melodious order an affirmation from each of the others.

Now, Peter, what I would like you to do is follow me once again, remembering the experience in Todd's realm. Are you willing?

Yes. Proceed and I'll follow. Though I don't know how I'll do it, I do know that I shall.

Very good.

Peter feels a sense of motion. He cannot determine how, but he knows it is Elizabeth in motion. Some aspects of sensory perception known to him as relevant to physical existence return, and instantly he begins to create the image of a great oak tree. Suddenly, it is before him, its massive crown stretched upwards towards an azure blue sky of incredible depth. Surrounding its base is a lush, green expanse, dotted by wondrously colored flowers. Awestruck by its clarity and beauty, and the familiarity of finiteness, he finds himself in a state of mixed emotion and thought.

Just follow me, Peter, as you said you would. Try to focus on where the thought is coming from.

Peter discerns that it is, surprisingly, coming from the tree itself. *Elizabeth, where are you?*

Here, Peter.

Peter focuses on the tree again and knows for certain now that somehow or other the tree and Elizabeth are occupying the same place. *Are you in the tree, Elizabeth?*

Not actually, but the tree and I are in harmony with one another, so that much is true. Would you care to join me?

Slightly unnerved at the concept of moving into a tree, Peter stammers, *Well, uh, how, I mean, what ...*

Don't worry, he hears from Zachary. *If you get stuck in the thing, I'll pull you out.*

Peter is softened instantly by Zachary's wit. *Okay, Zachary, I can always count on you.*

There is a perceptible motion of swiftness that Peter has nothing to do with except to the extent that he allows himself to move, and he finds himself in the same space as Elizabeth. Remembering what it felt like before, he knows this.

As he does, nothing is different except that Elizabeth is speaking to him. *Peter, you and I and the tree are one. We are not separate. The essence that is the life existence of the tree and you and I has come into harmony. The tree is still the tree, you are still Peter, and I am still Elizabeth, but we are one. If you would like, you can release your own thoughts of Peter, and know what it feels like, what the essence is, of the tree. Would you like to try?*

Stimulated by the thought of such an adventure, without answering, Peter simply lets go, and he can feel the essence of this mighty oak. Flashing by him with incredible rapidity is the entire life span of this oak, until, moving backwards, he perceives it as a seed. The seed, then, moving backward, brings forth an image of another mighty oak. And so it goes, back and back and back. *Wow!* He exclaims, *Incredible!*

Suddenly, as swiftly as it began, Peter is stopped short, as Zachary's voice calls to him, *Peter, hold up a bit here now. You could get caught in this and I'd have a hard time pulling you out. Don't get too caught up in anything finite. Move parallel to it, not as it. Understand what I mean?*

Zachary's words resonate within Peter as, to his wonder, he does understand. In an instant, he finds himself outside the movement of the lineage of the oak trees, and Elizabeth is at his side. Though both are yet formless, he can tell this because of the harmony that is produced by their conjunction of proximity.

Okay. Good, all hear from Zachary. *Time to return, now. We mustn't overdo on our first outing.*

David can be heard speaking next, though Peter does not know to whom or to what comment David is addressing, *Yes, I will lead them back. Thank you.*

At this point, Peter finds himself replicating the path back to the point of his exposure to the vibration and sound. Suddenly, there is the light again, and he is back within the membrane-like luminosity, moving at incredible speed, until there is an audible perception of a feeling or sound, and to his utter disbelief, there they are, all of them, right back where they started.

"Incredible! Utterly incredible! I like that one, Zack. Elizabeth, I am so grateful, and to you, Rebecca, and David. I never imagined anything could be so wonderful. And that oak tree experience! Could I really have been drawn backwards sort of infinitely in the oak tree's lineage? Would I have never ended? Surely there must have been a beginning."

Zachary explains, laughing softly, "Well, in a manner of speaking, yes, there is a beginning even for an oak tree. But it's difficult to explain, if you know what I mean."

Peter does not actually know what Zachary means, but somehow he understands that this is neither the consciousness nor the realm in which to inquire. He is also not all that certain that he wants to know any more just at this point, for he is fondly remembering his experience in formlessness.

As he does, Elizabeth compliments him, "Peter, I am so pleased that you find it as wondrous as I do. I had hoped you would, I believed you would, and now I know it to be so."

At this point, our group pauses, each one sharing their experiences with the other, remarking about the colors, the sounds, the music, and the wonder.

———————————

So do we, then, turn to each of you, to indicate that this experience of formlessness is available to each of you.

As you release habits, doubts, fears, or anything that limits you, infinity awaits you. Not to the loss of your identity, but to the enhancement of it. As you, a single note in the wondrous symphony created by God, join yourself with another and another, your uniqueness becomes more resplendent, not less, and certainly not lost.

So this, then, might be the ideal, might it not?

CHAPTER 5

Joining Paul and Todd

JUNE 20, 1991

It is our hope that we have provided some insight into the nature of your own being while you are in the Earth plane presently and for that time that lies ahead for all. For as surely as one embarks upon an experience, it is with the knowledge, at some level, that such experience shall come to a point of change or ending. It is to this that we would encourage you all to look within those works that have been observed by Peter and his colleagues, to discern that which applies to you now in the Earth and that which can serve as keys to unlock the passageway in the future for you to move into higher realms of consciousness when such time comes.

The group is gathered, as we make contact with them again, at a point in consciousness not too distant from where we last left them. We suggest that you not measure this by the scale known in the Earth as time, for as one can expand in awareness and comprehension, then that expansion can be not simply a straight line or a linear projection, but multi-faceted, simultaneous in direction and reference.

Peter has been and is questioning the others with regard to his recent experiences. Several points have been of particular interest to him. The first of these he commented upon was the mechanism for movement from their previous state of expression into a state of spherical light, and then from that to embark upon what he discerned as movement. He questioned thereafter with regard to the tube of luminosity (his term).

This could be considered what the Channel has called the tunnel or the tunnel of light. Then, he questioned, to considerable depth, the function of the state of formlessness. It is wise, we concur, for us to begin our commentary here, since we note in the hearts and minds of many of you considerable interest in this form of expression.

Peter is speaking. "You told me that the sound I heard was myself, right, Zachary? And you said that it was, in a manner of speaking, the same when I heard your individual ... Shall I call them notes? Tones? What?"

"It's not so important how you title them, what word or words you use to describe them, Peter. What's most important is that you comprehend their expression. Titles are finite, experiences are not necessarily so. Experiences are as vast as the expression might actually be, but titles tend to box that in.

"Here's an example: Let's say you're observing a sunset in the Earth, and as you study the colors and the movement of the sun's waning rays cascading across varying types of cloud formation, that may be what captivates your attention. In other words, that is what you remember. Yet at the same time, there might be landscape, an ocean, other people nearby. But if you called that a sunset, then the image brought to mind is specifically that, and what you remember will probably also be confined to a more narrow conception. However, if you were to move back to a memory of a sunset and we were to question you about the surroundings at the time, and we were to help you pursue that to greater and greater depth, you'd make all sorts of discoveries. Then, you'd have to tag onto, the title of *A Sunset*, something such as, *A Sunset on the Mountain, A Sunset at the Seashore, A Sunset at the Seashore with Charlie,* See? Get the point?"

Peter pauses briefly. "Yes, I have that quite clearly. But my question here is not intended to ... How can I put this? I'm not intending to focus on the outer layers of this, but to delve into the deeper parts of it. What I mean is, tone, as I know it in the Earth, is an element of music that is definable. In other words, there is the C note or the D note, or whatever. If you have a piano and you strike that designated note on the piano, a certain tone at a measurable frequency of vibration per, I don't know, second or something like that, is expected to come forth providing that the piano's in tune. So, what I'm driving at is do I always have that particular vibrational frequency that would be associated with middle C?"

"Good example. Consider this: Every time you strike that C note on the piano, can't you hear some slight echo or resonance from the surrounding strings that make up the piano, the ones the little mallets strike when you push the key?"

Peter pauses to reflect for a moment. "No, I don't think so. I don't think I heard anything but the note that was struck. Perhaps it did resonate, but I can't remember it."

"Okay, then, think of it in this way. If you throw a stone, a pebble, into a small body of water, it ripples out from where the stone strikes. True?"

"Sure, everybody knows that's true."

"Well, the striking of the string or pushing of the middle C key on a piano is the same. Do you agree?"

Reflecting but a moment, Peter responds, "In principle, I agree. I don't know the technical side of it, but I guess the sound goes out from the string and I hear it and perhaps it passes on somewhere. So, I guess that could be true."

"Okay. Well, what it does is, as it passes on and on and on and on, it loses its force, its primary energy. It moves into a state of expression that becomes less and less audible to the mechanics, as it were, of your ear. Now, since we are not dependent here on the mechanics of the ear, were we to strike middle C here, that force is, in essence, unending. Do you grasp that?"

"Sort of. Are you trying to tell me that if I had a piano here and I struck middle C, that that sound would never end?

Goodness, Zachary, if that were so, we'd be inundated with sound, wouldn't we? I mean, if every time a sound was created, like my voice, and that sound didn't diminish in time or space or whatever … I've never been very good at physics, remember?"

Zachary Nods and smiles, affirming that he knows.

"Well, how could it be that it doesn't diminish? It has to diminish, or we'd be barraged with sound, wouldn't we?"

"Good thinking, Pete, and to a degree that's so. But remember, you're comparing that to the Earth, where you'd hear mechanically. If you produced middle C electronically, so that holding down the triggering mechanism of the electronic device would perpetuate the force behind that vibration, it would, in effect, never end until you removed your finger from the triggering mechanism, the key. True?"

"Yes."

"Well, the difference here is that you aren't responding to the inner ear mechanism transmitting vibration to the nerves and being interpreted by the brain. Rather, you're intuiting, in a manner of speaking. You are becoming one with that level of expression. Do you hear the sounds now? Do you hear your note? Do you hear Miss Cherry Pie over there?"

Rebecca sparkles and smiles, and the others giggle, remembering Peter's earlier reference to Rebecca as cherry pie.

After overcoming his slight embarrassment, Peter responds, "I get it, Zack. So, in other words, the sound continues but one's … what would I say, uh, one's realm of sensitivity may not continue with the sound, and so the sound's vibration (or whatever) gradually moves out of the sphere of our focus or awareness. Is that reasonably accurate?"

"I would call that splendid. In fact, better than I might have given to you, for if you would look back a moment I used lots of words to try to give you that impression, and you got it right off. This is one of your talents, Pete, and one for which you will undoubtedly be recognized often." Giving Peter an exaggerated wink, as the others all smile broadly.

There is silence again as Peter reflects upon this and then comes forth, as the others anticipate he will, with several more questions. "So when my sound went out and it sort of echoed and came back to me, it brought with it not only my note but the note of each of you in succession?" Peter casts a warm glance around at the group gathered near him.

"Indeed. That's as accurate as any description might be."

"And then, afterwards, when you asked me to review the music (I guess you'd call it) that I had created, I found it to be utterly enchanting. But it seemed to me that I heard other notes in there, too. Is that true?"

"Of course, Pete. We weren't alone there. You know, we can't always have these realms all to ourselves." All chuckle gaily, including Peter.

"I didn't mean that, Zachary. It's just that I couldn't perceive anyone else, and yet by the tonal vibrations I was certain there were others there."

"That is excellent, Peter," offers Elizabeth, entering into the conversation. "That shows that your consciousness is expanding and becoming increasingly sensitive. That's a good sign, if you'll accept that term."

"What's good about it? I mean, why is that important enough for you to comment on it to me?"

Looking quickly at Zachary, who begins to get his rather impish grin and turns to the side, fidgeting, as is his habit, Elizabeth knows instantly that she has the ball.

Turning back to Peter, she smiles warmly, which Peter can feel, as though he has been bathed in a curious warmth, which he knows comes to him from Elizabeth but hasn't yet discerned how. "Well, Peter, the question is, how far one wishes to progress. That question is not idle, nor is it one that is very often put to entities who are as recently entered into these realms as are you. But because of your cumulative progression, your soul's tenacity for spiritual growth, and your accomplishment in terms of balancing the lesser vibrational essences, all of these things and more combine to bring you to a threshold of discovery that is somewhat unique. Not that others can't approach it but, so often, they don't even find themselves capable of considering its existence. Understand what I'm attempting to convey to you here, Peter?"

Shifting himself to gaze at Elizabeth in a manner he has come to know builds comprehension, he gains images, thought-forms, patterns. Essences pour to him from her as she attempts to convey understanding, not only verbally but in mechanisms that are less known to him. He has come to accept these and has grown less and less concerned about how they work, satisfied, for the moment, to simply use them, and to understand them later. "I think I have the image of what you are trying to convey to me. What I see is graduated bands of vibration that I perceive as both vibration and flavor, for lack of a better word, to each of these bands, and an essence to each of them of varying hues or densities of color with separation between these, progressively blending. It's quite a collage of sensation that I get. I get the impression that each of these is demarcated somehow or other. Is it correct for me to presume that those demarcations are, in essence, the delineation of separate realms of existence?"

"That is a correct presumption, an accurate assessment. As Zachary just told you, this is one of your finer qualities indeed. But turn now for a moment to the experience with the oak tree, and maybe that will help build an understanding within you that could be useful."

Without a moment's hesitation, Peter can, in essence, to his own amazement, relive the experience with the oak tree! As he begins to do so, Zachary abandons his fidgeting and turns to face Peter square on.

Noting this, Peter pauses for a moment in the memory. "No, no, Peter. Continue, please. Do continue on."

Encouraged, Peter visualizes the oak tree and instantly

finds himself immediately before it again. Glancing quickly about him, he cannot perceive any of his colleagues. Not knowing what else to do, he simply utters, "Hello?" to which there is a resplendent vibration of collective humor directed to him, in the same positions in which the everyone was located just before he reappeared before the oak tree. "Thank goodness. I had thought for a moment I was off somewhere by myself. You're all with me, then?"

"Right-o, Pete. We're all here. Proceed."

"Uh-h, proceed with what, Zack?"

"Proceed with remembering."

"Oh. Okay. I'm not sure what all you mean by that, but here I go … remembering." Instantly, the memory of the previous experience flashes by him with remarkable clarity, depth and breadth, to the extent that he reels slightly from its impact. Abruptly, he stops or, rather, the kaleidoscope of the experience pauses.

He hears from Zachary, *Hold up a bit, Pete.*

"Okay, I think I must be onto something here," at which point, there is a combination of sound, light, color, and a sensation of movement, and Peter instantly perceives his colleagues immediately back where he was before he began remembering the oak tree. Stunned a bit by the rapid movement from, and return to, this state of expression, he simply stares at Zachary, who is warmly returning his gaze with a smile of reassurance.

"Now, Zachary," Peter asks slowly and deliberately, "what is it in this that I cannot grasp? I know there is a valuable lesson here, and I know that all of you," as he sweeps a glance around his group, "are patiently awaiting my discovery and to, well, I guess I could call it, actualize it or make this knowledge real for me. So, what is it, Zack? How do I move so easily all of a sudden to an oak tree and back, and … You did say that this tree was in the Earth, didn't you?"

"Right, Pete. In the Earth, as far as you would associate

reality to be there, but not in the Earth in the sense of its potential, for reality can be co-creative and can transcend the points of demarcation between realms. For example, Todd's realm existed for Todd, and though he was existing within an image or a creation that was in the Earth, he wasn't actually in the Earth, was he? See what I mean?"

"I think so. Go on."

"Okay. Consider this: None of those entities in Todd's realm lifted a finger to build those buildings, or the street, or the lamppost that Todd was leaning against when you and Elizabeth found him. They didn't do a thing, manually speaking, to create them."

"So, was it like my table or butterfly or your bells?"

"Precisely like that. In a manner of speaking, it was automatic. It's the massing of the thought-form that is collectively focused at a point of intersection that formulates what you call, or what you remember as, matter. The reality of a substance is then proportionately an exponential value of the cumulative thought-form, the conceptualizing and agreeing to that thought-form, and then simply allowing it to exist."

"Wow! Imagine what a manufacturing firm in the Earth could do with something like that. Wouldn't need any raw material, no labor, just a group of people sitting around imagining and creating, and then someone to box it up and truck it off to market."

Unrestrained humor pours forth from the group at another of Peter's noteworthy comparative analyses to the Earth.

"Manufacturing in the Earth aside, Pete (which is not too far removed, mind you, from how it really works), consider this, as well: The potential for all creation exists in all realms. Now, before you ask me fifteen questions about that, let me emphasize for you that I used the term *potential*.

As he reflects deeply on Zachary's emphasis, Peter is visibly growing in luminosity. Golden-white and bluish-white rivulets of light are erupting here and there and cascading down over him.

Rebecca and Elizabeth smile at each other as they turn to observe Peter further, and Elizabeth turns to him. "That's a wonderful assimilation of Zachary's guidance to you."

Slowing down in his outward activity, Peter looks at Elizabeth and asks, "It is?"

"Oh, yes, indeed. For we can see that you are drawing that wisdom into yourself, and we can also see that as you are, you are bringing it into a position of understanding from whence you can actually use it. Knowing something and becoming one with that knowledge are often very far apart. The difference might be to simply have knowledge as opposed to experiencing the knowledge that, in turn, becomes wisdom. So, we are privileged here," and Elizabeth casts a gesture to the other members of the group, "to observe you assimilating this and to perceive you developing wisdom as the result. That is a gift to us all here, and we thank you for it."

Somewhat amazed, Peter turns to each of them successively, to observe their radiant smiles and nods in affirmation to Elizabeth's comments, and turns back to his trusted friend, Zachary, who is also nodding, terminating the bobbing of his head with a very exaggerated wink. "Well, Pete, I don't know about you, but that's about enough of this exchange for me. I do enjoy action, and I know you do, too, and I think we're being called. So, if you can hold the remainder of your questions for a time, and if you turn inward, you'll know that we are being called and we can discuss it."

Somewhat surprised, Peter obediently retraces Zachary's earlier exercises and guidance to him, and goes inward. Startled, he finds that he can perceive Paul's face smiling and radiating light to him.

Just as remarkably, he hears Paul. *Hello, Peter. Sorry to interrupt, but if you wouldn't mind, would you join us?*

Startled beyond the capacity to speak, he hears Zachary

commenting off to the side somewhere, *Paul, he's in a bit of a state. You know what I mean. Let me talk to him, and I believe we can join you straight away. Is that acceptable?*

Hello, Zachary. Yes, that would be just fine. You know where we are, then?

Sure, Paul. I have you locked in, as they say in the Earth.

As though there is a subtle poof, the image of Paul is gone and Zachary's perception is immediately before Peter. Just behind him, Peter can perceive the others smiling.

"Did you get the message, Pete?"

"Yes, I did, Zachary, as you well know."

"Well, then, any questions?"

"Well, sure, lots of them, as you also well know. I know that was Paul, but where is he, and how did he communicate with us? How is it that when I turned inward I could perceive him, but I can't see him now? And where is he? What is that, anyway, some sort of telecommunications system, in a manner of speaking?"

Without a word but with a broad smile, Zachary turns to the others who knowingly nod. He is so tempted to announce, *There he goes again. Questions. Wonderful questions,* but he simply nods to the others and turns his attention back to Peter. "Paul can communicate with you or me or any of us because we are one with him. Okay? Got that much?"

"I am one with Paul. Yes, I've got that much. I don't truly understand it, mind you, but I can intellectualize it."

"Okay. Well, then, because you intellectually understand," with good-humor, somewhat mocking Peter's comments, "that oneness creates a sort of link, a kind of connective fiber. Not unlike a telephone line in the Earth, but not made of finite stuff. More likely understandable to you to be like a fiber of light that connects you and Paul, and Paul and me, and Paul and me to Elizabeth, and Paul and me and Elizabeth to Rebecca, and so on and so forth, and all of us back to you, and you back to all of us. For that matter, you are also connected to Benjamin, to Todd, to Wilbur, and to a number of others. See?"

Pausing to reflect upon that for a moment, Peter envisions a network of light, like a luminescent spider web. As he visualizes this, he can imagine that little rivulets of light run along each of these lines, and that each of these little rivulets is some form of communication.

Zachary interjects, "That's close enough, Pete, good enough for you to understand."

Once again he is embarrassed, because he forgot that his inner thoughts are known to his friends. "Well, it was the best I could do, but I think I have a handle on it. So, where is Paul?"

"Where else, Pete? Where else would he take Todd?"

"Todd?"

"Yes, remember? Goodness, is your memory is fading? Perhaps you're aging here."

The humor that bursts forth at Zachary's comment is as fireworks in a Fourth of July evening sky. The group spins and rolls and shifts through the spheres of expression here, and when it comes to rest finally, Zachary continues, "Just joking, of course, Pete. You couldn't age much more than you have, could you?"

Chuckles come forth from again, and even from Peter. "You did say Todd, didn't you?"

"Hm-m, let me see now," again poking good-natured fun at Peter, "yes, I'm almost certain that's what I said. Anyway, Paul asked us if we could join him, remember?"

"Oh, yes! Goodness, I forgot my manners. I became so unsettled or curious by the appearance of Paul and the mechanism and all that. How do we go to him? Let's do it now."

Glancing at the others, having received a nod of affirmation from each of them, Zachary turns back to Peter. "Picture him."

"Picture him?"

"That's it. Picture him. Picture Paul in your consciousness. What's he feel like? What do you remember of him? Got the idea?"

"Yes, I've got it. Give me a moment."

Instantly, Peter is flooded with the memory of Paul, his kindness, his gentleness, his seemingly endless compassion and wisdom. Remembering how much he truly admires and loves Paul, in that instant, Peter finds himself surrounded by greenery. Though he realizes immediately that, once again, this has caused movement, he does not pause to question that aspect, but turns to look about and is pleasantly surprised to see each of his companions expressed in a form comparable to their physical countenance. Then, looking around, he thinks he is at some point between the Patio Realm and the Garden. Not absolutely certain of that, he turns to Zachary and perceives that Zachary is smiling and nodding gently. "Am I correct, Zachary, in my thinking?"

"You are correct, Pete. Well done. Let's go now. Paul is waiting."

Without another word, Zachary takes the lead and Peter falls in behind, with Elizabeth on one side and Rebecca and David bringing up the rear. In a moment, they find themselves in the Garden.

Peter is delighted to see it again. Off just a bit in the distance he recognizes, with a flood of warmth and familiarity, his beloved knoll. Then, to his surprise, he can see two figures, one of whom he immediately recognizes as Paul. The other he cannot discern quickly, but believes it to be Todd, though he looks different somehow.

Zachary is still moving, and with delight, Peter notes that Zachary seems to be bouncing along, ever so mirthfully, as though he is singing and bouncing along in rhythm to it.

Peter finds it such a delightful observation that, without realizing it, he himself moves into it until, in the next moment, he sees Zachary's hand rise up into the air and spin about, making a little circle, and instantly there is jingle-jangle-jingle. He turns to cast a look over his shoulder at Peter, smiling broadly. "You liked it so much, Pete, I thought I'd try it again. Who knows? This might be a hit tune."

Humor murmurs through the group, including Peter, who marvels at Zachary's uncanny ability to interject humor into any situation, even the most intense ones.

Presently, they are before Paul and the other entity. Peter rushes forward to embrace Paul, as though he is embracing a long-lost brother. After comments are exchanged, Paul takes Peter's arm and turns him, pointing to the other entity who is standing in a bit of awe at the presence of the group.

Peter looks at the entity and states, "Forgive me. I was simply caught up in seeing my friend Paul again, and …" pausing, he studies the entity carefully. As he does, a flood of memory comes back, and he knows instantly that this is Paul. No, it's not Paul. Turning back to look at Paul, Paul is still there. He looks again at the entity, and there is so much of Paul over and around the entity that Peter can hardly believe it. Looking back and forth from one to the other, he becomes aware of Zachary chuckling a bit to himself. He glances over and sees Zachary looking down and, having reclined himself, as is his custom, fidgeting with the grass and the flowers.

Realizing he's not going to get an immediate answer from Zachary about what is taking place, he again looks at the entity in front of him.

It is in that moment, that he hears Zachary's voice, very softly, *Use what you know to use, Peter. Don't just rely on what you're accustomed to. Rely on all of your abilities. Reach inside yourself, and extend yourself out to touch this entity. Then see what you discern.*

As Peter follows Zachary's suggestion, he suddenly becomes aware that the entity standing in front of him is, indeed, Todd. Now it is clearly, unmistakably, Todd. Obviously flustered, unnerved by this event, Peter turns back to Paul, who is smiling warmly and, in answer to the question on Peter's face, Paul softly explains, "I gave him my cloak, Peter. Remember?"

A flood of understanding comes over Peter. How quickly he has forgotten this very basic function, this action of extending one's own spirituality as a gift or blessing to one who might be in need of it. The realization of this cascades over him, with the slight embarrassment that he did not understand and that he could not perceive beyond Paul's cloak, which is shimmering around Todd sufficiently that he might have discerned Todd immediately within it. He puts his embarrassment aside to offer a greeting, "Todd, how wonderful to see you again. You must forgive me. I didn't realize it was you. You look so different, and so well."

As Peter studies Todd after speaking to him, he realizes that Todd hasn't heard him. Turning back to Paul, he asks, "What's wrong here, Paul? Is it something I have done, or is there something wrong with Todd? Can we help him?"

Paul smiles very broadly and warmly at Peter's concern for Todd. "Peter, you have just returned here from a realm of expression that is much more rarified. You could think of it as a much more intensified or liberated vibration. You obviously had activities there that you have grasped very well, and you are now communicating with Todd on a level of expression that he cannot comprehend. In fact, he is not aware of any of this conversation. Essentially, Peter, this entire time Todd has been, in essence, in a state of blissful suspension. He hasn't actually been such, but for purposes of reference, that's adequate. Do you comprehend?"

Peter is a bit bewildered, but he grasps bits and pieces of what Paul is conveying to him. As he turns to look at his friends, he sees smiles and nods of understanding, and Zachary, who is quite comfortably positioned on the ground, is looking up at him and shrugs, extending his arm as though

Don't look at me. I didn't have anything to do with it.

Peter cannot help but smile back at Zachary's silliness, which is made even moreso by Zachary's aloofness. It puts Peter at remarkable ease, and he nods a thanks to Zachary for that kindness, to which Zachary simply casts a gentle nod to him and returns to focus on the grass and flowers.

"In order for you to communicate to Todd," Paul speaks again to Peter, "you'll have to slow your vibrations to his level."

"Well, I'd be glad to do that, but I don't know how."

"You do know how, you just haven't given it enough concentration. Think about it for a moment, and think about the different realms we passed through when I first brought you into this realm of expression."

Visualizing, then drawing upon Paul's projection of the image, Peter perceives the bands of color and remembers the different feelings and essences he gathered from so doing. His consciousness races over the other events, and suddenly he realizes that it has to do with varying expressions of his own consciousness. Just as swiftly, he realizes, too, that his cloak can make him perceptible or imperceptible. Functioning almost as though it is automatic now, he remembers creating his cloak, and as he does so, he enacts that process.

Swiftly, he cascades himself with that luminosity and immediately hears a voice. "Hey, Pete! It's great to see you. I was wondering if I'd see you again. Look where Paul has brought me. Isn't this place beautiful? Gosh, I'd like my mom to see this. I was about to ask Paul if he could help me find her and bring her here. I know she'd like it. She loves flowers and rolling green hills. Always wanted to live in the country. Sort of like the old country, you know? But we could never seem to get out of the city. That city, once it gets a hold of a person, it never seems to let go! It's like there's glue on you and it sticks you right there, doesn't it?"

Zachary can be heard chuckling at medium volume, as he

glances at Peter, who knows instantly that Zachary is thinking, *Just like you, Pete, one question after another. Likeable chap, isn't he?*

Within himself, Peter responds, *You're right, Zack. Is that typical of new entries into the Garden?*

Well, not always. But listen, Todd's standing there waiting for you to talk to him. Maybe you should turn back to him and do so, don't you think?

Peter feels a rush of embarrassment and rudeness and, instantly, he can perceive David, *Not at all, Peter. Todd doesn't know about the communication between us. It's is in what you would call the space between time. In other words, you could think of the space in between as little segments where there are openings. We are communicating right now laterally to Todd's recognition of existence. For him, nothing is transpiring where we are. When you turn back to him, to speak to him, a split-second will have transpired, and that's all."*

That's incredible. How does that work?

More on that later, Peter. Let's tend to Todd here, for now. Is that acceptable?

Oh, yes. Forgive me! "Well, Todd, I'm glad to see you, as well. I wondered how you were getting on, and I missed Paul." He turns to gesture to his friend. "I might have known he'd eventually bring you here. This is one of my favorite spots, if not the most favorite spot I've experienced up until a certain point in time." He turns to wink at Elizabeth, obviously meaning that he now favors her realm. She illuminates in response to Peter's acknowledgement and his sharing of her fondness for existing in the formless state. "So, tell us how you are. Are you doing well here? Has Paul shown you around?"

"I feel wonderful. I can't thank you enough, Pete, for getting me out of that mess. I can't understand why I kept myself there. You know, Paul was explaining to me about how it was my own choice to remain there, and that seems, even now as I consider it, unbelievable. Know what I mean?"

Simply nodding, Peter smiles at Todd, which is enough for Todd to continue on.

"Paul told me that we'd be joined shortly by some friends, but I didn't know it would be you and the rest of your group," as he turns to acknowledge their presence. "And he also said that you'd probably have some things you'd want to show me. Is that so, Pete?"

Swiftly, he turns to look at Paul, who reciprocates with a nod. Peter intuitively knows this to be an encouragement to continue. "Well, I'd be honored to contribute what I can, Todd. I'm not all that knowledgeable, but what I have experienced I am willing to share totally with you."

"That's really great, Pete. Paul told me that's the way you are, and he also told me that you probably wouldn't claim any credit for what you did. But I do appreciate it, and I know that you are much more than you say you are or are willing to let others think."

Surprised at that comment, Peter balances with it without disrupting his cloak, which is at the moment rather awkwardly perched upon him. Peter reflects on that as he realizes that, coming from the other realms of purer vibration, the cloak now feels awkward and clumsy.

In that moment, he perceives Zachary rising and walking over to him. Without a word Zachary begins to brush Peter's cloak, as though he were adjusting it somewhat here and there. As he does so, Peter begins to feel more and more balanced. Zachary then walks over to Todd. "Good to see you again. Could I help you straighten your garment there a bit? I see you've got it ruffled just a bit off to the side."

After a vain attempt, Todd cannot see what Zachary is referring to, but as he looks into the warmth and depth of his eyes, he knows that Zachary is utterly trustworthy, "Why, I would appreciate that. Thank you very much."

So, Zachary busies himself behind Todd as Peter stands

facing him, and their conversation continues.

"Well, what can you show me here, Peter? Is there some way you could help me find my mother? I would truly appreciate that. It would be so wonderful if I could bring her here."

Somewhat disarmed, Peter studies Todd's face. As he does, he again marvels at the preponderance of Paul's essence over it. Looking over Todd's shoulder, he can see Zachary now, who has stepped to the side enough that he can project to Peter clearly. Zachary is nodding an affirmation, and as he nods, Peter realizes that something is also happening within him. Zachary is continuing to nod, and though his face is gentle, he can see that it is much more serious than normal, and it begins to gain in luminosity.

Peter studies Zachary carefully and, in that same moment, he hears: *When one accepts a commission, Pete, it's not like in the Earth. To a degree, we did fulfill the commission with Todd, but this is now an eternal bond, an eternal opportunity. Paul has done, as you can see, a great deal of work with Todd, much in the same manner as he did with you some time ago. Now, Todd is at a point somewhat different than you, for his path is not identical to your own. Todd has certain facets of his consciousness that are, I might call them, limitations. So we can't take him to some of the realms we took you to, at least not yet. For instance, he can't see the Hall of Wisdom over there. To him, it's not there.*

Peter glances to see if he can perceive it, and sure enough, it is there in its radiant shimmering glistening. Just looking at it, he feels a tug within him, and remembers the hand of the Golden One who gave him the commission in the first place. A sense of surety seems to awaken within Peter.

He refocuses on Todd and answers, surprised to hear his depth of confidence, "Certainly, Todd. We'll do all we can to help you locate your mother. If you'll give us but a few moments, I'd like to confer with the others on how we might go about this."

In that moment, Rebecca steps forward. "Todd, my name is Rebecca. If I might, let me show you the wonderful work that has been done over here on some of these benches and fountains. That will give the others time to organize."

Utterly melted by the warmth and compassionate depth in Rebecca's eyes, as he accepts, he glances over to Elizabeth to perceive if the same essence is coming from both of them (as he discerns them both in the feminine) and notes that it is.

Meanwhile, Peter asks Paul, "How do we go about this? I mean, where is his mother anyway? Do you know?"

"Yes, I do. And so do you. You simply haven't brought it forward yet. Zachary, what do you think? Can we take Todd?"

When Peter follows Paul's glance he realizes that Zachary wasn't merely straightening Todd's garment but was energizing it. For Todd's cloak, which was actually, in essence, from Paul, is glowing in a different way than it was when he first perceived Todd moments ago.

"Zachary, you've done something to him. Right?"

"Well, not to him. I just gave him a boost to protect him. Paul, I think we can proceed. Particularly with Rebecca and Elizabeth along, there shouldn't be any problem keeping the balance. I think he can sustain the trip, and it might be good for his mother and others in that realm, as well. Don't you agree?"

"Yes. I think it would be a worthwhile work, and I think there are two or three of them there who are ready."

Peter is amazed at this conversation. He thinks of it as sort of *shoptalk* between his two friends, Zachary and Paul. It's a side of them he can't recall having seen before, as though they are meticulously planning, comparing notes, not unlike a planned work in the Earth.

Zachary notes Peter's thought and turns to him. "Well, in a manner of speaking, Pete, it is very much like that. But it needn't be. Much of this, in the way we are doing this, is so that you can comprehend the mechanism we are employing. We wouldn't need to do it like this, but it places it in the appropriate perspective for you if we do so." He turns to wave at Rebecca, and she brings Todd back to the group.

What transpires next is very similar to what you have heard in earlier experiences with Peter. Todd is assured and strengthened, and they begin a journey somewhat ceremoniously and in the pattern of surrounding Todd and moving forward through the mist, through the cloud, if you'll recall it.

Todd is awestruck by this, of course, and as the movement progresses he begins to formulate questions.

Zachary again lightens the intensity by bursting forth into song, which is highly contagious, and Peter marvels at the mastery of Zachary, Paul, and the others as they seem to magically calm Todd and keep him in a state of balance, harmony and ease.

Suddenly, there is a transformation in the radiant white mist. It parts, and Todd gasps. In front of him is the very street on which he was born and the flat in which his family lived. There, sitting on the front steps, as was their custom around about twilight, are his mother and father.

───────────────

At this point, dear friends, we are unable to continue. Because of the intensity of what will follow, it will require a much fuller breadth of time. When Todd is sufficiently balanced with his current state of what you might call shock, the others will be able to proceed, but at this point, he is in a state of what we would call heightened energy. Therefore, there would be little that could be commented on or worked upon of significant value to you. Todd will be stabilized and balanced and will receive some foundational works. After that, we believe he will surely be presented to his mother and father, and a number of old neighborhood friends he knew during his childhood period.

Todd's mother and father shared such a bond of love that it endured and carried them over into a realm that parallels their joyous existence in the Earth. They are surrounded by many old friends they had known who have passed on to this realm, as well. Some of them were able to move to this realm immediately, while others went through other experiences and are now at this stage of consciousness.

There will be other works as well, and Todd will come to understand how various types of bonds, even some he would consider good, can also bind one and inhibit their progress.

For the present, then, we conclude. When we return, we believe that you shall learn much about the nature of other souls' experiences as they depart the Earth.

CHAPTER 6

The Control Tower
SEPTEMBER 7, 1991

We welcome all of you to the beginning of yet another chapter of experiences in these realms, as we continue to follow the soul we have identified as the man called Peter. As we further delve into these experiences, it shall be our continuing prayer that the events and the knowledge incurred by Peter be a source of illumination for each of you, that you might ever draw upon them to apply much more literally some of this knowledge in your daily lives in the Earth.

To more or less recapitulate the experiences that have transpired since our last observation, Todd has enabled himself to balance with the realm in which his father and mother now exist. During the course of the experiences that followed, he also met and rejoiced with a number of other members of his immediate and distant family who have also come to be gathered here, as well as a number of friends, neighbors, merchants and so forth that chose, either knowingly or unknowingly (the latter, by way of their spiritual acceptance level), to dwell in this realm.

Included in the group is to be noted the presence of Mikey, also known to you as Paul. His presence is several-fold. Namely, he did accept an incarnation of brief tenure as Todd's younger brother, in the knowledge that that lifetime would be brief and constructive in helping this soul group, namely, Todd, Todd's family and friends, and perhaps a few others on the street.

T odd is relating to his parents many of his experiences, as they sit casually reminiscing on the front stoop leading to the flat in which he was raised.

Zachary, Peter, Elizabeth, and Rebecca are standing off to the side as Peter looks up and down the street, studying the structures and the entities. He turns to Zachary and observes, "This doesn't look all that different from the realm in which we found Todd in the first place. The structures look cleaner, brighter and more vibrant, but, in essence, they look the same. I can see that the people certainly seem to be happier, but basically they look the same, too. So let me ask you, how much … what shall I call it? How much higher or better, is this realm than where Todd was?" Pausing to await Zachary's reply, he notes a familiar twinkle in Zachary's eyes, which resonates within Peter such that he gets the growing feeling that he's about to engage in some further learning, compliments of friend Zachary.

"Let's take a walk, Pete. How about you, Elizabeth? Rebecca? Care for a stroll down the avenue?"

Nodding knowingly, our group begins to walk.

"In answer to your question, Peter, I'd like you to begin to do some exercises. Before you argue with me, understand that the exercises are intended for multiple purposes, which you'll understand better as we go along here. So, for the moment, trust me. I will answer your question or, rather, you'll answer it yourself. Acceptable?"

Peter glances over at Zachary, himself smiling, and nods.

As they move along down the avenue, Peter notices, over his shoulder, that none of the group around Todd seems to pay much attention to the fact that they've begun their stroll. Nonetheless, he can see Paul's, or Mikey's, eyes on him, and he feels a sense of communication, which he interprets to mean, *See you later.* He nods and smiles at Paul, and then turns to focus on Zachary again.

Zachary gestures with a sweep of his hand, "Look around

here, Pete. What do you see?"

He follows Zachary's sweeping motion and then turns back to him. "Could you narrow that down a bit? What do you mean by, tell you what I see? I think what's here is apparent, isn't it?"

"Yes, it is apparent, but it's also *trans*parent. Take a closer look."

Puzzled, Peter looks over to his left where the multi-storied, rectangular, irregular shapes loom over them, thrusting upwards like the fingers of a giant lying upon the ground. As he concentrates on a particular corner of one of the structures, he is taken aback when the structure begins to dim and fade, and the upper portion creeps into the background of visual perception, the structure actually disintegrating before his eyes. The more he allows his eyes to follow the disappearance of the upper portion of the building, the more the fading continues until Peter pulls his gaze away, as the building shrinks, literally, to just about the windows of the first floor. He swiftly turns back to Zachary. "Good heavens! Did I just destroy that building?"

Giggling, the group waits for Zachary's response, which is measured.

"In a sense, you destroyed it. More accurately, you have regained a sense of reality."

"Reality? What do you mean by 'regained a sense of reality?' Isn't this realm, this city, or whatever we're in, real? I mean, as real as anything is here?"

Zachery nods. "Yes, it's real, but reality has much more to do with those who are perceiving it and accepting it than it does with true reality. True reality is almost indefinable. But this reality is limited, and it is defined and accepted by the entities, the people, if you will, who dwell here." He turns back to motion to Todd and his family and a few others scattered here and there.

As they continue their stroll, Peter, somewhat nervously,

turns to glance back over his shoulder at the structure he just caused to vanish and perceives, to his astonishment, that the structure is every bit as "real" as it was moments before he saw it disintegrate.

Puzzled, he turns back to Zachary and asks, "You are saying something to me that is difficult for my consciousness to grasp. Let me say it back to you, and you tell me if I heard you the way I was supposed to. You're saying something like, that when I look at these 'real buildings' they are only real because the people who exist here believe in them. Is that much correct?"

Silently, Zachary nods, stepping up his pace a bit so that Peter has to accelerate his movement in order to keep up.

"And so, as I, who do not live here, concentrate on any of the real matter (if I could use that term) here in this realm, my reality is different, and, therefore, it begins to, well, not be there. Am I right so far, Zachary?"

"Very good, Pete. Continue on, if you'd like."

Peter is beginning to feel a bit annoyed that Zachary is both talking and walking when he, Peter, is very intent on understanding this new lesson. He then remembers that Zachary understands his thoughts, and realizes in an instant that Zachary has some purpose for moving so quickly.

At this point, Zachary turns to smile at Peter and nods, "Good work. That's using what you have. That's very important. Very good work, indeed." Abruptly slowing, Zachary turns to Peter and stops. "Okay, Pete. We'll pause here. This is far enough. I want you to realize something, and then we'll talk about it. Look back down the avenue. What do you see?"

As he turns to look at where they have just walked, Peter perceives only the structures, the same environment as he had been observing for some period of time now, and relates that to Zachary.

"Okay, now turn and look in front of us, where I was leading you."

Peter casts his gaze in that direction, away from Todd and Paul and Todd's family, and is startled by the fact that the buildings begin to fade off into a sort of mist-like substance. Not quite the same as the cloudlike essence that they traveled in to bring Todd to this realm, but similar, in a strange way.

"What do you see, Peter?"

"Well, it looks like a kind of fog, like a veil of mist, is hanging over this end of town."

"Care to walk into it?"

Peter turns to study Zachary for a moment. "I suppose it will be of value to me. Is that true?"

"I would think so, so let's go."

Moving again, he notices that the buildings on both sides are fading noticeably and quickly, as are the sidewalks, the pavement, the light posts. The entire city is ending in a cloud of mist until suddenly there is nothing around of finiteness at all. Only Peter and his colleagues remain definable here. "What is this stuff, Zachary? I can't see a thing. Just you all."

Zachary pauses and then responds very slowly for effect. "There is nothing to perceive Peter. So you are, as it would follow, perceiving nothing."

"What do you mean? How can it be that I walked down a street, and suddenly it ends and there is nothing, nothing at all? Are you are saying, if this mist-like cloud were to dissipate, there'd be nothing here?"

"Exactly. But, in fact, this mist-like cloud, as you call it, will never dissipate because it's the only existence that is possible here. This is like a separating veil or a buffer between realms. If we were to continue on beyond this, we would probably run smack into another realm."

"Wait a minute! Are you telling me that this is like a cocoon or …"

Zachary interrupts, "No, no, Pete. It's not that at all. It's just the end of the definition of their collective thought-form. It does exist in what you would consider from the Earthly perspective as time and space, but it exists here in this finite sense because there are those who want the existence to continue. Therefore it is here, sort of suspended in consciousness at a level that is the equivalent for it to exist. Follow that?"

"Well, I think I comprehend what you're giving me, in words and thoughts, but I can't put it into perspective in my logic. Know what I mean?"

Zachary laughs softly, "Only too well. Actually, I had anticipated that reaction, as did our colleagues," looking at Rebecca and Elizabeth. "So, I have several ideas that I'd like to offer you."

"Go ahead."

"Well, now having been in several, and I'll call them for sake of example, finitely defined realms and, as well, several non-finite realms, perhaps you would like to go to what I'll call, for purpose of reference, the Control Center."

Staring at Zachary for a moment, Peter cannot keep from laughing. Of course, as he does, the electrical display of lights, sound, and color begins to spew forth.

Knowing that Peter would probably find humor in this, Zachary responds in kind, as do Elizabeth and Rebecca.

As they continue their laughter, with Peter amused at the concept of a Control Center in these realms, they grasp arms and begin to roll through this mist-like cloud until they are surrounded in light and color, spinning, rotating, into the Realm of Laughter. After the passage of some time (as you would measure it in the Earth) they pause.

Well-balanced from the exchange of love, joy and humor, Peter remarks, "Where you come up with these terms is a wonder to me! I am always so tickled by these references. No doubt you know, before you give them to me, that they'll tickle my funny bone."

Half mocking Peter, Zachary cocks his head off to the side. "Bone? Funny bone? Where have you hidden that, Pete? I'd like to see the anatomical depiction of that at some time when we have nothing else to do."

Chuckling a bit, the group then refocuses on Zachary, who obviously, having lightened things up with his attempt at humor, is about to say something that will be significant. Enjoying this moment of focus upon him, he deliberately straightens and brushes his cloak, then leans over to brush Peter's cloak up on the shoulder, as though flicking off lint.

"For goodness sakes, Zachary! You and I both know I have nothing on my cloak. Let's get on with the Control Center stuff."

A ripple of laughter can be heard from the group.

"Ah, yes, the Control Center. You'll love it there, Pete. So many people have lost sight of the fact that it takes a great deal of work here in these realms to watch over all of the happenings in the Earth and other realms. You've just seen some that we have a responsibility to assist with. Imagine, with all these entities and all these realms, what it takes to coordinate all that."

Striving to grasp Zachary's thought-form, Peter leans back, visualizing rooms filled with charts and schedules, computers, filing cabinets, many entities busied about desk jobs, just as though he might be in New York at a large headquarters building, peering in room after room full of people busied by, what is called in the Earth, work.

A tinkling sound of laughter comes from Zachary, "That's a good depiction, Peter, but I have to tell you, that's not at all how it works here. Let's go, and I'll show you."

Dutifully rising, Peter follows along with the group. There is a series of beautiful flashes of light, each followed by a period of, as Peter can best define it, a sense of tranquility, ease, like the total absence of any thought, as though one were perfectly attuned, meditatively or prayerfully, to something absolutely pure. Light after light is experienced, followed by a kind of veiling of all consciousness and peace, until Peter notes that the next light they experience doesn't pass.

He studies the envelop of light in which he finds himself, and perceives it to have a yellowish-gold tone, but basically a soft white, not in any sense irritatingly bright. It is like the whiteness of a fluffy summer cloud. Moving into this, it clears, and Peter can perceive a number of entities, one of whom seems to be lounging back, doing nothing at all. As our group approaches, the entity leans forward, smiles, and waves vigorously, apparently at Zachary, and Zachary returns the gesture with equal vigor and perhaps a whit more.

At that point, the entity rises and moves directly to Zachary and embraces him. Peter notices that this collision between Zachary and the other entity seems to be more like striking a masterful chord of music and light. As they stand at arm's length from one another, obviously communicating in some way that Peter cannot clearly perceive, the entity then extends an embrace to Elizabeth and Rebecca, each in turn.

He then turns to look at Peter and moves deliberately to stand immediately in front of him. As he does, Peter marvels at the sense of, as best he can define it, eternal warmth and understanding. The depth of the entity's eyes as they peer at Peter makes him feel as though he is an open book. Peter's thoughts trail off as he hears the entity speak.

"Ah, yes. So this is Peter. My, my, Zachary, he's everything you told us he is, and more. Hello, Peter. How are you doing in your travels and experiences with Zachary here?"

Peter stammers just a bit, and then recovers, "Quite well, sir, thank you. And I am very pleased to be a visitor here in what Zachary calls the Control Center."

The entity's laughter is likened unto thunder booming. Not disruptive, but it seems to echo off the envelopment of the white substance in which they are now contained.

As it does, Peter notices that lights flash up in the distance as though a silent firework went with his laughter.

After this subsides, he thinks to himself, *That is remarkable.*

Zachary responds silently, *Not at all, Pete. Just an outgoing sort of a chap. Know what I mean?*

Abruptly, Peter hears the entity, *Why, thank you, Zachary. That's the nicest thing you've said about me in centuries.*

The laughter bursts forth again, as though racing to join with the other laughter, as the entire group now finds themselves caught up in the humor of the moment.

Peter, of course, is noting all of this and is also unnerved by the "intrusion" of this new entity's consciousness into his heretofore private communication with friend Zachary.

He communicates audibly to Peter, "Not at all, Peter. Not an intrusion, at least I hope you won't take it as that. But, you see, that's part of my chosen work here. You could think of it as being a commission. Therefore, I am merely doing what comes naturally, if you'll forgive the Earth-oriented cliché."

With that last comment, he motions for the group to follow, which they do. "Come, join me. I was just doing a bit of work with a few entities in a realm that is beginning to fade. Maybe you'd care to help a little, Zachary, Elizabeth, Rebecca, and too, you, Peter, if you'd like."

Mystified, Peter looks from Zachary to Elizabeth and Rebecca, and finally back at the entity, "Well, sir, I have no idea what's involved, but if I can be of assistance I would, of course, be glad to help."

He smiles broadly, "Your help would be particularly beneficial here, Peter, for, you see, this realm is quite close to the Earth. It's been some time since I've been in the Earth, and though I can call up memories as vivid as a printed book, I hate to trouble anyone to do that. If you could help, well, it would just make things easier, and perhaps we could settle this quickly and get on to other matters."

Peter looks at Zachary for an indication of what to do. Zachary smiles and nods, encouraging Peter to accept.

"Okay, sir. I'll be happy to help. Tell me what's expected of me and how I can do whatever it is you want me to do."

"Oh, of course, Peter. I wouldn't leave you in the dark on any of this. There's enough darkness out there without me creating any more."

Chuckles can be heard from the two females.

"But, please, forgive my manners, Peter. I don't feel entirely comfortable with anyone calling me 'sir' anymore. Why don't you just call me … Well, let's see, what's a good name, Zack?"

Literally choking to hold back his laughter, Zachary stutters and stammers, "W-well, I-I don't know. How about … Zeb? I always liked Zeb."

Surprisingly, Elizabeth steps forward, "What about Rose? Rose is a nice word. It conjures up all sorts of wonderful things, and God does love roses."

The entity seems inspired by Elizabeth's thought and, as he turns to look at Peter, smiles even more as he realizes that Peter is trying to fit the name, Rose, with this entitly.

He laughs, "Well, Peter, I see that would trouble you a bit. I've never thought of myself quite like a rose, anyway. They're too perfect, and I have a few steps to go in that direction, if you know what I mean. So why don't you just call me Zeb? That seems to feel okay with me, if it suits you."

Puzzled, Peter looks back and forth from his group to the entity, now offering the name of Zeb, "Well, sir, or uh, Zeb, but, uh, don't you have a proper name? Why are you all trying to pick a name? Doesn't everyone have a name?"

Some of the humor fades from the entity's countenance as he responds softly, "Indeed, everyone has a name, a sort of unique identifier. But it's difficult to express that in terms that you would consider to be a name. It's not a word, this identifier. It's more like a vibrational frequency. Each entity has its own vibrational frequency that is unique.

"This unique identifier is probably thought of in some realms to be a sound or an array of sounds that might sound equivalent, in your Earth terminology, to a chord, though probably a considerable distance away from the usual expression of a chord on a piano or harpsichord or something of that sort in the Earth. Nonetheless, the point behind this little exercise, if you will think of it as such, is to make clear to you something which Zachary was trying to express to you back there in Todd's realm." He pausesand studies Peter.

"You mean, you know about Todd's realm and what we were doing there?"

"Yes, Peter, I do. I am what you might consider to be the controller or supervisor of that realm. My responsibility or, our term is *commission*, as you know, is to keep things on an even keel. We couldn't have one realm floating off and running into another, now, could we? I mean that would be like an earthquake. Buildings would be falling down, and entities might become dislodged from their consciousness. Then we'd have to go around and re-awaken them all, and it would be just a mess, you see?"

Struggling to keep up with the thought-forms flowing to him from Zeb, Peter nonetheless does comprehend every word he is relating. He can feel himself expanding as the entity speaks. Peter leans forward with his usual eagerness and asks, "Please, sir, tell me more about this. I understand what you are saying better, I think, than I have understood many things." Turning quickly to look at Zachary and the others, "No offense, of course."

"None taken, Pete, by any of us. Our colleague here has a talent at this sort of thing, or he wouldn't be in the Control Center. See what I mean?"

Smiling broadly, the entity turns back to Peter to resume his comments. "So, each realm has, in a manner of speaking, its own uniqueness, and the entities therein have the right of their existence in that unique realm. But, I'd like you to come over here by me, Peter. And why don't you just be satisfied with calling me Zeb for a moment or two. Then, if you'd like, we can get back on that issue later. But for a little thumbnail, just to satisfy your curiosity, which I see dangling off there in space, yes, I've had many names, but I no longer have a need for them or a use for them. So whenever Zachary, or someone like him, comes to visit, we have this little exchange until we find a name that seems to fit me okay for the entity or entities and the situation."

He leans and glances past Peter, "But you know, Zack, I'm getting a little weary of Zeb. Couldn't you come up with something more creative?"

Giggling can be heard from Elizabeth and Rebecca, as Zachary, feigning embarrassment, looks down, shuffles this way and that, and, quickly recovering, looks up with a smile.

"Now, then, Peter, if you'll follow my guidance here, I'll show you what I mean and how you can help."

Following his gaze, Peter perceives it as a shaft of translucent energy that projects from Zeb and enters into the white mist in front of them, so that Peter is looking down a bit and forward. He marvels that it is as though he's looking at a gigantic television screen, though there is no indication of any screen per se. But, Peter realizes that he is looking into another realm.

The first thing he notices is that everything seems to be faded, almost to the point of blurring. He strains to look about and to perceive the entities. He notes a few, but very few. Zeb gently interrupts him, as though he's placing a hand on Peter's shoulder, "Don't bother to strain, Peter. It isn't that you need to adjust your fine-tuning or anything like that, for this realm is, indeed, fading."

"Could you explain more about that, Zeb? I can perceive the realm, and they seem to be losing their definability. They don't have the density I would expect. And there aren't very many of them. Why is that?"

"It's good that you noticed that last bit, for that's exactly what's happening here. Remember what you've been told about when a group of entities come together in agreement on a certain way of existing, that that literally creates a realm in which they can exist? Remember when Zachary took you down Todd's main street and it began to dissipate?"

"Yes, I remember that well."

"Well, look here again. There are only a few entities left in the entire realm, and that's not enough to provide strength to the thought-form to perpetuate it. In fact, while we are here talking, in the equivalent of several Earth minutes, this realm will be down to only three entities. Get that, now, only three souls to focus their consciousness on this one entire realm. What do you think of that, Peter?"

Peter, reeling from the realization of what he is being shown, responds rather weakly, "I-I don't know what to think, Zeb. I've never experienced anything like this, as I suppose you know."

"Well, as Zachary would tell you, you have. You just don't know that you have. But that's not important for the moment. What is important is that I need your help right now, if you can."

"Well, sure, Mr. Zeb, I mean Zeb, What do I do?"

"If you'll follow my gaze, I'll put an illuminator on the entity over there, second from the right. Look at them now, there's only three of them. The second from the right is the one I want you to help me with. Okay?"

As Peter observes, he can see Zeb's, whatever he has called it, somehow or other brightening up the entity. The entity straightens up, obviously feeling this illumination. He begins to look about and, in an instant, Peter finds himself standing face to face, right in front of the entity, with his Mr. Zeb at his left.

The entity is startled, "Who are you?"

Peter looks at Zeb and then back to the entity. "Are you talking to me?" he asks, unnerved.

"Well, whom else would I be talking to? You're the only one here besides me."

Peter turns to look back at Zeb who smiles at him, *Sorry about that, Pete. He can't see me. No way I can make myself visible to him. Just impossible at the moment, so it's up to you. I'll be right here and will help, but he won't hear a thing we're saying to each other. All he'll perceive is you standing there in front of him, staring at him.*

Well, what do I do, Zeb?

Do whatever comes naturally. You've got experience now. Remember Todd and the others, and give him some help. Use your own internal guidance. Remember, you've got a connection to your group always, so call upon them if you need them.

Remembering this, Peter feels a flood of warmth and, to some degree, confidence come over him. Looking squarely at the entity, he states, "I'm sorry. Let me introduce myself to you. I'm called Peter."

"Well, holy cow! Are you Peter? You know, the Pearly Gates Peter?"

Peter cannot contain his laughter and shock at the reference. "No, I don't think so. At least if I am, I don't know about it."

"Well, then, who are you?"

"Might I ask, before I go any further, who you are? What's your name?"

"You mean you've come here to visit me and you don't even know my name?"

Somewhat embarrassed, Peter turns and asks his colleague, unseen by this entity, *What can I call him, Zeb? I'm at a disadvantage here.*

Never mind. He won't tell you the truth, no matter what you ask him. He's a compulsive liar. He'd rather tell you a lie than what time of day it is, if there was such a thing here.

Peter is stunned as he considers what Zeb has just said. "Well, certainly I know your name," Peter answers as he turns back to him, "but that's not the issue," becoming more bold now, fortified by this information. "What I want to talk to you about is, what are you going to do now?"

Looking down, the entity shuffles about a bit and states rather remorsefully, "I'll tell you, uh ... What'd you say your name was? Peter? I don't have the faintest idea. You can't trust anybody. We had this place going well. We were about to take over the next town and I don't know what happened. People chickened out and went this way and that and, well, there's not much left here anymore, and I'm tired of fighting to hang onto it."

Suddenly Peter realizes that the key word in the entity's statement is *tired.* Hearing an affirmation internally from Zachary and an encouragement from Elizabeth and Rebecca, he states, "Well, if you're so tired, why do you struggle?"

Abruptly, he turns to Peter, "What do you mean, struggle? I'm not struggling. Nobody struggles here. Things just happen. Who knows why? But I am tired of it. It's gotten to be a big bore. You know what I mean?"

In an effort to move into harmony with the entity, Peter says, "I think I can comprehend that one. Look, tired, bored, whatever it is that you are, why do you stay here?" He glances around, "There's not much left. I only see those other two guys over there, and you. That's not much of an exciting existence, I would think."

The entity looks down again, "You're right about that! We had a real group here. I mean, quite a gang. We used to do all kinds of things. They never lasted very long, and things'd always go back to the way they were, but ... I don't know. It's just, like I said, nothing much worthwhile in anything any more."

Peter detects an opening. "There are worthwhile things if you're open enough to hear about them."

Ever so slowly, the entity turns his head to glance sideways at Peter, and Peter can tell that the entity is going to lie. He doesn't know how he knows, but he can feel it. Looking out of the corner of his eye, the entity bitterly spits out the words and thought-forms, "I suppose you'll tell me about those same places again. I never liked 'em. Why would anyone want to go to them? They're boring. Worse than this place. I'd rather stay here and fade away into nothingness."

Peter is aware that the entity has no idea what he's talking about but, somehow or other, has developed the use of his intuitive consciousness for lying or distorting truth. So much so, that everything that the entity experiences is distorted back to him.

Softly, Peter points out, "Well, we are what we think, you know. And what we say is what we experience."

"Just what do you mean by that?"

Unwavering, Peter returns the entity's glare with a look of warmth and compassion. "Just this … I know you have no idea what I'm going to tell you. And I *am* going to tell you, because your very existence depends on your movement to another realm. If you don't move to another realm, then you're going to go back into what you'll recognize, I think, as a period of sleep or restful contemplation."

Obviously stunned by these comments, the entity states, "How'd you know about my confinement?"

Peter is puzzled. "Confinement?"

That's how he looked at it, Peter hears from Zeb. *His time of rest and re-balancing, he thought of as confinement. The guy's an ex-con in the Earth, a real rowdy. But you know there's hope in the worst of them, isn't there?"*

Peter is now stunned, as he realizes the magnitude of the task before him. Re-focusing himself, he states to the entity, "Look, I can more easily show you than tell you. What do you say?"

The entity obviously draws back into himself. As he does Peter is buffeted with heavy, sluggish bolts and jostling, and he realizes that this is the counterpart of the emanation of light, sound, and color that normally radiates from him and his group. Only this entity's vibrations are slowed to such a point that they have this dull, heavy impact on him. Peter shrugs himself intuitively and, as he does, he feels as though splotches of a muddy, gloppy-like substance fall off his cloak.

As the entity looks at Peter, he is surprised. "Hey, Peter, how'd you do that? How'd you get rid of those?"

"Nothing to it," responds Peter, truly out on a limb with his commentary and his understanding of the situation, but following the guidance from Elizabeth, Rebecca and Zachary on their "private line."

"Well, could you show me how to do that?"

"That's what I was talking about. But, as long as you'd rather move back into confinement or stay in this realm and fade away, who can show you anything?"

"Well, now, wait a minute! I didn't mean it like that. You know, it's just that that's the way everyone thinks here, and whenever one of you guys floats into our realm, it makes us nervous. We don't have any idea what you're up to or why you're here. Frankly, we know that you think you're better than we are."

"Oh, not at all," responds Peter as casually as he can muster. "We're all equal. It's merely our choices that separate us. It's not the old Earth caste system. It's just choices."

"Caste system?"

Peter realizes that he did not know the meaning of the term. "You know, like the rich folks and the poor folks, the haves and the have-nots."

"Oh, yeah. Got that one."

"Look, we're wasting time here. Your realm is fading. Either I help you or you can move into your confinement, as you call it. But you don't have a lot of time."

Glancing around nervously, the entity states, reluctantly, "Well, okay, then. Show me."

Peter turns to Zeb, *Now what?*

That's it, Pete. Good job. I'll take it from here.

As swiftly as he speaks, Peter is instantly back with Zachary, Elizabeth and Rebecca. He looks at them with amazement and breathes a sigh of joy and relief to be free of what he thinks of now as a realm of incredible weight or burden, sluggishness, as though he'd been in a quagmire of a murky, mud-like substance. He remembers wading through the muck of a swamp when a friend took him duck hunting earlier in his just-previous life in the Earth.

"Yep, it's like that, Pete, all right," comments Zachary. "And the reason you were the best choice here is, you have the most recent experience with thought-forms like that, that are carried over from the Earth, and this guy certainly has a bunch of them."

Peter listens carefully, then asks, "Zachary, you are infinitely more qualified to deal with (in my mind, at least) virtually any situation. Why on Earth, or shall I say *in heaven,* would you have me do this job instead of doing it yourself?

"Appreciate the compliment, but take a look at this from another perspective. Look at me."

And Peter sees his friend.

"No, I mean really look at me, Pete."

At this point, Peter goes inward and looks at Zachary, not from the sense of perception, but from the sense of knowing. Instantly he perceives a brilliant, brilliant light.

"That's what I mean, Pete. It's that light. It takes me a long time to slow it down and to bring it to the level of vibration to enter into a weak realm like that. One misstep and the realm would be gone, simply because I goofed a little here or there and let out a bit too much light. On the other hand, you have the capacity to remember the Earth and, therefore, automatically can balance your cloak with those heavier vibrations because the thought-form of those vibrations is still vivid in your consciousness. I would have to work to re-build the memory of such thought-forms, and we just didn't have that as our time or opportunity. The event was happening, literally, as you perceived it, and if you'll look back now, you'll understand what I mean."

Turning to look back at where Zeb had made the opening, Peter sees clearly that the realm is no longer there. In its place are two dull spherical-shaped objects, hovering.

"What are they, Zachary?"

"Those are the two remaining entities of the three. They didn't make it."

Sadly, Peter gazes at them.

It is Elizabeth who speaks next. "Please don't worry or be saddened, Peter. They're all right. They are where they have chosen to be, and their period of rest, as you will see in moments, will be watched over."

As she speaks, Peter can see several very beautifully glowing and wonderfully colored orbs of light move in to position themselves around these two spheres of dull, grayish-brown light.

"What are those?"

"Peter, you know what *those*, as you call them, are. Don't you remember?"

Immediately he intuits in his memory and his consciousness that these are balls of light like he himself had taken the form of earlier.

"How beautiful. Are those entities going to help them?"

"Yes, indeed so," she responds, and in the softness of her commentary Peter is reassured. As they watch and Elizabeth continues to comment, Peter sees the entities and the two denser, darker-colored spheres slowly move off and away from them.

"Where are they going?"

"To a place of rest and non-involvement, like the areas between the colors that we passed through when we came here. I have a friend in the Earth who calls them the Inter-Between, and that rather describes them well, wouldn't you think, Peter?"

"Hm-m, Inter-Between. Well, yes, that sounds good. Good title for it. So they'll stay in the Inter-Between, then, being the state of rest, a sort of suspended animation?"

"Yes, they will, but it's not suspended animation. They are growing, balancing and shifting and being helped the whole time. They are neither being expressed in a form nor in a realm, because at the moment they haven't got the comprehension or the ability to attune to another realm that is equal to or beyond the one in which they just existed. And we can't have them going down or backwards, can we?

Without thinking, Peter answers, "No, indeed. I wouldn't want anyone sliding backwards. Goodness, that realm was not at all pleasant. Are there many like it?"

"More than we'd care to express to you," comments Zachary softly.

From his reserved tone, Peter can tell that this is not a topic of joy to Zachary. "Gosh, Zachary. Can't we do something about that? I mean, why would entities want to dwell in such a realm? I couldn't understand why Todd was living where he was, but these folks … This is awful."

Zachary shrugs his shoulders. "It's their choice, Pete. What can you do about that?"

"You mean to tell me with all the things you've shown me you can do… your jingle-jangle, and creating flowers and butterflies and benches, moving into formlessness and into balls of light, moving with, I don't know, the speed of light or greater from one place to another … you can't help a few folks stuck in the mud down there?"

Zachary similes gently, "Can help, in terms of our capability, can't help, in terms of the Law."

Peter reflects on this and, as he does, the others note his cloak demonstrating the intensity with which he is attempting to assimilate this information.

"Look, it's like this," Zachary continues, "we do not violate the right of others to choose, and these entities have chosen. Even though we might think they've chosen rather misguidedly and inadvertently, chosen they have. As long as they are putting greater energy or consciousness into their choice than in the willingness to see something different, or know something different, we can't interfere. By the way, Peter, the same thing is true of the Earth."

Peter now is changing outwardly in his coloration, and the others simply observe as he reflects back on experiences in the Earth. Flashing incredibly rapidly through his consciousness are many experiences of the just-previous incarnation that he couldn't understand or grasp that existed under the watchful eye of what was purported to be an all-knowing and all-loving God.

"Yes, Peter, all those things you've just re-lived also fall under the auspices of Universal Law."

"And I suppose there is a reason for the Law working like that. Is that right?"

"Well, if you give it some time and some thought, I'm certain that you will understand the answer to your own question. Think about it just for a moment. Would you have God make all the decisions? Or would you give the children free will, free choice, and then stand back, even if (in your eyes) they make the wrong choice?"

Peter colors up again as he remembers his own children and the times they experienced making decisions and then had to bear the less than joyful burden of those decisions. "I see. So what you're saying here is that as long as these entities choose to dwell there, and to be only conscious to the extent that they are, we can't do anything about it. We can't interfere or help them or anything?"

"That's true, Pete, but we aren't utterly helpless, and I'll try to explain to you why as we go along here. But for now, I want you to move to the Control Center at a point where we can perceive the Earth. Is that acceptable to you?

"Sure. I'd like to leave this little area. I feel like I need to go to a dry cleaners and sort of be spiritually cleansed."

Laughter abounds as Zachary leads again, and they find themselves in short order at a point that makes Peter feel marvelous. "Look." Zachary points to a mass of white, mist-like substance and, as he does, with a wave of his hands it begins to clear.

Peter suddenly has a thought and interrupts, "Zack, before we go on, what about that fellow I left with Zeb? Is he okay?"

"That's what I like about you, Pete. All of us do. You always have time to think of the other person, the person who has less than you. You are concerned about them and want them to be well. That's a quality that endears you not only to our group, but unto God Himself."

Embarrassed, Peter glances down and, adopting one of Zachary's own habits, begins fidgeting with his cloak.

Noting this, Zachary states, glancing good-naturedly to the area of the cloak Peter is adjusting, "You studied well, Pete. But no need to be embarrassed. God loves us all." Turning back to the area in the mist-like formation, Zachary again concentrates.

As he does, Peter can perceive the Earth. First he perceives it as though he is off in space. Then it slowly begins to become more and more visible in a finite sense, until he sees a beautiful, vast forest covered with magnificent trees that have a radiance of green leaves on the tips of each branch.

Peter stares in wonder at the beauty. "That is lovely, Zachary! I always loved the forests and nature. That is just beautiful. But may I ask why you're showing it to me?"

"Certainly. I want you to learn to observe."

Puzzled, Peter looks back at the forest. "Can you not tell if I see the forest? I do see it. It's lovely. What else would you have me observe?"

"Listen, look. Observe for a moment."

Obediently, Peter focuses his consciousness. As he does,

he hears a very subtle tinkle, a little chime-like resonance, as though someone had just struck a thin piece of glass with a soft mallet of some sort to create an enchanting tinkling rivulet of sound.

"Did you hear that?"

"Are you talking about that little tinkling sound?"

"So you did hear it. Do you know what it was?"

"I've no idea. What was it?"

"A leaf just fell from one of the trees in that forest."

In disbelief, Peter stares at Zachary, beginning to laugh … no, to giggle. "You're kidding me. A leaf fell in the forest and created that sound?"

Just as serious as can be, Zachary nods. "Now, I want you to develop your awareness, and look at the forest.

Peter does.

Then Zachary asks, "Tell me, Pete, from which tree did the leaf fall?"

———————

In order that one can find their way into truth and into all realms, there must be the ability to observe.

As the observer, one can learn the answer to any question, the solution to any problem or challenge. As we proceed, we shall attempt to assist you to learn how to observe and to use the tools God has given you in order to advance yourselves spiritually, mentally, physically and emotionally. That shall be, in part, some of the work of the commission being offered to you.

CHAPTER 7

The Inner Light
OCTOBER 10, 1991

Peter has been contemplating the questions Zachary posed to him. "What would be the purpose, Zack, for my being capable of identifying precisely which tree dropped a leaf? In the past you've provided some, forgive me, strange opportunities for learning, but this one I believe tops them all."

"We can come back to the *why* of your question later, if you still choose, Peter, but for now, if you would, simply try to do as I asked, and tell me which tree dropped the leaf?"

Puzzled, but trusting his friend Zachary without question, Peter pauses only a moment, looks into Zachary's eyes, and then turns his attention to the forest that is before him and upon the Earth.

Reaching out with his consciousness, as he recently learned to do, Peter tries to establish a oneness with the forest. Remembering his experience with the oak tree, he finds to his surprise that this is easily done. Wherein the experience with the single tree seemed to draw him into that specific form itself, here he has a feeling of completeness. Compared to the essence of the single tree, there is now a sensation that the forest itself is functioning or vibrating as one collective entity comprised of many singular components.

So quickly that it actually startles him, he detects the same tone, the same resonance as that small tinkling sound like a soft mallet striking a glass. Peter simultaneously notes that one tree, off to the left and up a bit, seems to be illuminated, and the illuminations of that single tree coincide perfectly with the tones. He finds the experience most absorbing, and as his attention is drawn more and more into what lies before him, he hears Zachary's voice, as though coming to him from a great distance.

"Hold on a bit, Pete. You're slipping into that again. You wouldn't want to become a forest for ten or twenty years. Or would you? Not a bad place to be, I suppose, but we do have other things that we might rather focus our attention on."

A bit startled at his movement into the consciousness of the forest and specifically this singular tree, just as swiftly Peter finds himself back with his small group and, looking from one to the other, sees them smiling at him. He looks to Zachary who is, at the moment, considering him carefully, looking him over from head to foot exaggeratedly, until their eyes meet.

"Why is it that after each one of these adventures, you to bring me to something like this? Like interacting with the oak tree and then this forest. It's almost as though you are doing this deliberately. And, while we're at it, why am I so attracted to trees?"

Laughter ripples through the group because of the way Peter states this.

Peter finds humor in his own intense tone and shuffles a bit, "Well, I didn't mean it quite that way. But anyway, what is it about the oak tree, and now this forest and that singular tree? And, I wonder what would have happened if you hadn't called me, or uh, awakened me, or whatever it was. Was I sleeping? I mean, it sounded like you were miles away, or realms away. But …"

Musical laughter spews forth from Zachary, echoed by all, including Peter as he realizes what he has done.

"Well, that's good, Pete, you haven't changed. Your

questions still pour forth like the fountain of eternal youth. Just wonderful. Let's see if I can do as well in answering them. But perhaps, if you don't mind, I'll separate those questions and try to deal with them one at a time. They should be more understandable that way."

Looking down with just a touch of embarrassment at his old habits, Peter simply nods.

"When you move from a state of consciousness, essentially defined as being 'centered', and then into an activity as you just experienced with Zeb in that dissipating realm, we bring you to a subsequent activity, such as this forest or the oak tree to, in effect, re-center you, or, re-balance you.

"Whenever one is asked to concentrate or to focus, the process itself requires that external or extraneous influences be cast off. In other words, one needs to go within oneself, take control of one's own individuality and uniqueness, and then perform the activity requested. In this way, should there have been any last vestiges of those globs or splotches (as you might remember them from the dissipated realm) clinging to you anywhere, this would give you that spiritual dry-cleaning that you felt you needed. Just take a moment now and think about it. Don't you feel better?"

Peter takes an inventory of his sensations, his own awareness, and concludes that, indeed, he feels perhaps a bit lighter and brighter somehow than he did back when they were strolling in Todd's realm. "I do, indeed, Zachary. In fact, I feel better somehow than I did before we got to the Control Room, if that makes sense. Do continue. I'll hush now. I want to hear the answers to those questions. They seem important."

Smiling, Zachary extends a hand to Elizabeth, and Peter notes that apparently it is she who is to continue.

"To follow up on what Zachary has explained, each entity constitutes, in essence, their own reality and their own perspective of that reality to the degree that they permit themselves to do so. In each of the instances that you have experienced with us, and in other experiences such as in your just-completed sojourn in the Earth, you have always been in command of your own awareness and your own reality.

"As Zachary has identified to you, as have Zeb and the others, Universal Law is a blessing given to all existence by God. This primal Law cannot be violated, unless you allow it to be violated for yourself. In other words, you have a kind of holy of holies within you, a *sanctum sanctorum*. However you would call it, it does exist. It is the core of your being. It is that point at which the light of your existence is the brightest and purest. As you turn inward to focus on, for example, Zachary's guiding suggestions, you approach that light. When you do, you are purified in all aspects of your being. This is the benefit obtained by entities in the Earth through the practice of what is called meditation, wherein they go within themselves to find a place of silence, of joy, of peace, of oneness. Have I made myself clear to this point?"

Nodding, Peter is obviously absorbing all of this at a commendable rate, and like one who has just emerged from an intellectual desert, Peter thirsts for more.

Glancing at Zachary, who gives the subtlest of nods and looks away, Elizabeth realizes she is to continue. "So, then, Peter, if you consider this as an activity available to you at all times, you will never be in a situation that you cannot deal with. You'll never find yourself without the presence of what you have come to know of as the balancing joy or the lifeline (as you visualized it often) between us, your friends and others, and yourself. But in truth, the greatest of all lifelines exists for each of us inwardly and is that which connects us directly to God."

Reflecting heavily on these last few words, Peter turns inward and his cloak radiates, sparkles, and becomes highly illuminated.

The members of his group quietly move into positions of

balance with Peter's activity. After just a moment or two, his cloak regains a state of harmony and balance, and he emerges again in his consciousness. "I think I have absorbed that, Elizabeth. Let me try to re-state it to you so I can be certain I have grasped it in the manner in which you intend."

Nodding approval, Elizabeth smiles.

Peter goes on. "You are saying that no matter where I am or what I'm doing, I always have this lifeline to make me well or give me … What? Strength? Courage? Faith? Can it also guide me? Can it give me needed information? For example, when I was in that realm that was dissipating, as you know, I called upon you all and you answered, to help me understand how to deal with that guy, and that was successful. Can this inner light do the same? In other words, can I speak to it and receive an answer, like I'm speaking to you, and expect to hear an answer back? Can it work that way?"

All three smile gently at Peter in a manner that seems to surround him with a soft pink luminosity. He feels this as the love, support, and encouragement coming from them, an essence that he has come to know very well. As this continues, he realizes that the answer to his question is that, indeed, there is much more available to him than he is presently capable of comprehending. "Is that true, Elizabeth? Zachary? Rebecca? The thoughts that just came to me, are they true? Do you hear them?"

All three nod an affirmation to him, indicating that they were aware of his thoughts and that the thoughts are true.

Peter pauses for a prolonged period of time, obviously grappling with this concept of inner guidance, to determine whether or not he can feel comfortable with it, whether he can believe in it as he believes in the friendship and truth that his three colleagues and others have demonstrated to him.

Zachary interrupts his thoughts, "You have no way of truly knowing that until you try. When we are placed in situations or interactions that call upon us to produce our highest and best, therein do we find the mettle of which we are made. Therein do we find the truth of our nature, and that which we have believed about ourselves must now be proven. It is good because it causes us to become truthful. For in order to gain guidance from the eternal light within, one must have a sort of communication line of truth between the consciousness of self and the eternal consciousness of the light within. Wherever there is falsehood, wherever there is the shadow of habit building an illusion, things distort and create static along the communication lines. But again, Peter, we all concur here (and I believe that you do, as well) that experience is always the best teacher, with only a few exceptions here and there."

Peter looks from one to the other of his group.

Rebecca seems to become luminous, "What you are hearing from our friends, Peter, is truth. Truth has a way of coming into one's reality as one becomes familiar with its expressions. You have, in the past recent events, been granted numerous opportunities to become familiar with truth. As a result, you have learned much about your less limited nature than you would have believed possible when you first entered the Garden and began your works. Now the position that you are in, if you would like to consider it from that vantage point, is whether or not you would like to continue and to further your understanding of truth through more experiences and more of what you and Zachary call adventures." Rebecca smiles broadly to Peter in a way that resonates within him to a remarkable degree.

Peter pauses for a time to absorb the emanations from Rebecca, which, again, he finds, to be delightful, warming to his heart and …

"Just a minute, Pete, we're not going back to the cherry pie thing here, are we?

The group erupts in luminosity and tones, and they roll about in laughter.

Coming to rest after a goodly passage of joy, our group

finds itself upon a high knoll, looking down over a vast valley, with high mountain peaks surrounding this valley, up and behind them. The peaks reach up into an incredible luminosity of blue and silvery-white, periodically dotted here and there with brilliant flashes of small spheres of color.

Peter glances about in awe. "This is a beautiful spot. Where are we now? The last thing I recall is all that laughter and joy. Did I fall asleep?"

Zachary looks down, rubbing his hand against the blades of up-stretched grass, "Yes, in a manner of speaking, you fell asleep. But as you already know, it's not sleep like in the Earth but a time of spiritual re-balancing and re-orienting. In these realms of expression, these periods of time are to sort of realign, to balance with awareness, to integrate new truth into the sum and substance of being; and to cleanse and purify, to rid the temple of light (as we call it) of unneeded habits. Some in the Earth call it drosses."

"You mean I have drosses?"

There is a tinkle of laughter as Elizabeth quickly answers, "No, Peter. Zachary doesn't mean it like that. He's talking about the vestiges of thought-forms, attitudes, emotions, maybe even a fear or two, or a doubt. Not the kind you're talking about."

"Oh, good. You had me worried there for a moment, Zack. What can you tell me about these drosses, the vestiges of old thought-forms and habits, and all that? Why aren't I pure, now that I am no longer … alive, you know, like in the Earth? Aren't I in …" looking around, and feeling a bit awkward with this question so he asks barely audibly, "Heaven?"

Fountains of laughter come from the others and Zachary rolls about on the slope.

For a moment, Peter is concerned that Zachary might roll all the way down and end up in the valley. Having noted this, Zachary begins to roll upward, and then down, and then stops. Brushing himself slightly, he looks at Peter, "You see?

Believe in the illusion and it's yours. If you thought I was going to roll down the hillside here into the valley, then you believe in gravity, and you believe that we are in something paralleling the Earth. But if you are unlimited in your belief, it's as easy for me to roll up the hill as down. Get the meaning?"

"I grasp it, but not completely, obviously, for something inside me seems to be calling out."

"Oh, well, we can't have that," and with a tone of light-hearted mockery, Zachary leans forward exaggeratedly, cupping his ear with his hand. "Let's all be quiet and see what they're saying in there."

Peter chuckles and then decides that he'll turn this around on Zachary for a change. He quiets himself swiftly and then, from within, forces this communication to Zachary, *What's a thought-form, anyway?*

"Yep, I heard the voices. They want to know what a thought-form is. I'm going to show them, but you'll have to explain it to them, because I can't quite reach them. They're somewhere down in the murky depths of your being."

Elizabeth and Rebecca are struggling to contain their laughter at the antics of Peter and Zachary and at the rather odd manner of Zachary's teaching.

Standing quickly upright, he extends his hand, palm upward, and a burst of flame jumps from the palm of his hand, burning strongly and extending upward.

Startled, Peter jumps back. "Good grief, Zachary. Watch yourself there."

Instantly, the flame is gone, and Peter, regaining his composure, realizes what Zachary is doing. In that split-second, Zachary turns his hand over, palm down, and Peter sees that rain is falling from the underside of Zachary's palm. With a twinkle in his eye and an impish grin, he remarks, "I thought I had better put it out, just in case. You know, I can't be starting some sort of errant fire."

Peter is flabbergasted by the rain falling from the underside of Zachary's hand.

The rain stops, and Zachary is standing there, arm outstretched. "What would you like next? You need a dove or two?" As he turns his hand over, it appears to Peter that two, no, three radiant white doves fly upwards from the palm of Zachary's hand and, rising together, circle and soar down to the valley below. "Or maybe you'd like a rainbow, Pete. I've always liked them. Let's see if I have a rainbow in there today," and there springs forth a miniaturized rainbow. With a snap of his finger, Zachary sits back down, and the rainbow dissipates. He looks at Peter steadily. *"That's* illusion."

Peter fumbles for words.

"A bit dramatic, I think," remarks Rebecca softly, coming to the rescue, "but effective, if I am judging Peter's reactions clearly. Those theatrics, Peter, are to prove a point. Do you believe that Zachary created those things?"

Nodding, Peter swings himself about to look full on at Rebecca, who is seated just a bit up and to his right.

"If you believe them, they are so. They are your reality. But how did Zachary create them? Have you given that any consideration?"

Puzzled, Peter turns himself sideways to look at Zachary.

Zachary, is, as you might expect, fidgeting with his cloak, brushing it off, picking at it as though it has lint, "Goodness, all that activity requires a bit of tidying up," as though this discussion is of no concern to him.

"You see, Peter," Rebecca continues, "illusion is dependent upon the perceiver and those who are perpetuating it. Those are key ingredients that will be very important to you and to us and our works together in the future. To answer your unspoken question, Zachary can create, as he just demonstrated, because you agree with the creation. For example, you have known and lived rainfall, fire, rainbows, and doves. So they are, in effect, thought-forms within your consciousness, and, therefore, Zachary's seemingly incredible feats are nothing more than summoning forth the agreed-upon images or 'realities' as you have known them.

"But now, as you are expressed here in your current form that is far less limited, summoning or remembering is no great accomplishment. It is merely the demonstration of an agreement upon a given thought-form. So, while we are here in this expression, this realm or dimension, we would not be violating any of the constraints of the three-dimensional expression called Earth. Understand?"

As usual, Peter is drawn almost magically to Rebecca's comments as though she is somehow imparting at the core of his being an understanding that goes beyond the limited nature of words and sentences. She is communicating to him in experiences, shared living expressions, rather than descriptive words. He responds, barely audibly, "I think so."

The group pauses for a moment, awaiting Peter's next comment.

He turns slowly to look at Zachary and asks, softly, "Who are you, anyway?"

Without wavering, without a moment's hesitation, Zachary responds, "I'm your brother, Pete, pure and simple, just as Elizabeth and Rebecca are your sisters. But I am brother, and Rebecca and Elizabeth sisters, because we are polarized in this expression as male-female. Beyond that, we are kindred souls. We're souls of an harmonic, you might say, that have vibrated together in the past, and shall again in the future. You are asking who I am because you associate such works, as I just demonstrated to you, with something beyond your comprehension. Yet, I could, in the next moment, show you that you yourself can do the same. Remember the butterfly?"

Nodding now more vigorously, Peter acknowledges the memory.

"Do not think, Peter, that I am greater than you, or harbor for a second that little thought in the back of your consciousness that *maybe Zachary is an expression of God* or some such as that. We are all expressions of God, and I have no greater command over God's power than you do. I simply allow·myself a bit more latitude than some," and the impish grin appears once again on his countenance.

More relaxed now, Peter asks, "Well, tell me, dear friends, what's this all about? Let me sort of recap here, so I might comprehend this better."

All nod approval and quietly adjust their positions to await his commentary.

Peter looks down for a moment and turns inward.

(*Understand, what we are giving to you is in words. Peter is speaking in multiple expressions now, as he has learned to do quite well.*)

"Not that long ago I was in the Earth plane. Were you all with me there somehow or other?"

Nodding, each affirms that this is so.

"So then, when I, you know, died ..."

The group smiles warmly, encouraging Peter to continue.

"I remember when I died and I went through all those colors and the different feelings and all that. Somehow, when I was in that dissipating realm, I felt that tug again. And back when we were working with Todd, remember, Elizabeth? I felt it there, too. And a couple times with Wilbur, though much less. Now here we sit on this lovely summit before this radiant valley ... only God knows where, and I have no idea of what lies ahead or where we are going, or why I'm even participating in all these things. When I was in the Earth, I had always thought that ... well, when death came, something would happen. I believed that life would continue, but I sure didn't visualize it like this."

Peter's group continues to send him encouraging warmth.

"So, what's it all about? Why am I here? Why are you here with me? Does everyone experience as I have? I know the answer to that in a sense, because I now have our friend, Todd, and perhaps even some sort of a bond with the fellow in the now dissipated realm and, of course, Wilbur. But, what does all of this mean? Somehow it seems idle, as though it has no real purpose. Is this what all people in the Earth can expect? Or will some experience as Todd and others have, like his family, and some like Wilbur, who seems to have a bond with the Crystal Workers Realm? Is there a plan or an outline that we are following that you could share with me that will help me to comprehend this?"

Pausing and looking earnestly into the eyes of his companions, he turns from one to the other and then looks down. "I don't know what it is I am trying to convey to you. I guess I would ask you at this point to look within me and to hold nothing back. For I would like to do all I can and be the best that I can, because I now know that life is continuous … at least to this point, anyway. But who knows, in the next turn of a corner, I might find out there is an end to it all."

At this point, he sees Zachary shaking his head and hears, *No, Pete. Eternity. A wondrous, joyous, continuity of existence and unfolding experiences too staggering to grasp and too immense for me to attempt to convey to you.*

"Well, then, if that's so, after we've broken free of realms like Todd's earlier one and the now extinct realm of the entity we just worked with, do we all move into this? It all seems strange, just sort of bouncing around and rolling in the Realm of Laughter. There just doesn't seem to be much point to anything in the long-term. Please help me with this. It's been a growing concern within me, as I'm sure you might have detected."

Looking back up at his companions, Peter notes that each of them has become more luminous, and he admires their beauty and brilliance. He turns to Zachary, whom he has come to think of as his mentor of sorts, and notes that he is increasing in luminosity at a remarkable rate.

Zachary turns to Elizabeth and Rebecca and asks softly, *Do you concur with me that we are now at the threshold.?*

They smile, looking at Peter as they do, and respond inwardly, *We do. Shall we proceed, then?*

He turns back to Peter, *Look at yourself, Peter.*

Still conditioned by the familiarity of sight in the Earth, Peter looks down and perceives that he, too, is brilliant. Then looking back up, in his countenance he seems to be saying to Zachary, *What do you mean? How do I look at myself?*

Look at yourself in me. And don't question the mechanics of that. Just follow what I have given you. Move to me and look back.

Strangely, Peter finds it remarkably easy to move to where Zachary is. The feeling of turning and looking back at himself jolts Peter, as he sees a brilliant light directly across from where Zachary is.

Look at it, Pete, he hears within, *carefully now, and describe what you see.*

Joyfully, Peter allows his awareness to flow over the orb of light, which he knows is he himself. He notes, here and there, little variations in color, subtleties of continuity that seem to change sporadically, but overall he finds that the luminosity of his being is most radiant and beautiful.

Go back, now, he hears from Zachary.

Instantly, he is once again looking at his friends. *I am formless, Zachary. Have we shifted to the formless realm, Elizabeth?*

Yes and no. You are always formless, but what you are willing to perceive, and what you need for your perception, is always that which you have. You always are, and you always have been, formless and unlimited. But as long as your consciousness perceives from a finite perspective, you are given and we work with that which is acceptable to you.

Marveling at this, Zachary feels the urge from within Peter to return, and simply nods. Peter repeats this process over and over again.

He next hears an invitation from Rebecca and moves to her position and looks at himself, and then to Elizabeth, until he has a consciousness of his entire being. Every facet of his being is now in his own consciousness.

Then, softly, Zachary can be heard stating, *We are being called, Peter, and we must answer this call.*

Immediately, they gather together, link up, and move with a breathtaking swiftness that Peter can only discern because of the passing of realms of light, color, and sound that, again, utterly transfix him with their beauty and majesty. Periodically, there is a sensation as though they had popped through some membrane-like space of existence or consciousness, until suddenly Peter realizes that they are in the Great Hall of Wisdom.

Better balanced now, and more aware of his own being, Peter adapts to this change quickly and does not move out of balance.

Zachary notes this, and observes, *Doing well, Peter. Indeed, very well. We are proud of you, all three of us. But come, we must join the group.*

Peter turns to perceive that the vast beautiful table he had seen earlier is aligned with entities. Now understanding that his perception is directly related to terms of references that are comfortable to him, he cannot help but wonder what the other realms of perception of this gathering might be.

Finding the group positioned before the table in their familiar places, he feels a surge of warmth and leans forward to glance past Zachary and sees Paul sitting at Zachary's side, beaming brilliantly, pouring thoughts of greeting and encouragement to Peter.

Turning to his other side, he sees David and others now familiar to him. From a short distance away Peter can perceive what looks like an up-stretched arm waving vigorously in his direction, and notes with great joy and excitement the familiar countenance of Zeb, also at the table. He wonders, *Was he here all the time and I just didn't know him?*

With that thought, Zachary interjects in Peter's thoughts, *Could be, Pete. One just never knows, do they?*

Peter then feels the radiance of a loving smile directed his way. In that instant, the area before the table begins to glow with a lustrous golden-white orb of light, and he knows that the Entity is returning.

He begins to perceive the Entity in a radiant blue-white light, as the colors shift and polarize and seem to become focused. He perceives the Entity … a beautiful, loving, sweet face looking upon him and the others, and he feels the issuance of a greeting to all of the entities, as though each one is named, recognized, encouraged, and supported.

He hears his own name being called, *Welcome again, Peter, and, of course, you Zachary, Paul, David, Zeb, Rebecca, Elizabeth … all of you. We are most joyful at your service and your charity for those in need. We have come together in this meeting because we would like to extend to you an opportunity to further your own joy and to contribute the light of that joy to others.*

Peter understands that the Entity is meaning something in the nature of a commission, and he feels himself beginning to draw inward with a slight bit of apprehension.

The unknown, continues this radiant, soft voice, *is always to be looked upon with an attitude of question, perhaps even with doubt or fear. But as we all know, the growth of our own consciousness unto our Father is enhanced by such experiences. The contributions thereof are many-fold and long-enduring. Unto each of you gathered, I offer a continued work.*

With that, Peter can perceive communication taking place between this great Entity of Light and all of the entities gathered, as though each one is receiving some special blessing and work. To the marvel of Peter's awareness, he can perceive some of this and is aware of a somewhat misted conversation between the Entity of Light and each successive entity, seemingly an infinite array of them, who are here in this moment in the Hall of Wisdom.

And so, Peter, he hears, *we have a commission, if you would accept it, that would bring great joy to many realms, and, indeed, unto God. It is one that would be shared between you and others and, in that sense, you would know it to be a group effort. Nonetheless, you will identify with it in a more singular sense, perhaps from the individual aspect of each. Others may as well so do.*

This is a commission that comes to you in the highest light, and, as such, it is to be taken under advisement with the guidance of your colleagues and for which no immediate response is expected. Though I know, as I am aware of you, that you will accept it, it is also my wish that you know of it in its entirety to the best of your comprehension before you do so. For this is our Father's will and, thus, I give this to you in His Name. Take as long as you wish, and your dear friends here and my brethren will be with you and help you until you are of that decision to proceed.

For this work, Peter, I shall give unto you a blessing intended to be as a cup from which you might draw whenever you, or those you are seeking to serve in the name of this commission, might be in need."

After this communication a sphere, small but radiant, seems to move from this great Entity and hover out over Peter. He is drawn to look upwards to perceive it. As he does, it descends upon him and dissipates, leaving him with a wondrous feeling of tingling and warmth.

He now perceives that the Entity has moved back into the sphere of light. He hears softly, almost melodiously, *Ever know, friend Peter, God's Light is with you.* The light then turns in upon itself, shifts in its pulsations, reverts to the golden-hued colors, and is gone.

Peter has no concept of how much time has transpired when finally he feels a touch upon his being, and looks up into the radiance of his friend Zachary. "Ready to go, Pete?"

Nodding feebly, he mumbles, "Uh-h, yes, Zack. Are … are we through here?"

Zachary looks around with a sweeping motion, "Well, unless you'd like to hang around and tidy up a bit. Everyone else is leaving." Then he chuckles.

Peter realizes immediately that Zachary, in his loving nature, is trying to soften the impact and re-balance him. Rising and moving with Zachary, he notes the presence of Elizabeth, Rebecca, and to his joy, Paul, as well.

They move out and find themselves back upon Peter's most familiar and most welcome little knoll in his Garden.

"I must say that looks good on you."

"What looks good on me, Zachary?"

"Well, you know … the new radiance … the new you. I think it really fits you. Of course, I'm only half jesting here, Peter. You have certainly earned the gain in consciousness, and therefore your cloak should reflect that."

Puzzled, Peter looks down to perceive himself, and he hears, "From over here, Pete. You'll get a better view."

So, he moves out of himself to look back from the position of Zachary. When he does, he is awe-struck by the golden radiance that is dancing around his cloak, or his outer being, little issuances of silver-white light here and there upon the soft golden, almost phosphorescent, color over his cloak.

"Very nice, Peter," says Elizabeth.

"Indeed so," echoes Rebecca.

Moving back to himself, Peter responds, "What is it? What did I do? I don't understand this. It seems to be understandable within me somewhere, but I can't quite grasp it.

What's it all about? I seem to be at some stumbling block within my consciousness."

As softly as he can ever recall Zachary speaking, Peter hears, "It's not a stumbling block. It's a stepping-stone. What's causing you difficulty are habits. You're familiar with thinking in terms of the Earth. You're familiar and comfortable with being Peter and using forms and words and the verbal, visual, tactile, smell … you know, all those sorts of senses. You've come a long way in using your other senses, but there's much further that you can go. If you'll let go of some of your limitations, you'll find that obstacle moves into proper perspective and becomes a stepping-stone."

"How do I do that, Zachary? Precisely how?"

"Go within yourself. Remember? Find that light. Look in truth and you'll know what to do once you do that."

Gaining the understanding by way of a kind of transference from Zachary, Peter, now somewhat familiar with the activity, turns within himself. This time his cloak does not sparkle or crackle but becomes radiant--a steady, pulsing glow.

Zachary turns to Elizabeth off to the side and remarks, "Isn't that truly lovely?"

Both Elizabeth and Rebecca nod their joy and approval.

Peter only half hears this, and as he tries to follow what he perceives as a path to the inner light, he suddenly feels a radiant, warming sensation, as though he is a flower bursting free from bud to bloom. He has visions of the forest in the Earth bursting its buds to form leaves. He sees the butterfly emerging from the cocoon. He observes these and many other paralleling things that are like being born, or re-born, as he remembers them from the Earth.

Then, suddenly, all of this converges and becomes light. He sees the light evolving in a way he understands as the parallel of the tree budding and becoming leaves thereafter, and the flower blooming from its bud, and on and on, until he comprehends that the evolution of his being from a state of expression in the Earth is now quite the same, only expressed in different mechanisms. Less limited, he knows, than those he is familiar with in the Earth, but by the measure of something beyond his current comprehension, not nearly as unlimited as is his potential to be.

Peter, inside himself, in close proximity to his inner light, now has the answer to his question: Once he can merge with this inner light, he reaches his destination and his goal, and all of the activities shared between himself and his new wonderful friends are intended to bring him to this point of realization. Suddenly, as swiftly as a gentle breeze, where there was question and doubt, understanding now falls into place.

Finally, when Peter ultimately emerges from this movement within himself, he looks to find his friends Zachary, Rebecca, Elizabeth, and Paul radiating light to him, not as in their finite forms, but as great and wondrous spheres of living essence. Light? Yes. Sound? Yes. Color? Yes. Vibration? Yes--but much, much more than this.

"Welcome back, Peter," he hears from the sphere immediately in front of him.

"Zachary, that's you, right?"

"Indeed so. One and the same. Well, you've crossed the threshold, we see. How are you? What is your state of being?"

"Well, I think I have nothing really to compare wellness to, so I suppose I'll just answer that by saying I feel exceptionally good. But I don't know what I'm feeling *with*. I just know that I do."

Peter feels from his friends the familiarity of the essence of energy he recognizes as laughter, which he revels and basks in, and joyfully absorbs.

"The commission ..." Peter then comments, "I think I understand. By doing the commission, by helping in this way, somehow that will enable me to move closer to that light within. Now I know that's what we're striving for, isn't it?"

"Yes, that and more, Peter. But that's sufficient for the present, wouldn't you think, Paul?"

Peter is overjoyed to hear his friend Paul again. "Yes, I do concur with that, Zachary. And, Peter, as you may or may not know, I have been with you and following you and our friends here all the while. I have admired and been joyful for those things you have accomplished in our Father's Name and those blessings you have imparted to souls in need. The commission will do what you stated, and much more."

"Very good. But now, tell me, what is this commission and how do we go about it?"

Here, dear friends, we shall have to conclude, but you know the answer to Peter's question. Soon, so shall he.

CHAPTER 8

Many Lessons
NOVEMBER 11, 1991

Paul is explaining the commission to Peter. "This would be somewhat different than those you've experienced to the present. In some regards, it may seem to be straightforward. In others, it could appear to be complex. So, rather than have this be unnecessarily complicated for you, we have discerned that perhaps the wisest course of action at this time is to proceed to a different position from which we can literally view the commission, and discuss it from that heightened vantage point."

"You're saying that we will travel to the location of the commission?"

It is Zachary who explains further. "This seems to be the best of all approaches for you, Peter, for, as you reach out and comprehend, you might draw upon all of your abilities and come up with just the right questions and, we hope, answers about this work. So, does everyone agree that we should get going?"

A round of silent affirmation is directed toward Zachary, and in that moment Peter becomes aware of the emergence of another brilliant sphere of light, familiar to him in some way, though he is not quite able to identify it. After a ripple of some re-balancing passes swiftly through him, he breaks the brief period of silence with, "Greetings. Uh, let's see now, you are ..."

Muffled laughter can be heard coming from the luminous

sphere that is Zachary, and a whisper, "That's Zeb, Z-E-B. Got it, Pete?"

Now a ripple of laughter can be discerned from the entire group, including Zeb himself. A few rivulets of light dance outwardly from him, to Peter's delight, and one of them moves, wave-like, over to Peter. Upon contact, it is as though Peter can perceive Zeb in every possible way, visualizing him as an image in physical-like form, discerning him in color, then in light, in virtually all aspects, some of which Peter is as yet unfamiliar with.

"I pulled the short straw, Pete, and that means that I get to lead everyone to the point of commission. Of course, that depends on your approval. After all, you are more or less the forerunner of this commission since it was, as you may recall, given specifically to you."

Taken somewhat aback, but detecting a note of humor from Zachary, Peter remembers that he had come to realize that Zeb's humor is not unlike Zachary's and that, with it, he can sense the ever-present ring of truth in what is given to him. Peter summons his confidence and answers, "I suppose that's correct, although I do remember that we were told that this would be a group effort. True?"

"Duly noted," responds Zeb. "But the others have already agreed, so you're the only one left to vote yea or nay."

Still detecting the flow of loving humor from Zeb, Peter realizes that this is true and, to his surprise, he hears himself say, "I consent, then. Let's go."

Zeb gradually but gently increases his movement and, as Peter observes this, he feels himself drawn along behind Zeb, as though he is a tiny bit of debris being pulled along by the wind current of some rapidly moving vehicle in the Earth. It's a delightful sensation that permeates his entire being, as though a great exhilarating, silvery wind is passing through him, charging him like a wet cell. He casts his awareness around and notes that his friends all around him are also aligned with Zeb's movement as he becomes aware of another communication from Zachary.

"Pretty nice flight, wouldn't you say, Pete? I told you that Zeb is quite a fellow, a real adept. Has this sort of thing down real pat." He pauses for any comments from Peter and hearing none, asks, "Do you have any questions while we're in motion here, Peter?"

As he draws his focus away from the sensations he is experiencing during the movement, Peter comments ever so softly, "I don't seem to be able to think of any at the moment but if I do, you know you can count on me to express them."

"Very well. Enjoy the trip, then, and I'll be right here should you come up with anything or have any needs."

Upon the conclusion of Zachary's comments, Peter is aware of one directed to him from Paul, whom he now discerns to be on the opposite side of him. The comments are merely gentle communications of re-affirmations. Upon their conclusion, he receives other communications from Elizabeth and then Rebecca, as well. Each of these seems to illuminate some portion of Peter and that, along with the flow of energy that streams back to him from Zeb, delights him.

After some passage of experience (you would call this time) Peter shares, "This is a simply marvelous experience, Zachary, similar to the activities in the Realm of Laughter, though more purposeful and specific somehow. Is this due to the presence of Zeb?"

"To a degree. Zeb is, of course, a unique entity and, being a member of the Control Center, is heavily experienced in such activities as we are now embarked upon."

Zachary's comments are interrupted by what Peter experiences as a loud pop. Only slightly jostled, and kept in harmony by the continual flow from Zeb in the forefront, Peter asks, "Zachary, what was that?"

"Merely passing through what we will define for you, at the moment, as a plane of existence, or a point of division between certain levels of consciousness. In the past, you have noticed various bands of color as we've moved in this manner, remember?"

He recalls those experiences and indicates an affirmation.

"Well, this is similar to that event, only on a larger scale. It's a major point of demarcation and it is ..." Once again Zachary is interrupted by a popping sound.

(While our interpretation and description of the sound is woefully inadequate, it is the best we have before you. Peter is experiencing beyond the three-dimensional, and therefore what is sound is also light and also energy and other types of expressions that you would not comprehend in the present.)

With this second perceptible change or pop, Peter asks, "Was that another major level? What is this? Where is the commission, anyway? How far are we from my Garden? And what about the Hall of Wisdom and the Crystal Workers Realm ... Where are they?"

Warmth cascades all over Peter and, intuitively, he realizes his group is sending loving laughter to him. He himself finds humor in his barrage of questions.

Before Zachary can respond, there is another pop, and this time Peter does feel jostled a bit.

The movement slows, and he hears from Zeb. "Peter, are you well? Are you still balanced and in harmony?"

"I believe so, Mr. Zeb ... I mean, Zeb. But this certainly is a strange experience. I think we look like a flock of wild geese in the Earth. We're in a V-shape pattern, with me in the center. Is there significance to that? I'll try to constrain my questions, but what are those dramatic changes in energy that I discern as a sort of pop, like a membrane bursting? What are those?"

"If you don't mind, Peter, I'll resume the travel, and have Zachary explain it all, since he can do so as adequately as I can, and perhaps better, in some respects." Without waiting for confirmation from Peter, Zeb resumes the movement that was slowed for a time.

Peter again feels exhilarated by the flow of the energy stream that is passing through him as Zeb continues on, and asks, "Well, Zack, will you continue?"

"Certainly, Peter. Here's the way it is: Each of the realms, which are definable by collections of consciousness that agree upon a certain reality, is preserved under the auspices of what's called Universal Law. Therefore, each realm or group of realms exists in sort of stratified layers. Now that's a rather coarse depiction, but it is graphically correct for the purposes of your comprehension.

"Each of these, then, reaches a place wherein their expression of consciousness or reality begins to diminish. That's why I took you to the edge of Todd's reality. Remember? You saw that, when you concentrated, truth caused the illusion to begin to fade. What you are experiencing is the passage through numerous, we could call them, sub-realms of thought or consciousness or reality, supported by and agreed upon by the group of souls therein. After those, there are others, and others, until we reach a point where the transition from a certain level of thinking is so significant that the next level of thinking can only exist in juxtaposition by being buffered by some sort of neutral zone. A friend I know in the Earth has titled this a *veil of separation* and that's as good a name as any. The audible sounds you hear, and some of those you haven't noted, are caused by the movement of our group as we pass through."

Zachary's words begin to trail off at the same time Peter notes a definite slowing down of the group, very quickly. He senses a heaviness, a significant increased density in his being, similar to the effect he recalls when jet airliners raise the wing flaps to slow the air speed upon approaching a landing.

In a matter of a few moments, he hears a communication

from Paul off on what he discerns to be his right. "That heaviness can be eliminated, Peter, whenever you want. Of course, we could have prevented it from having any impact on you whatsoever, but we did not for a specific purpose: It is good for you to be able to note this sensation and to keep it in the back of your consciousness for reference. In what might be termed on a gradient scale of the realms of existence, we are in consciousnesses that are very low on the scale. They are neither good nor bad. They are merely basal. In these basal realms, the potential that is within each entity is virtually in all stages of expression or, perhaps more accurately, *non*-expression.

"This is where our commission is located. We are identifying this for your comprehension and understanding, that you might relate this to your memories, or thought-forms, drawn from the Earth and that you can compare and relate this to other experiences which you have had here and some that lie yet ahead."

In that moment, Peter realizes that they are no longer moving, and that Zeb has, in essence, turned back to face him. Suddenly, he becomes aware that he is perceiving Zeb in a physical-like form once again. Quickly glancing around, he notes that all of his colleagues are expressed in a somewhat finite form, and that he is, as well.

His eyes meet Zachary's, who is looking at him warmly as though anticipating and, indeed, inviting his question.

Peter obliges. "Why have we shifted forms? Has it something to do with where we are? Will we be dealing with entities who are in physical-like forms?"

Zeb glances quickly to the others in the group and seems to receive a silent affirmation, at which he turns to look back at Peter. "We thought for the time, at least, that it would be good to revert to these expressions. Our reasons for so doing are quite simple, quite straightforward. Even though there could be the acceptable expression of the balls of light, as you've referred to them in the past, we would like you to become adjusted to the essences in this realm from multiple levels of expression. We have no way of knowing what sort of mechanisms might be needed, nor can we even discern at this point which would be the best approach towards our commission."

He pauses and allows Peter to ask his question.

"That brings me back to the question I asked when we were in the Garden area. Could someone tell me what the commission is? Is another realm about to vanish? Is this one going to go poof?" adding his note of obvious humor.

Enjoying Peter's good cheer, Zeb turns to Zachary, "I'm not aware of any planned poofs, are you, Zack?"

"Nope. I have no poof scheduled here."

All this lightens the atmosphere in the group considerably. Little multi-colored rivulets of light stream in and out from all of them and are reflected from one to the other.

"That bit of humor is just what was needed to lighten this discussion. We have no intention of evading your question, Pete, but as indicated to you previously, these things are not easy to explain. However, the essence of the commission is to attempt to help a soul who has more or less *moved into* this realm here. She truly doesn't belong here, yet is here of her own free will or choice."

"Her?"

"Well, *her* to the extent that the energies, the potentials, the essences, are familiar to you as feminine, and therefore the reference of the feminine seems appropriate."

Reflecting and nodding, Peter studies Zeb for a moment, then Zachery. "There's something different about this one, isn't there? I mean, from the entity in the Great Hall, I could tell something was unique. And the gift … What did He call it? God's light, I think. Well, that gift He gave me makes me feel so good …" Peter visibly takes on the countenance once again as the golden light cascades all about him.

Zeb pauses until this subsides. "Look, Peter, again, we're not trying to be evasive, but we do believe that the best way to explain this to you is to approach the commission and then offer explanations that will make sense to you because we are in her proximity."

Reflecting but for a moment, Peter understands that this makes sense and nods, his eyes bright in joyful anticipation of the unknown.

"Ah, good, Pete," Zachary notes. "Your sense of adventure never ceases to rise to the surface does it? I like that. You know, we're two of a kind in that regard. Adventure! That's the ticket. Let's go, then, Zeb, can we?"

Zeb smiles broadly at Zachary, and the group begins what Peter discerns to be a movement from an upper to a lower level, though the movement is slow enough that Peter feels that Zeb, who is in the forefront again, is being cautious.

Feeling this caution or care, Peter whispers, "Zeb, is there some reason for your reduced speed?"

"As a matter of fact, yes, there is. You see, this entity or soul, whichever suits you, is in this realm by choice."

"Well, weren't the others? Weren't they in their realms by choice? Wasn't Todd in that realm by choice? And his parents? What's the difference?"

"The difference is that this soul knows where she is and knows where she can be. She knows that she has the potential to dwell in a realm of considerably higher consciousness than this one. Therefore, we have no right to interfere with the free-will choice this soul has made. So we are proceeding in what I will call guarded neutrality, that not only do we not disturb her, but we use care not to disrupt any others who are also in this realm."

"Others? Goodness, I guess I hadn't thought about that. There usually has to be … what did you say to me before… at least two or three others here in order to make a realm and perpetuate it?"

"Yes," responds Zachary, "but in this case, what Zeb is saying is that this entity has sufficient consciousness to support a realm in and of her own consciousness. In other words, she has that much power, you might say."

"Power?"

"Yes, power."

"What kind of power, Zack? Are you talking about *zap* kind of power? Butterfly-creating power? Or rainbows or fire or rain, like your earlier demonstrations? Qualify that for me so that I can grasp it."

There is a pause, which heightens Peter's attentiveness.

Finally, Zachary explains, "Just power, Pete. All of those examples you mentioned direct and make for finite power. The source of the power is God, but the power is unlimited. So what we're talking about here is unlimited power."

This strikes Peter internally. "Is this like the inner power, the inner light? Does she have that kind of awareness? Has she gained possession of her inner light?"

"That's very good reasoning, and you are right on target. Yes, she has."

"Goodness. What is she doing here, then?"

It is Zeb who responds, "In a manner of speaking, you could say that she has fallen."

This throws Peter, in his consciousness. "Fallen?" He has the image of slipping on a banana peel in his consciousness.

A slight wave of mirthfulness ripples from his comrades at this.

Peter's countenance, his cloak, remains static but the intensity becomes brilliant.

"Take a look inwardly," he hears from Zachary.

Without effort, Peter turns as though he is about to walk back into himself, and easily does so.

As he moves inward, he begins to feel, to sense, to become conscious of a warm, glowing feeling. With this feeling comes a sense of ease. An incredible attitude of trust, of faith, sweeps over him, as though some wondrous cleansing balm had passed all through his being. He becomes remarkably crisp in his consciousness. His reasoning moves rapidly, more than he can ever recall previously. As his consciousness races over the potential, the power described to him by his colleagues, a vision of the wondrous entity in the Hall of Wisdom comes into his consciousness. He hears the words once again: *Ever know, friend Peter, God's light is with you.* As swiftly as it appeared, it fades somewhere into his being. Peter emerges, again aware of his colleagues and aware now of what it means to have such power. "I think I comprehend what you're saying. But I still don't grasp how she could fall. I understand the power, the potential. But how did she fall? You said she is here by choice?"

"More or less, yes, that's accurate. It couldn't be put in terms more accurate than that. At least, none that we know of," answers Zachary.

Looking about him now, Peter notes that something else has changed. The others, in their finite forms, are posed in various positions as though resting, leaning here and there. Peter is striving to discern what they are leaning on.

"Good, Peter. Keep reaching out. This time fine-tuning is appropriate. Perceive and survey the surroundings."

Following Zeb's cue to him, Peter continues to reach … reaching, reaching. As he does, he feels his consciousness pass through Zachary, and a small murmur of humor ensues as he light-heartedly remarks, "Whoops, pardon me, Pete. I'll get out of the way here."

The reflection of humor reminds Peter of Zachary's wondrous nature and how he can be so continually joyful and light-hearted, how he stands with him side by side in any challenge, in every growth opportunity. His humor, his cheer, never wavers.

"Thanks, Pete, nice compliment. But follow Zeb's suggestion and reach out."

Returning to his effort, Peter suddenly feels an impact. Solid. *Solid as rock*, he thinks to himself. Instantly he is back in his own form and viewing outward from himself, as though reaching out with his consciousness, establishing the contact, providing the depth of field for vision or perception. He can discern that, indeed, it seems that they are surrounded by solid rock. Everywhere Peter can see, it appears as though there is rock.

He looks over to Zeb, who is now perched rather casually upon a large boulder, and receives a warm smile. "So, you see it is as rock, do you?"

"Well, isn't that what it is?"

"Probably so. Now, if you'll look about, you'll note that there are quite a few fellows here, *he's* and *she's*, but *fellows* meaning fellow Children of God. See? But as I was saying, there are quite a few fellows here, and they prefer it that way. In fact, right where we are at the moment, you can become aware of several of them, along with some of my colleagues who are more or less *monitoring* them, we might say."

Looking about here and there, Peter strives to make out what it is Zeb is referring to, and discerns nothing.

"Perhaps a little more fine tuning, Peter," he offers in half-hearted humor.

Peter makes a sweep with his consciousness, and still perceives none of these others. "What did I do wrong?"

"Try again, Peter. This time, why don't you have Zachary over there point to them as you pass over them, and see if you can distinguish them from the background."

Zachary moves swiftly. He nods, extends his arm and flexes his forefinger mirthfully, implying that some sort of act, with which Peter is entirely familiar and often comes to expect from his friend, is about to be performed.

Zeb's rippling laughter can be heard off to the right and slightly behind Peter now as he is turned to follow Zachary.

Zachary's eyes are solely on Peter as he turns his body

halfway to point his arm and a finger in a direction in which he isn't even looking.

"Zachary, are you certain you're pointing to something? I mean, you're not even looking."

"Well, if it'll suit you, Pete, I can look at them too, but I thought pointing would be enough."

The group sends a note of humor to Peter and Zachary.

"Okay, Zack. I get your message. Lighten up. Right?"

"Right-o. Lighten up. Flow easily. Not too intense. After all, you're not going to be graded on this. It's not a test. It's just a commission, you know?"

"What do you mean *just a commission*? I thought these sorts of things were, you know, almost holy." After having blurted that out, Peter is shocked at his own words. This time, none of the others come forward with the laughter Peter might have expected.

It is only Zachary who smiles and nods and gives Peter a wink. "Probably more to that statement than you realize, Pete. But, come on. Let's look for them. They're not hard to find."

Trusting his friend, Peter allows his consciousness to reach out in the direction of Zachary's pointing finger.

Very, very subtly, Peter can now make out a faint gray orb on the dark murky background that he earlier defined as stone. "Good grief! You're not telling me that's an entity!"

Zachary only nods, continuing to point at the entity.

"How can that be? The energy, the light, is barely perceptible."

"Perhaps from your perspective, Pete, but not from theirs. From their perspective, they feel normal. See what I mean?" Then he twirls his finger a bit, and the outline grows in density and intensity, still with a very dull color, but now looking more like a cocoon of the dull silver-gray webbing that Peter remembers caterpillars weaving.

"Gosh, Zachary."

"Now the other one, Pete. There's another over there to

the right. Look where I'm pointing now."

As Peter does, his eyes, his consciousness, his awareness, all attune to what it is that Zachary is striving to help him perceive. This time, he can more easily distinguish the entity. This one has a dull, sort of reddish-brown hue, and as Zachary again twirls his finger, Peter sees the entity becoming more dense, appearing almost like an oversized rusty doorknob.

"A doorknob, Pete? That's the best you can do for an analogy? A rusty doorknob? We'd best not tell the entity. Might drive him even deeper into his own remorse."

"Remorse? They're here because of remorse?"

"Well, sort of. You might say yes, and you might say because of other factors, but that's pretty good, particularly for this one here. Notice the reddish hues?" Zachary thrusts a probing finger outward.

Peter, alarmed, calls out, "No! Don't touch him. You might … wake him up, or something."

"Good, Pete. Good response. Why'd you make it?"

Peter looks at Zachary squarely and puzzles, "I don't know. It just came from somewhere within me."

"Good. That's just the ticket. You allowed it to come forward and to terminate an action. And you did so because …" Zachary's words hang in mid-air.

Peter derives from this that an answer is expected from him. "Gosh, Zachary, I don't know what you want me to respond with here. I just somehow knew that you shouldn't touch them. Didn't you tell me that at one point? Or didn't you say they had the right to do as they want? That we all have the right to choose?"

"Very good, Pete. Zeb?" Zachary nods at Zeb's.

Zeb turns now to recognize Elizabeth and Rebecca, who have been, Peter now realizes, silent during this exchange. As he turns to perceive them, there is a feeling of warmth and reassurance. Now in this dark abyss-like level of consciousness, he experiences an incredibly delightful counter-balancing force flowing from Elizabeth and Rebecca.

"Peter," Elizabeth smiles, "you are doing so very well. I cannot begin to tell you how much I respect your courage, your faith and willingness to trust and place your well-being in the care of us, your friends."

Peter returns Elizabeth's warm gaze. "I thank you for those comments, but they do not seem to be, if you'll forgive me, meaningful. Why would I not trust you? Why would I not place myself and my well-being in trust with you? Were it not for each of you, where would I be? In one of those bands of color? Had it not been for Paul," with which he nods to his dear friend Paul, "would I not be stuck in that mess of red? And if not for you, Elizabeth, would I have known the joy of formlessness? And Zachary, and you, Rebecca, always there to give me that last ounce of needed certainty and of an eternal flow of love."

Each of the group then turns to one another, smiling and nodding, as though Peter's comments had confirmed his readiness for the commission at hand.

From Elizabeth, he hears, "Well said, Peter."

And from Rebecca, "Indeed so, Peter. Carry on."

Peter turns to confirm her communication, for the uniqueness of Rebecca's expressions always brings some special note of resonance into Peter's being. He turns back to Zachary, "I can perceive them clearly now. Thanks, Zachary. Once you identify them, it's rather easy. It's like trying to see quail in the underbrush in their season. Unless they move, which they rarely do, you just can't find them unless you know what you're looking for."

Zachary nods and shrugs at the same time. "Quail? Well, whatever. Let's get on with it here." He throws another wink to Peter who realizes that Zachary fully comprehends but wants to lighten the energy. Understanding this, he swiftly inventories his own status and realizes that he is a bit out of balance. Then, in just a hair's-breadth of a clock-tick in the Earth, he completely rebalances himself.

"Splendid!" comments Zeb. "Now, come forward with me just a bit."

Peter sees that his group has formed a circular pattern, within which is light. Beyond it is the other essence that Peter had detected as solid rock. Following along, he discerns Zeb moving in a straight line away from the group. He stops and turns to look back at him.

"Take a look from over here, Pete." He steps back so that Peter can take that position.

Peter is aware of Zachary on the other side of him, as he does.

"Oh, excuse me, Pete. I'll just get off to the side here. Thought I'd take a look, as well."

Peter smiles. As he turns to look forward, he hears Zeb. "This will be different for you, Peter. We don't know for certain how you will perceive this. So, I'll stand here and Zachary is on the opposite side of you. Should you need any assistance or balance, we are here. Behind you now, you will note, are Elizabeth and Rebecca. Don't let this positioning heighten your concerns any. It's just a matter of convenience in the event that you need us for a bit of balancing."

Nodding, Peter turns forward again.

"Now, if you will listen to what I am communicating to you, Peter, and follow along, I believe I can assist you in perceiving. As you reach out, don't reach out a great distance. Think only of yourself reaching out, let's say, five or six feet as measured in the Earth. Get the meaning?"

Still peering straight ahead, Peter nods and thrusts his consciousness out and stops it at what he would imagine would be the equivalent.

"Now, as you are extending your awareness, like you're extending an arm, try to feel what's there."

As Peter follows these words, he begins to feel something strange. "Sticky, it feels sticky, Zeb. Almost like I've put my hand on some … like a gigantic piece of jellied toast."

Muffled laughter comes from Zachary, and he hears in muted tones, "This guy's descriptions are really something."

Finding humor in his own comment, Peter continues on, "Well, I guess that does sound a bit odd. Let's see … it feels soft and spongy … and, by the way, Zack, that's what buttered toast with jelly on top does feel like."

"Uh, thanks for that, Pete. I'll file that away."

Still smiling, Peter continues, "But this sticky sensation feels like it has depth."

"Ever so slightly, now, Peter," directs Zeb, "extend yourself slowly forward and tell me when you feel anything different. Any different sensation or awareness."

Slowly, Peter feels himself moving forward in his consciousness. The sticky sensation feels very strong now. "This stuff is like super glue in the Earth!"

"Just for a moment now, see about pulling your consciousness, your *arm,* back."

"Okay, Zeb," and he immediately withdraws his *arm* of consciousness. As he does, he notes clearly detectable resistance. "Goodness, this stuff is really sticky. I mean …"

Pop! There is a sound. Red is everywhere, moving, undulating, flowing all up and down in all directions.

Peter is startled to the core. *What is this? Zeb, what's happening here?*

You've opened a level of consciousness. How are you doing? he hears from Zeb.

Well, I-I guess I'm doing okay. I admit to being startled. Goodness, this is very, very intense, isn't it?

Peter now hears Zachary on the other side of him, *Yep, Pete, that's heavy-duty stuff there. That red is first class thickness and density, I'd say.*

Again, the essence of Zachary's light-heartedness comes to Peter's mind.

From directly behind him he hears Paul. *Pete? Remember the colors we passed through? Remember them now. Recall them.*

Warmed by the comments from Paul, Peter now turns his consciousness back to the red. As he does, he remembers he and Paul meeting the red.

Good, he hears from Paul. *We passed through the red. Remember? Do it again.*

How, Paul? What should I do? I mean, should I thrust my consciousness further or pull it back or what?

Do what you know to do.

Peter turns inward on that comment, and as does, he feels, knows, and perceives the essence of a golden light. Inward, inward, he travels. As he does, the sensation of the red, its heaviness, its stickiness, its intense level of basal energy, begins to be greatly diluted, almost as though it were particles of paint pigment now separating by a media added to it. Onward, onward he moves, ever so rapidly, until he hears again, *Friend Peter, God's light is with you.*

The golden light basks Peter in its shimmering radiance. He immediately emanates this golden light, and the red is swept away in waves. Only particles remain where there was density, until outstretched before him is his spiritual arm of consciousness and a soft mass of what he can only describe as a gray, clay-like substance so immense that he cannot discern its beginning or its ending, its upper or its lower definition.

Slowly, without awareness, he pulls his consciousness back, still facing this immense grayish mass. As he does, he is awed by its size and by some properties he cannot find an understanding within himself to use as a definition. "What … is … that?" he asks softly and deliberately.

As though echoing Peter's style and nature, Zachary answers, "That, Peter, is … your … commission."

Peter is stunned. He stands speechless before this incredible mass, looking like gray clay, no breaks, no cracks, no surface disruptions, as though something had spun itself into a cocoon-like shelter so vast and so incredibly perfect, yet dense, that it exceeds the capacity of Peter's comprehension.

He hears Zeb softly explain, *Perhaps now, Peter, you can understand why we were reluctant to attempt to describe the commission to you, and why we felt it wise to bring you here so you could experience the nature of the commission. Now, we can explain some of this to you. The commission is within this great mass. It is true, as you have discerned, that this mass is purposefully placed before you by the will of the soul within. The entity in this sphere has built this of her own will, and we, you see, must find some way to accomplish communication in order to do those works that will fulfill the commission given to our group.*

Peter is suddenly aware that he is in near disbelief of the incredible hulk of this gray mass before them. He then hears himself saying, *It won't do any good for me to go within. I know that. I don't know how I know that, but I know I, or we, have to find the answer here. But what an immense barrier it is, if that's what it is. You're saying that she created this, and supports this by herself?* Peter turns his focus to Zachary.

Zachary sends forth a gentle affirmation, *All by herself, Pete. Sort of awesome, isn't it? Can you imagine the potential of an entity who can create such as this and sustain it without a flaw, without a single opening, not even so much as a crack, and mind you, we've been over every inch of this.*

You have? You have been over every inch?

A sigh comes from Zachary.

Unusual, for Zack to sigh, Peter thinks to himself.

Yes, Pete. Every inch, if we could call it by the measure of your Earth nomenclature. But that's of no concern, and Peter notes an immediate brightening from Zachary, *for we know that we wouldn't be given the commission unless there was an opportunity. Right, friends?* Zachary makes a bold, sweeping gesture to the others.

They all brighten and nod their affirmation, directed half at Zachary and half at Peter, who has turned to observe their response.

Is that true, Rebecca? Is there always an answer when a commission is given? Always a way to accomplish it?

At the least one way, Peter, and perhaps many.

Well, how do we find it?

There are several ways, he hears Rebecca answer, *but in this situation, there are factors that are unique.*

You mean there is more uniqueness here than what I've already experienced or become aware of? That seems almost impossible.

Gently, but not wavering even for a moment, Rebecca continues her soft warm focus upon Peter. *We believe you will know the answer before any of us, Peter, because you have certain talents, just as we each do. We believe that yours are the right ones for this commission. Not only do we believe this, but those from the highest light also have chosen you, in case I need to remind you.*

Peter is warmed and encouraged by Rebecca's countenance as well as her communication, and then by a second wave of warmth from the memory of the experience in the Great Hall. He pulls himself up, in a manner of speaking, *Very well. I accept that and I have already accepted the commission, as have we all. I guess what we need to do, then, is identify some sort of plan. Do you all have one and are simply waiting for me to ask about it?*

It is Rebecca who answers, *We have some possibilities, some alternatives, and certainly we know some things at this point better than you, but we have no real plan. This we shall need to evolve together. We value greatly your perspective, your thoughts, your ingenuity and creativity. These are valuable assets we very much encourage you to share now with our group.*

Without question, I will share all that I have, all that I know, and you know this. But tell me, what do you know of her? Peter points to the hulking gray mass now behind him.

What do you mean by that question? Elizabeth asks.

Well, I mean, you know, like in the Earth. If I were going to try to establish a business relationship with someone, I'd try to find out more about them, their likes, their dislikes, maybe where they were from, and their background. See what I mean? What do you know about her?

Elizabeth states softly, *Well, we know that she used to be an angel.*

Peter stops, utterly aglow. *A what?*

She was a part of the angelic host.

Th-the angelic host? You mean she came from those who are, like, at one with God?

That's correct, he hears from Rebecca softly.

Turning incredulously, Peter gazes at the gray mass. *Why in the world ... I mean, why in the, wherever we are, is she here?*

(We shall conclude for this gathering and invite the Channel to return in short order, perhaps after an appropriate rest period, whereupon we shall continue.)

CHAPTER 9

A Group from Earth
NOVEMBER 11, 1991

(We thank the Channel in humble joy for his willingness to return here, and we now rejoin our group, continuing from where last we were with them.)

Z eb is explaining, *Before we attempt to answer that and other questions for you, Peter, let's all draw back to our previous point of consciousness. Before we do, we would like you to take one last observation of our commission, that you will have this committed to your awareness, your consciousness, and that you might be able to reclaim that memory or image whenever you should have the need. If you don't mind, would you do that now?*

Still in awe of the commission's position, Peter rather numbly but dutifully attempts to respond to Zeb's request. Refocusing his awareness upon the vast mass before him, he attempts to grasp the scope of what he perceives. But he finds himself unable to do so, and hovers in this thought and effort.

From Paul, off in the background, he hears, *Never strain, Peter. Don't labor or create an attitude of intensity. Simply allow your intent and your will to flow freely through you and from you. Let it be an easy work and, before you know it, it will become precisely that.*

Without shifting his point of focus, Peter issues a *thank you* to Paul and returns his concentration to the immense mass before him. Striving now to do so in the manner as suggested by his dear friend, he looks within himself simultaneously to comprehend what is before him. As he does, he notices with curiosity some portions of his being seem to be charged with a unique amount of energy. He is able to discern these by their intensity of color and the perception that he has of a sort of pulsing, crackling-like emanation that he relates to memories of static electricity in his recent Earth sojourn.

As he focuses upon these, uncovering each one, he attempts to soothe them in a manner he does not fully understand technically, but by surrounding them with his own faith. Nearly instantaneously, one by one, these seem to blend back into his own light. *There, Paul, I believe I have settled all of those somewhat unbalanced energies, and I feel now as you have urged me to feel. If you offer further suggestions for correction as I go along, I will attempt to do precisely as you have guided.*

Feeling considerably lighter, Peter again allows his awareness to grasp what is before him. A subtle flow of information about this entity starts to emerge. Delighted and amazed, he lets this flow into his consciousness without question and without slowing them by trying to examine them one by one. Intuitively he knows he can do so later, so he is like a librarian, stacking up on some shelf within him this continual flow of information and awareness about his commission.

He begins to feel the emergence of something unique. As he does, he allows himself to be a neutral, passive observer. Even though at times this seems to be a bit of an effort, he manages to retain his neutrality.

You're doing fine, Peter. Continue, he hears from Paul.

He finds himself being drawn to the grayish mass before him, and comes immediately before it, almost to the point of being immersed in it. A tingling sensation begins to resonate within him, and he feels he should expend some effort of control over this motion.

Once again, he hears softly, *Do as you feel guided. Do not question. Have faith in the guidance you are receiving.*

Again encouraged by the message from Paul, Peter draws

himself up a bit, as though he is in control of some sort of throttle which, by moving this way or that, could enable him to accelerate or decelerate his movement. He adjusts accordingly, until he feels himself within a hair's breadth of the mass before him. Immediately, he can make out that this is not a solid or an inert substance, but, rather, that it has motion and depth and that it appears *alive*. He assumes from this observation that the grayish mass is unquestionably projected by the individual within. Now he is aware that the potential of the entity is even greater than he had presumed just earlier.

He allows his consciousness to flow over the periphery once again, just a few millimeters above its surface. As he does, he notes several reactions. The first is a sense of wonderful calm and tranquility. The next is a sense of individuality about this mass, while being so timeless or eternal, that it is difficult for Peter to fathom in the moment.

After the passage of an indeterminate amount of time, Peter is suddenly aware that he is back to the point of contact, and that Zeb has maintained some sort of continual flow or spherical chamber over the surface of the vast mass.

How are you? he hears from Zeb.

Peter responds quickly, I *feel just fine, Zeb. I explored this, if I might call it, 'object' to some degree, and I feel I have a better understanding. I can't put it in specific terms yet, but I have gathered some interpretive information, I believe in considerable detail, though I haven't analyzed it yet. I felt that wise, and so, as Paul suggested, that's what I did.*

Excellent. And do you have a sense of the outer periphery of the entity?

Only to the degree that I traversed the surface.

Well, you have covered it all, Peter.

Peter is surprised at Zeb's comment, for he was not aware of this. *Truly? Have I truly covered it all?*

Indeed so. Now, if you will, let us draw back to our earlier point that we might review and carry on, focusing on what you've gathered and working together to answer your questions, such as why she is here. Is that agreeable to all?

Each communicates an affirmation and, somewhat more eagerly than the rest, Peter's can be perceived above them all.

Zeb notes with good humor, *Very well, Peter, I can't fault you for your eagerness to return to what you now think of as a more neutral ground. So, without further delay, if you would simply turn and follow the path of light back, I shall as you say in the Earth, bring up the rear.*

Peter perceives Zeb smiling warmly behind him and, with Paul just ahead, Peter moves easily and swiftly until he notes that all other motion has ceased. He realizes that they are at the earlier point of gathering, where their discussions and his discoveries of the other entities in this realm took place.

Looking around, he notes that all his companions are once again expressed in what he perceives as a finite form, and looks down at himself to discover that he, too, is now expressed in the physical appearance known as Peter.

Rebecca perceives this. "Peter, in case you're wondering why the group has reverted to being expressed in a physical form, it is for several reasons. First, while in this type of expression, it is easier to communicate and function within this realm without as much concern that we might inadvertently do something to disrupt the harmony here, thereby insuring that we have conformed to Universal Law, which, of course, is always all-important."

Nodding his understanding, Peter studies Rebecca for a few lingering moments. Many things about her are still curious to him, and yet he cannot help but feel the beautiful sense of wellbeing that this particular one of his friends always emanates towards him.

Breaking away from that thought, he turns to look at the others and they return his gaze with their own of warmth and compassion. Finally, resting his sight on Zachary, who is now standing immediately next to Zeb, Peter marvels at the similarity he sees in them and feels a sense of unique bond with them both. "How curious," he muses, "that I feel such an affinity to the two of you," and quickly turns to the others, "not that I don't with all of you, but there's some quality about Zeb and Zachary that seems to resonate within me."

Paul answers for the others, "Not at all, Peter. We understand better than you might think. You do have a similarity that is traceable back to some earlier mutual works, which you could easily recall at any time should you so wish. But rather than move off on that digression, perhaps it would be well if we all now review and determine how we shall proceed with the commission. Is that agreeable to you?"

Peter looks at his friend with fondness and a great depth of compassion and love. "You know that it is. There isn't a thing that you could suggest to me that I wouldn't accept."

Simply smiling and nodding, Paul steps back a bit allowing Zachary to speak.

"Well, Pete, you collected quite a bit of awareness about our commission, and I commend you for not allowing your curiosity to intervene during the gathering of that awareness. You exercised your control and allowed it simply to be accumulated within your consciousness. Now would be a good time to review that and to return to your earlier question, and your unspoken questions, about our commission. So, speaking to your question of why she is here, I would like to suggest that we go to another realm and review this. It's familiar to you and should be an easy journey. But before we do, we would like to explain several things to you here. This is to insure that they are in the right perspective in your consciousness, and that you can have a clear comprehension of all that is taking place and of what we shall do in that time ahead, so you won't be hindered by questions or doubts while the work is progressing."

Not knowing what Zachary has in mind, Peter simply

nods.

"Where we are now is indeed in a realm that could be defined as very low, if one were to place it on a diagram that would show lower levels versus higher ones. Without belaboring these points specifically at this time, let us just say that this is one of the lowest levels of expression in the creative scale of potential for all who engage in the incarnative cycle. Yet, our commission has not incarnated, and this is a point of some importance that we would like you to make note of. In other words, she is not one who has been born into physical body in the Earth, had experiences there, and struggled with them. She has not, therein, created choices of her own free will that would bind her in the incarnative cycles, in what is often referred to as karma which might have caused her to be cast into this, one of the lower realms."

Zachary pauses to allow Peter to absorb that communication and noting that he has, then continues, "The method of travel here was not truly necessary. As you might have already realized, we could have used other means to reach this point than the one that was chosen. Therefore, it's probably obvious to you that we did so for a reason. That reason was, quite simply, to create a kind of tunnel of light, to use the colloquial term. This tunnel can be used by others to travel into and out of this realm without disrupting other realms through which they pass.

"So, an entity in your Garden realm who is capable of moving to a realm such as this could now simply move to the point of light we have created and follow it (actually, within it) to arrive here. Conversely, anyone who had been working here could use the same pathway to return. In this way, any number of entities can move to and from this place and contribute in whatever way might be deemed beneficial to the commission. Do you have all that?"

"I believe so, Zachary. Do continue, for I am, as always, fascinated with this sort of thing."

Zachary smiles. "Well, then, Zeb, more or less, volunteered for this mission."

Peter hears Zeb utter a low murmur of feigned dread.

Zachary smiles again and continues, "With his background in the Control Center, he established this area in which we are now expressed." He sweeps his hand broadly before him.

Peter follows Zachary's gesture and realizes that it is a large area of light not unlike that of the first Control Center where he met Zeb.

"So now we have established another Control Center here, in this realm. It's a sort of neutral zone, Pete. It is enveloped in a sphere of energy undetectable by entities in these realms. Should one or more entities who are within this Control Center react too strongly with energies that might be thought of as little errant outbursts, the outer periphery of what we have established will contain that and sustain Universal Law. Zeb has agreed to remain here and continue to sustain this along with the tunnel of light to other realms. Now, do you have all that?"

"I believe so, Zack. It seems straightforward, though it's most curious."

"Why is it curious, Pete?"

"Well, you told me that all I had to do was think of a place or remember, and I could be there."

"That's true."

"Then why did we need the, what did you call it, tunnel of light and this Control Center here? If I am capable of making such a journey, I would think that I would also be capable of being in this realm and maintaining the harmony or conformity to Universal Law. Wouldn't I?"

Smiling with obvious pleasure at Peter's grasp of the earlier lessons, Zachary nods. "Yes, that's true for you, Pete. But how can you be certain that it's true of anyone else? You can presume, certainly, that all of us gathered here can probably do this, but we don't know who else might choose to be a part of this work and what their various levels of consciousness might be. So, just as an added measure of caution, or dedication to God and His Law, this is the method we have incorporated. Understand?"

Peter nods without speaking.

"Well, then, since you have expressed your understanding of how to move from one realm to the other, in a moment I would like you to demonstrate that for us, if you will."

Somewhat embarrassed now, Peter again nods, this time looking down a bit, thinking that his comments might have been a bit bolder than he is usually comfortable with.

"No, no, Pete. Not at all. You were correct and accurate in all that you said. Don't back out of it now. Once you claim a truth, don't let a little challenge cause you to release it. Truths are difficult enough to acquire. Have the strength and faith to believe in truth as you find it."

Bolstered by Zachary's encouragement, Peter resumes his former stance with a bit more confidence and more aware of his own equality with his companions.

"That's much better, Pete. Don't become wishy-washy now. Know what I mean?"

Peter smiles and nods.

"Okay, then, here's what we suggest: Zeb will remain, for that's his choice and he loves this sort of work."

Peter glances at Zeb, to see him smiling and flexing his arms, mimicking someone who is trying to indicate a strength worthy of a task. He then gives Peter a big wink.

"Zachary," Peter laughs, "you two could be brothers. You're so much alike."

Zachary grins. "That could be so, Pete, couldn't it?"

Peter laughs as he realizes Zachary's meaning to be that he, Zachary, Zeb, David, Paul, and Elizabeth, Rebecca, and all the others, are all brethren.

"Well, as I was saying, Zeb will stay and operate this

Control Center, and Rebecca has chosen to remain, as well. Paul, will you remain or return with us?"

Peter turns to look fondly at Paul, who smiles. "I prefer to remain here with Rebecca and Zeb, if this is acceptable to the rest of you."

A thought suddenly occurs to Peter, and he expresses it. "Paul, what about Todd and his family?" A smile crosses Paul's countenance, which raises some point of curiosity within him.

"Don't be concerned, Peter. That is being tended to, more than you could understand at the moment. We can get into that later, if you'd like, but just be assured that Todd and his family are well cared for and that my remaining here will not diminish or moderate that one bit."

Peter nods at Paul, and then turns to Zachary, "Well, then, I guess it will be you, Elizabeth and I who'll be going?"

Elizabeth smiles warmly, "Yes, I have chosen to remain with you and Zachary, if that's okay with you, Peter."

"Sure it is. Always."

"Okay, then, Pete, if you're ready," teases Zachary. "I don't want to interrupt, but we have lots to do. And you know me, I'd like to get about it. So, if you will, come stand here, and Elizabeth, you on his other side. And, dear friends?" he calls to Zeb, Paul, and Rebecca, "we'll be back shortly. If you need anything, let us know and we'll respond immediately."

Looking at the companions he is leaving behind, Peter receives an indication of support and encouragement, and returns to each of them an expression of joy and blessing.

Now, with Zachary on one side and Elizabeth on the other, Zachary instructs Peter, "Very well, Peter, I would like you to remember your Garden. Close yourself down, go within, and draw forth the memory of the Garden."

Peter follows Zachary's suggestions and swiftly finds himself able to remember the Garden. It becomes incredibly vivid, to the point where Peter is startled at its reality. Without thinking, he turns to his left and there stands Zachary.

To his right is Elizabeth, smiling at him. "Well done, Peter. You've mastered that quite well."

"You mean we're in the Garden already?"

"Quite so, Pete. Nice bit of work, I would say. Doubt that we could top that, eh wot, Elizabeth?"

"Hardly so, Zachary. I think he has performed as adequately as any of us could have."

"Okay, then, let's not waste any time. Come, Pete. Let's go to the Great Hall of Wisdom."

Intrigued, Peter follows Zachary without question. Soaring easily, the three of them are almost instantaneously within the Great Hall. Peter looks to the great table and notes that there is no indication of a gathering. Although he can perceive entities congregated within the Great Hall, they are not, as he is accustomed to, assembled about the great table. Puzzled, he turns to Zachary, "Why are we here?"

"Well, you know this place as a very special location wherein we meet the Entity of Light and such, and you remember our earlier gatherings. But what you haven't remembered, or aren't aware of at present, are some of the other aspects of this Great Hall. You'll learn those quickly enough if you'll simply follow along here."

Zachary turns, and Peter, feeling the presence of Elizabeth at his side, casts her a somewhat grateful glance for her presence. She confirms her presence with a smile, and he can feel her urging him to follow Zachary.

Within the twinkling of an eye, Peter finds himself before a small group of entities.

One in the midst of the group before him speaks, "Greetings, Zachary. Welcome."

"Hello, again. How are we doing?"

"Quite well. Greetings to you, as well, Elizabeth, and you, Peter. Welcome."

"Uh, thank you, sir. I'm pleased to be here, though I must

admit I don't know why."

Peter receives the emanation of warmth and understanding from the entity and from the entire group.

To the extent that he has become familiar with such warm emanations, he knows the entity and the group to be of some significant stature of spiritual accomplishment. As he observes the group, he notes with interest that each of the entities seems to be unique in some specialized way. As he continues observing them, he feels himself being greeted by each as though he is receiving some sort of blessing in turn. Finally, he returns his attention to the spokesperson.

"We know a great deal of the works you and your colleagues have been involved in, Peter, indeed, all of them since you left the Earth."

The impact of the entity's statement moves through Peter like a brisk autumn wind would in the Earth, as though his Earth clothing could not stop the penetration of the wind so that his body underneath would react immediately. Simultaneously, he is aware that these entities would not, and did not, do so merely to eavesdrop or because of idle curiosity. Therefore, he returns the spokesperson's gaze with his own and asks, "May I inquire, sir, what your purpose was for observing my progression? Of course, I have no objection to that, for I have felt ever since I left the Earth that all of my being was like an open book."

Zachary can be heard chuckling off to the side.

The spokesperson acknowledges Zachary's humor and returns a warm look to Peter. "This is true, Peter. We have, in a manner of speaking, been participating in a way with your progression for the purpose of helping others and, as well, to contribute what little we might, wherever we might, in accordance with our Father's will and purpose."

At that statement, Peter realizes they indeed could contribute a great deal, though he knows not why.

The spokesperson continues, "We have these works with

you and your companions, and other works defined as our purposes and goals in accordance with our Father's Will."

Warmed by such sincerity and honesty, Peter allows his consciousness to rest upon the entity.

"Peter, while you are aware of communicating with me as the spokesperson for this group, I wish you to recognize that I am speaking primarily as an instrument of the entire group, all of my colleagues here and a considerable number elsewhere."

"Elsewhere?" Peter looks about. "Where would that be, if you can tell me in references that I would understand?"

Peter is aware that the entire group has now focused their attention upon him. Somewhat uneasily, because he is aware that he is the focal point of all here, he makes a brief effort to keep himself balanced.

Zachary offer reassuringly, "Don't be concerned, Peter. There is no need. These are friends. These are colleagues."

"Indeed, that is so," adds Elizabeth, "very dear friends."

"I'm sure of that," nods Peter, "I can feel that to be true."

"But to answer your question, Peter, we are a part of a greater group of those who would serve, who are in accordance with a common purpose and work. Even so, the number changes, now and then, of those who come and go, in a manner of speaking. We have a basic group, but welcome all those who would come forward to contribute to the works at hand. Some of our group express themselves in realms well beyond this, the Garden Realm you are so fond of. You would think of those realms as being 'higher' than this."

Peter is amazed at the thought that entities from a higher realm would be interested in him and his progress.

As though observing his thoughts, the spokesperson continues, "Their choice of works is one and the same which you have been given, Peter, and therefore, they are like brethren unto a call that has come from God. Is that clear to you?"

"Yes, sir. I grasp that completely."

With a subtle nod, the spokesperson continues, "Well, then, others of our group are expressed in realms that are not identified as 'higher' realms, but realms familiar to you, in the past and even now as we speak."

"Might I inquire, sir, what these are and where they are?"

"Most assuredly, Peter. Among them are those realms you have already visited. Some you would remember clearly and some less clearly. To specifically answer your question, there are those among our group expressed in the formless realm; some who serve in the sense of being guardians, functioning through, and in accordance with, our Father's Will unto His Law; and others who are keepers of records, who strive with their consciousness to assist any who would seek from that often referred to as the Akasha; and others among our group who are expressed in a realm familiar to you, called the Earth."

Peter stares at the spokesperson, then glances quickly at the others. "Excuse me, but did you say, in the Earth?"

"Yes, Peter, in the Earth."

Allowing his thoughts to flow freely, Peter assumes that the spokesperson means that these are entities who have moved in spiritual form to do some work in the Earth, as he has in past occasions.

Again, aware of Peter's thought, the spokesperson responds, "That is true, Peter, there are those. And there are others, as well."

Peter studies the speaker further. "What are these other expressions?"

"Physical body, Peter."

"Physical body? Do you mean, uh … people? I mean, well, you know, like I was? I mean … *alive?*"

Peter can hear Zachary's good-humored chuckles, flowing to him.

Then Zachary steps forward, asking the spokesperson, "If I might be permitted, perhaps I could help a bit here."

"Please do."

Peter feels Zachary's typical easy nature wonderfully flowing to him with a mix of humor, love, and understanding, all intertwined with forthright energies. "You see, Pete, lots of us work in multiple ways, and as we do so, we often work in many forms of expression. You already know this. Right?"

Peter nods, but still has his consciousness focused on the spokesperson's comments about entities who are living in the Earth being a part of their group.

Zachary speaks to Peter's unspoken thoughts, "Why not, Pete? I mean, you're aware of the group, and you've been lots of places and done lots of things. Why wouldn't it be possible for others to do the same, even in physical bodies?"

Peter chooses his words deliberately. "Yes, Zack, I suppose anything is possible. I'll be the first to accept that, with all I've experienced recently. But if I hear accurately what you are both saying," turning to look at the spokesperson and then back to Zachary, "you're saying that this group, here, is composed of entities from higher realms, other realms, this realm here in the Hall of Wisdom, *and* living, breathing people in the Earth?"

"That's it, Pete. That's it exactly."

"Well, how is such a thing possible? I mean, I just came from the Earth not that long ago, and I never heard such a thing while I was there. And, forgive me for questioning you, but if that were so, I would have thought it would be, well, you know, headline news. Like 'So-and-So Communicates with Other Realms,' and that sort of thing. So, please explain that further, because I can't grasp it."

"You can, Peter, but not if you keep the framework intact that was derived from the Earth. You have to think of this in unlimited terms, and then allow your consciousness to explore those unlimited terms to the extent that you can understand the full potential of all entities, no matter how they are expressed. This is an important point that will become clear to you as we continue on in the commission. So, let's get this understood clearly here so we can get on with our work.

"Quite simply, when you were in the Earth, you actually communicated with this and other realms. Often. And before you interrupt with your question, I'll answer it. You did so in your sleep. You also did so occasionally here and there when your mental framework was relaxed enough for thoughts to be communicated to you directly and received here directly. So, this is simply a group of entities who have dedicated themselves to recognizing reality in the Earth to be what it is and, at the same time, to also affirm their eternal nature. As they exercise this awareness, they become better and better at it, more and more adept. Understand?"

"I actually do understand that. So," turning back to the spokesperson, "these people in the Earth who are a part of your group … Do they, you know, do they know about me?"

Nodding, the spokesperson sends Peter a warm smile.

"*All* about me?"

He shakes his head, "No, Peter, not all about you, but enough to understand where you are and what you are striving to accomplish, and to be willing to contribute what they can to help you complete your commission."

"No kidding!" states Peter, amazed. They are willing to help me with the commission from the Earth?"

"That is so, Peter."

Zachary, smiling and, more or less bouncing around, having difficulty containing himself, comes to rest in front of Peter, looking him straight in the eyes. "Peter, nothing is impossible. The only limitations we have are those we accept. If there are people, as you call them, in the Earth who have allowed themselves to significantly release their limitations, wouldn't it logically follow that they would regain an equivalent amount of their limitless nature?" He steps back, pleased with his statement, and smiles radiantly at Peter.

Peter returns the smile. "I see what you mean, and yes, I

assume that is true. I have had enough experience recently to know what you mean by that."

"Good, then ask whatever questions remain, and we'll get to work."

Sensing from this comment that some expediency is advised, Peter turns to the spokesperson. "Well, sir, I admit to being somewhat astonished, and that's putting it mildly, to discover that there is a group of people alive in the Earth … and I guess they're alive right now as we're speaking, right?"

The spokesperson smiles very broadly, "Yes, they are quite so, Peter."

"And, uh, well, can they hear us speaking? Right now, I mean?"

Nodding, the spokesperson responds softly, "Some can. Some cannot, clearly. But all will have an awareness of this conversation."

"That is amazing! I would certainly like to know much more about that and maybe even become involved somehow because I would like to know about how such a lack of limitation in the Earth can occur. It truly is amazing."

"You are always welcome in our group, Peter, and anything we can offer to you that is in accordance with your desire, you have but to ask." The spokesperson turns to look at Zachary, "We have prepared the information that you are seeking and can provide it to you whenever you wish."

Elizabeth now steps forward, "We are grateful for the retrieval of the information, for we're aware of the complexities involved in so doing. We wish to extend our gratitude to your entire group in all realms for their dedication during this time of concentrated effort."

Zachary nods vigorously, "Yes, please communicate our gratitude to all."

The spokesperson then slowly makes a motion, and the group reassemble themselves in a curiously ordered fashion.

Peter cannot fully comprehend what he sees, but it is as

though each entity has a place and a function within the group. As they move into what seems to be predefined positions, he begins to feel a very pleasant energy or vibration flow from them. In the midst of this flow, he, Zachary, and Elizabeth can hear and feel a cascading essence of color, sound, vibration, and emotional sensations, as he would describe them from his memories in Earth, and an additional array of energies that he finds difficult to define.

Without thinking, he shifts himself a bit and becomes less structured, finding himself now in a formless state. As he does, he notes that his companions have also shifted their focus and are formless now, as well. He feels himself in motion. It is as though he is striving to tune into the flow of consciousness that is coming to him from the group by continually adjusting his own awareness. He thinks of this as though fine-tuning a receiving device in the Earth.

Finally Peter finds himself expressed very joyfully, just as he was after the Entity in the light in the Hall of Wisdom gave him what he thinks of as a blessing to use in the commission. In that moment, in his radiance and in the glow of that gift given earlier, he perceives the group before him as a collection of similar light and essence, so very beautiful that he is moved by the brilliance of what he beholds.

Coming to the forefront, he recognizes the essence of the spokesperson of the group and hears this communication, *What you have come to understand regarding the commission, we would now like to convert for you, in a manner of speaking, into knowledge, adding certain other aspects of information you have asked about earlier, and those unspoken questions within you, as well.*

A few moments later, Peter hears, feels, and experiences the answer to his question: W*hy is she here?* The flow of the information is as though he moves simultaneously to many different places and to many different points of view, as though each entity in the group was, for a moment here and there, in direct communication with him, offering what they had in terms of perspective, background, awareness, and wisdom. This continues for an indeterminate period of time by Earth measure, until Peter, now in a state of realization and feeling utterly magnificent, realizes that the group before him considers the communication to be complete.

Slowly, he feels himself turning his concentration back to a more formed expression, and he perceives peripherally that Zachary and Elizabeth are doing the same.

Before him once again are the expressions of the group, and this time he perceives the spokesperson clearly. "Peter, we have given you that which we have collected in answer to your questions, spoken and unspoken, and what we have anticipated to be that which you shall need as the moment is appropriate. Therefore, it will remain in and/or about you until it is needed, and only when needed. The reason for it operating in this way is so that in all works, such as a commission or other works performed in God's Name, it is never forgotten that the development of all souls involved under Universal Law is also assured. Therefore, the *mechanics* of this activity have been structured to allow your individual consciousness to progress in accordance with your free will choices. The information will be available, but until needed, it won't flood your consciousness and divert your individual progression on to a path that might in any way usurp that. Do you have questions at this time?"

Peter can feel the constraint of Zachary near him, knowing intuitively that he would like to say, *Does he have questions? This guy has an inexhaustible supply of them.*

Without responding to Zachery's silent communication, but amused at this realization, Peter nods to the spokesperson, "Sir, as my friend Zachary would tell you, I am rarely without questions. But for now, I will place my faith totally in the greater wisdom and judgment of you and your group, for I sense that there is some need for expediency here. Apparently some sort of schedule is before us, and I wouldn't want to be the one to disrupt it."

"Wisely chosen, Peter. So, then, if you'll permit us, we'll withdraw and return to a position of observation regarding you and your works. Remember that you can call upon us at any time and we will joyfully respond. Also, we would like you to know that all of our group, including those in the Earth, have attuned to you and your works during a special time of prayer and meditation."

"Really?"

"Really, Peter."

"Do please communicate to them my gratitude for that. Somehow, the involvement in my progress and in this mutual work with people in the Earth," turning to also acknowledge his gratitude for the involvement of Elizabeth and Zachary, "has special meaning. I sense it and I feel it, and I am warmed that somebody in the Earth would care about anything beyond the Earth. My memories of it are that only rarely did I find anyone who was even aware of anything beyond the finite, beyond that which was necessary for them each day, you know, their jobs and the need to provide for their families, and competing to get ahead, and all that sort. Sometime, I do truly want to find out more about your group and that portion of it in the Earth, so if I could make an appointment for a future time of discussion with you all," motioning to the others, "I would consider that a great honor."

"We have noted your request, and we shall be at the ready as you deem appropriate."

"Well, then, I will look forward to that with eagerness. But as you said, your group in the Earth is on a schedule, and I can remember those only too well. I don't want to disrupt the effort that's being expended, if that's so."

"It is so, Peter."

Peter turns to Zachary, "What next, Zack?"

CHAPTER 10

Preparing for the Commission
NOVEMBER 12, 1991

Peter, Zachary and Elizabeth have moved out of the Hall of Wisdom and have taken restful postures upon Peter's favored little knoll.

Peter is speaking. "Wow, Zack, that was quite an experience and, I might add, it's inspiring to consider that people living in Earth, and elsewhere, might be a part of this work, and even observing my progression, as you call it. And those in that group that we met were awesome! They have an understanding beyond what I could have imagined possible. Are all of those people or entities, or whatever we are here … Are they all continually working together like that, or have they come together just for this commission? Are they always listening or observing what we're doing? And how do they do …"

"Hold up, Pete. Let's slow down and take this bit by bit." Zachary's warm smile centers Peter, and he turns to Elizabeth, "Perhaps you'd like to fill Peter in while I just enjoy listening for a while."

Nodding with an understanding smile to Zachary, Elizabeth turns to Peter, "Well, as you may recall, anyone can join us at any time when what we are about is in harmony with their own ideal and purpose. As far as observing or communicating to or with us is concerned, so long as they don't violate or interfere with your right of free will, they are welcome. And I feel certain that that's your feeling, too, isn't it?"

Peter, simply nods, studying her, hopeful that he'll gain

as much insight and information as possible. It is as though he is afraid to comment, that he might somehow inadvertently prevent that information from being given to him.

Smiling knowingly, Elizabeth continues, slowly and deliberately. "The group, as you perceived them, is comprised of a dedicated group of souls or entities who are working with and under a common ideal and purpose. They had already anticipated this commission. In fact, so much so that their observation of your activities began shortly before you departed the Earth."

Peter blurts out, "You mean they knew about me when I was still back there in … in … in my physical body?"

"Yes, but only to the degree that it provided understanding for the group. No invasion of your personal life or privacy was ever made. For that matter, they know you only as Peter. They know of your background to a degree, and of your family and so forth, but they didn't, what you call, eavesdrop," pausing, with a twinkle in her eye.

Peter reflects the same qualities back to Elizabeth, obviously understanding what's being communicated between them.

Little rivulets of humor can be detected from Zachary, who is now in his familiar reclining position, brushing the lush green beneath him, the grass that had been created here for Peter.

"In order to be of the greatest possible contribution and service with you and our group, in this and possibly future works," Elizabeth continues, "that bit of background was important for all of them. Also, some who are with that group, that you call *alive* … though I don't know what you'd call us, then."

Peter adjusts his position a bit, embarrassed at his reference, since he knows now that life is continuous and that only the expression of the life-force changes.

Elizabeth understands Peter's realization. "Remember

that each soul progresses, no matter what the work is. So all the members of that group from the Earth, from the most spiritually unlimited one to the one who might be expressing limitation, they'll all progress. That is the beauty and joy of service in works under God's spirit and in His Name. To a large degree, a number of them, still in physical expressions in the Earth, learned a great deal along with you. When you struggled, they observed it and identified it with their own struggles there in the Earth. When you made discoveries, they shared in those and strived to apply your discoveries to their own potential while they are yet in physical body."

Peter is incredulous. "What a wonderful opportunity. I am pleased to hear that greater benefits came from my trial-and-error activities in these realms than merely the ones to me. But how do they do that, Elizabeth? I mean, how do they, you know ... how do they communicate with these realms? Are you saying they have the ability to observe us here, so far away from the physical expression, or finiteness?"

"They do, but in a different way than what you might anticipate. Each of them possesses the ability within them to communicate and move about here, just as you have learned to do. As you might expect, while they are in physical body, it is difficult for them to truly do that. Whether they know this limitation as illusionary or not, it is very real for them. In fact, it's not that they truly are illusions. Remember, where two or more agree, reality is formed out of that agreement, and when you have so many souls involved, as are within and about the Earth, you can imagine the degree to which that reality is expressed. Things appear three-dimensional, and the tendency to let it all rest at that is quite strong."

Peter nods, remembering only too well his experience in the Earth of which Elizabeth speaks.

"So, back to your question, their communication is quite similar to what we have just structured in order to connect this and other realms with the realm in which our commission is located." She pauses to allow Peter to absorb that.

"So, it's like that pathway we made by moving as we did? What did you call it, Zachary?"

Zachary continues to brush the grass. "Well, there are several terms for it. We gave you the reference of a tunnel of light, a pathway of light. Sometimes, from the Earth, it's called a channel, or something like that."

"That's right, Peter," adds Elizabeth, "that is the mechanism with which communication is maintained, though not always to the conscious awareness of all participants. What happens is, at periodic intervals, the experiences we have had are assembled and given to the Earth through the group we just met … primarily through the spokesperson, who acts as a link for the collective consciousness of all involved."

"I see. So there's a sort of parallel with the Earth?"

"Yes, and those who have the dedication, or you could say those who developed the ability to communicate through past experiences or a number of different things, can act as the counterpart of the spokesperson of the group here to the group in the Earth."

"Fascinating! Too bad I didn't know more about this while I was there. I can't help but wonder what I would have done with that …" His words trail off.

Zachary explains, "Well, you did know, somewhat, as do many in the Earth. But things being as they are there, there's rarely time in the thoughts of most people to dwell on such things. The intensity of their agreed-upon thought-form often encroaches heavily upon the viability of such a 'possible reality' (and you'd have to put that in quotes, wouldn't you?)" winking at Peter as he looks up. "So, you did, here and there, know a bit about it but it seemed so foreign, so *unreal* from your perspective there, that it didn't have the strength to be sustained as a reality."

Peter realizes that Zachary and Elizabeth are allowing him time to absorb and digest their comments, and to place them in a sequential order in his awareness along with all of the other information he has recently gathered from his experiences with this commission. "Well, I have to admit that I have many questions, as you know, since that's my nature, as you often point out, Zachary," which earns Peter a knowing nod from Zachary. "But I guess we'd better turn to the information we've received, thanks to the group, so that we can get about our work."

"Wisely stated, Peter," comments Elizabeth.

"Well, let me go back to my last question. I had asked why she is here. I understand now that something happened that caused her to become involved with the energies that are prevalent in finite realms. Do I have that much straight?"

"As accurate as we comprehend it, "Elizabeth answers.

"So then, it seems that we have a situation here where … well, I'm not sure what to call her, or even why you call her a *her*, since you've told me repeatedly that once beyond finite expressions we are neither male nor female. Let's see if I have the information about that." Peter pauses to review. "What I find as I search this, is that her basic nature is that, in finite realms of expression and form, she would be defined by the souls involved there as being of that side of polarity. Right, Zack?"

"You're right, Pete. Continue."

"Okay. So, having the essences or energies that are defined as feminine when in finite realms, she is defined as a *she*. Correct?"

Elizabeth and Zachary nod.

"Well, let me see if I can locate specifics as to why she came into finite realms in the first place. Maybe that would give us some clues as to how to proceed to help her." Reflecting on the knowledge he has gathered, it is as if Peter just acquired a set of encyclopedia or reference books and is now taking the time to use them. He realizes he has been given a vast array of information, and the potentiality of it intrigues him greatly. But sticking to his task (as was his nature in the Earth, self-discipline having enabled him to become quite successful there) he offers his deductions. "It appears that she was looking for someone, a colleague, someone who had moved into the realm of finite expression and who did not return. Curious ... I see this as several lines of light. I guess this must be how the tunnel of light that we created must appear to one who can see from this perspective."

His companions nod again.

"Let me try to follow the primary one backwards, as best I can."

Zachary is seated upright, paying more attention now, and Elizabeth, as well.

"Can you see this, Zachary and Elizabeth, as I am experiencing it?"

Peter hears and feels their affirmation.

"Look, here, at the light. I'm approaching such an incredible intensity of light. Wow! That is beautiful! And, oh, my, a thought just occurred to me about the group we just met and the spokesperson who said they were observing us. Can they hear us now?"

"Affirmative, Pete."

"That ... is ... a strange ... feeling. I'm okay with it, but it's a strange realization. One tends to think of experiencing privately." He laughs a bit, reciprocated by Elizabeth and Zachary.

"Don't worry, Pete. It's all within the highest degree of courtesy and in strict accordance with Universal Law. Not to worry."

"Okay, Zack. But it is odd, isn't it?" He continues his observation. "The light seems to be of a sort that I doubt I could penetrate, and somehow I know I'm not supposed to. But as I observe it, I get the impression that I can relate this to what was described to me earlier as the angelic host. So this is where the, as you called it, *fallen angel* must be located?"

"It would seem so, Peter," Elizabeth responds. "Might we turn, now, to follow the other line of light?"

Looking off to the side, he immediately realizes that this must be the companion who was being sought by the fallen angel, and with ease he moves to focus in on its light.

"Try to express what you detect, what you feel. That might be helpful to all involved."

"Okay, Zack, I'll do my best. Well, I get this incredible feeling of beauty, of peace, of harmony. It's just wonderful to experience. It reminds me of the formless state, though this seems far beyond that. As I follow it a bit further, more in the direction of finiteness, it's almost as though I would be following a trail of my own curiosity. So I deduce from that that this entity must have traveled into these realms, maybe out of curiosity?"

"That feels right, Pete. Go on."

He moves and moves and continues to experience growing degrees of what he remembers as emotions and, perhaps, a series of discoveries. As though the entity, who had moved into finiteness, was bit by bit discovering the alluring nature of finite expression, the awe of directing the power of God towards something specific. Peter can detect the amazement and the wonder experienced by this entity as the journey continues into finite realms.

He notes here and there that the entity paused at this point or that striving to actually experience what was found there. As he continues to follow the line of light, things seem familiar to him and he comments to Zachary and Elizabeth that this is similar to the movement of his earlier experience through the colors. It is as though he's passing through points of demarcation or veil-like areas of consciousness that seem to be preserving, or enveloping those individually structured arrays of experience. He notes, further that with each successive movement, these seem to be more and more defined, more and more finite. They become heavier, more sluggish, denser and, to his utter amazement, he realizes that they are getting what he calls *stickier*. "My goodness, Zachary, Elizabeth, look here! Right here at this point where the soul passed through this, there is the definite feeling of stickiness. You remember like I talked about the jellied toast?"

Both Elizabeth and Zachary giggle.

Peter also finds humor in his own comment, remembering the brief exchange that took place about this. "Well, this is what that feels like again, only more moderate than I felt around the commission."

"Good, Pete. Keep relating your experience."

As Peter continues to move, he describes the various sensations and emotions. "Say! This feels like an emotion I remember from the Earth called envy! And here's sadness. This one feels like guilt, and this one over here feels like joy. And here's one that feels, somehow or other, like growth. Wow, look at this one … it's out of tune, out of balance. What can that be?"

"Something imbalanced, I would think, Pete. What do you think, Elizabeth?"

"Yes, it would appear so. Look how the colors are improperly balanced and how they are moving one against the other, and then that one against the other. And on the periphery, you can see a few other colors. See that, Peter?"

"I do, Elizabeth! Looks orange-ish, doesn't it?"

"Yes, I guess you could call it that."

"Let's see where this leads … Goodness, this is getting more and more dense, heavier and heavier."

After some passage of time with all this, the three find themselves back upon the knoll in Peter's garden.

"Well, I have a clear idea now of why the fallen angel came here. Don't you both agree?"

Receiving approval from his companions, Peter continues, "So the first entity who entered into finite realms … and, goodness, they are vast, aren't they!"

"Oh yes, indeed," responds Zachary. "Far more vast than a mind on Earth could comprehend. Almost unlimited."

"All that emotion the entity was collecting, it looked to me like that first entity actually became lodged in it."

Zachary and Elizabeth exchange glances. "Agreed. I think they went so far as to enter into what's often referred to here as the incarnative cycles."

"This one must have taken on a physical form. It seems to be the only logical explanation. If that's so, aren't there records of all of that? Didn't you tell me that at one point, Zack?"

Zachary nods.

"Could we get those records?"

"Certainly, Peter," offers Elizabeth. "We have access to them right over here in the Hall of Wisdom if we want them."

"That would be very interesting, but before we do that, could we take another look at the other line of light? The fallen angel?"

Receiving approval, Peter moves inwardly to retrieve the awareness, and picks it up at the point of the emergence from the great Light, which Peter understands to mean the realm of God's expression, in a much purer state than he could grasp at the moment, such as a realm of angels.

Certainly the outer band of it, he hears Elizabeth comment to his thought. *Rebecca has told me much of that.*

This startles Peter. "Rebecca has told *you* of it?"

Yes, Peter.

Making a mental note to check on this later, he continues on, but only with extreme difficulty, for now his curiosity about Rebecca is raised another notch or two. "Look here, then. It appears to me that this fallen one has almost paralleled her companion's path. But her light is much brighter. Look at that. See here? Here's a point where the first one's light was already considerably obscured by the *absorption* of, I guess I'd have to call it, emotion and finiteness. And here's the point where that one must have stopped to actually experience that. From here, the light is considerably dimmer, but our fallen angel's light remains bright." Continuing to follow the two lines almost parallel to one another, Peter is in wonder at the discoveries. "She sustained her light all the way into this great depth of finiteness. That seems to be quite an accomplishment."

Indeed. I would agree with you, he hears from Zachary.

I, as well, Peter, echoes Elizabeth.

Continuing to follow this light, Peter suddenly comes to a point where there is a convergence of many different colors, and both the dimmer line of light and the very bright line of light seem to flow into it.

"This must be where the trouble started," Peter offers, based upon his intuition and also upon some subtle knowledge or memory from the Earth. "Look at all that orange color. To me that means intense activity. Am I right?"

Right, he hears from both of his companions.

"Let's try to get around this and look on the other side." Peter sees that the first light, the soul's path who first wandered into the realm of finiteness, has changed dramatically. "That's a line of light that enters into finite expression. There's no question about it. Right, Elizabeth?"

You are right, Peter. This first one moved into physical form. We can follow that later, and I'll get the records if you want them or if you think we need them. Now let's follow the other light, our commission, and see where that goes.

Curiously, Peter cannot find the other path. After some considerable effort, he states, "I can't find it. It comes into this, but it doesn't seem to go out."

I agree, Pete. How about you, Elizabeth, do you see it?

Not in my present form, Zachary. If you and Peter would help me, I will try to attune to it in what's called the feminine expression in this finite realm.

Puzzled, but responding, Peter moves with Zachary to

stand adjacent to Elizabeth, side by side. He looks at her with admiration and wonder as he perceives her now as a sphere of light, first changing into a very bold color, then into another, then another and another, on and on, until Elizabeth emerges again in the form Peter can clearly identify as she.

He inquires, "How are you, Elizabeth? Are you okay?"

Pausing for enough time that Peter is concerned, he finally hears, *Yes, Peter, thank you. I am well. It just takes a while to regain balance from that. I'm not as accomplished at it as I'd like to be. Perhaps we'll have the opportunity to do more with that and I can gain greater ease later. But I think I've found the path, so if you'll both follow me and stay close by my side, I think I can make the path open for all three of us to move within it and follow it.*

Zachary motions Peter to take a position adjacent to him, immediately behind Elizabeth, and they begin to move.

Peter is awestruck by the flashes and essences of energies and colors he notes just on the periphery. He begins to feel a reflection from them.

Center now, Pete, Zachary instructs softly. *Balance. You know, intensify your cloak. But keep it pure. Don't be reactive. Be neutral. That's important, or we'll slow down Elizabeth. She'll have to stop to tend to us, and that will take away from her ability to move.*

"I understand, Zachary. I'll watch that carefully."

As though he had moved into a peaceful sphere of light, Peter finds that they are moving easily. Like a vessel moving through the sea with a well-trimmed bow versus one that is barge-like, he feels no resistance. The movement becomes accelerated, until he notes that Elizabeth has suddenly stopped her progress.

"That's it, Peter, Zachary. Here we are."

Peter detects ever so slight movement and is delighted as he realizes he is in the presence of Zeb, David, and Rebecca. They are back, within their recently constructed Control Center, in the Realm of the Fallen Angel.

"Welcome back," he hears from Zeb. How'd you do?"

"Remarkable. Wouldn't you say so, Zachary and Elizabeth?"

They both smile and nod indicating their agreement.

"Peter has done very well, Zeb. I think we have enough to go on now that we can proceed. But, Peter, there are several things I want to tell you, because they are important at this point. Remember the group in the Hall of Wisdom?"

"Are you kidding, Zack? How could I ever forget them?"

"Well, in a manner of speaking, we have opened a line of communication with them or, rather, you have accepted one, since the rest of us have had such a line of communication for some period of time now. At any rate, as a result of this contact and your agreement to continue working with them consciously now, under Universal Law this always affords you a blessing in return. In this case, that blessing is, quite simply, that the group that you were so interested in, make that *are* interested in, is going to communicate with their counterparts in the Earth very soon to aid them in their inquiries to better understand the nature of our work."

"What are you leading up to, Zachary?"

"Well, what I was about to say was, now we can listen in on *their* works just as they can listen in on ours."

"What do you mean? How do we listen in on their works? What works?"

"You'll know more about this when it happens, but basically, they have opportunities to ask questions about your work, just as you do. They have asked for some considerable information about angels, their nature and so forth, which should be very useful to you as well as to their understanding. In a short period of their time, those questions will be answered, and you'll be permitted to have knowledge of that question-and-answer work."

"Wow! This gets more exciting all the time. There certainly are lots of perks taking on a commission, aren't there?"

The group shares laughter and merriment as the impact of Peter's comment finally resonates within him as well.

———————

And so, the work for this three-day period called by the Channel at our gentle urging is, to a degree, complete.

Next, we would ask for and try to respond to all of your questions* that deal with angels, their nature, and such. For the present, then, we conclude, thanking, with great admiration, the Channel ... and all of you.

*Note: Throughout this series of readings called the *Peter Project*, those following the series at the time were permitted to ask questions along the way. This reference is to the questions submitted by those members at this junction. The Q&A readings for the *Peter Project* are available in separate works.

CHAPTER 11

An Angel's Song
DECEMBER 20, 1991

We are now at the newly constructed Control Center, which is within the immediate vicinity of our commission: the fallen angel. Peter, Zachary, and Elizabeth have been discussing and reviewing all of their recent experiences. As we join them, we find Peter commenting about his experiences with what he calls the "new group," that, of course, with a note of loving humor, means you members and the Lama Sing group here.

Peter asks, "Do you suppose, Zachary, that the new group and those who are in the Earth are observing us at this point?"

"I wouldn't be a bit surprised."

"Incredible! For some reason that gives me a good feeling. Sort of an added boost of something or other, though I admit I'd have a hard time defining what that is."

Warm smiles are directed towards Peter, with nods of understanding.

"Well, Pete, why don't we move closer to our commission and see if there is any difference. Perhaps, while that yet might be difficult to explain, it will provide you with some interesting insights."

"Great. I probably should mention that I feel a sort of inner longing or something pulling at me."

Zachary nods at Zeb, who is with David.

A number of others have joined the group in the Control Center, which seems to have expanded greatly to accommodate them all. As Peter observes Zachary speaking with several of these other entities, he notes the expansion of the Control Center and also notes the presence of some other essences. Something that is almost definable but just barely beyond his grasp to do.

Before he can delve into that further, Zachary turns back to him. "Very well, Pete, everyone's ready. Let's proceed." He, more or less, sweeps Peter forward, accompanied by Elizabeth and Rebecca, and the four of them now move into what could be described as a large, luminous tunnel, a kind of living energy. The tunnel appears to be similar to what he remembers from his experience in the tunnel of light, but this is different in the sense that there is that essence flowing through it as well as through the four of them that is indefinable. He begins his series of now familiar exercises, within himself, to attempt to attune to the flow of the essence that he knows is there, but which he cannot quite define.

Zachary assures him, "Don't be concerned about it, Pete. You'll have the answer to that in just a few moments."

So, Peter directs his attention forward, and then comes to an abrupt stop as he sees the commission in front of him.

Where there was previously a rather dull, large, cocoon-like object, Peter is now awed to see what he believes must be this same spherical form but over its entire circumference are wondrous splashes of light, moving as many rivers of beautiful, melodious color. Here and there they swirl and join in beautiful blues, reds, yellows, lush greens. Peter can hear sounds, as though each of these is unique and each bears some sort of wondrous blessing. Utterly awe-struck, he is riveted to his position. Only after an indeterminate amount of time, by Earth measure, does he become aware on the periphery of his consciousness that Elizabeth, Rebecca, and Zachary are calling his name.

Struggling to balance himself, he recovers and slowly perceives his colleagues. They are all smiling at him, though there is no humor, for these are smiles of warmth and understanding being sent to him. "What has happened here? What is all of this magnificent color, light, energy?"

It is Zachary who responds, "It's that essence you were wondering about in the outer Control Center and in the passageway to the commission here."

"Yes, but what is it? What's causing all of this? Where is it coming from? What has happened to the dull, inert form of the commission? Is it underneath all that? Is it still there?"

Softly, Elizabeth explains, "It is still present. What you are perceiving at this point is something we had intended to discuss with you at great length, and this is as good a time as any." She quickly glances to Zachary and Rebecca, who nod their agreement. "This, Peter, is the help being given to you from the new group and from the group in the Earth, those you recently listened to in the questions and answers about the topic of Angels. This is the result of their loving thoughts and their prayers."

Peter cannot respond. He is still awe-struck. He studies Elizabeth's countenance with an intensity beyond measure, and turns to Zachary, incredulous, searching for some … something we cannot define to you here as interpreters. Perhaps it would be some untruth or incompleteness, for we, ourselves, do not fully comprehend Peter's search.

When Peter finally turns to look at Rebecca, she is aglow, which causes him to center on her.

Accepting this as an invitation to comment, she begins, "Peter, this is what the result of prayers from the Earth looks like or from any realm, for that matter. For prayers, just as thoughts, are living things. When one seeks to do a work in accordance with God's Will and strives to do their utmost to send that thought, that hope, under those auspices, the result is what you are perceiving now."

Peter manages to express one word, "Incredible."

He turns back to look at the commission and then returns

his focus to Rebecca, "Might I inquire, Rebecca, why it is that you are so aglow? Not to slight you, Zachary, or you, Elizabeth, or myself, for that matter, as I perceive me. But none of us are glowing like you are. Could you explain why?"

Rebecca radiates warmth to Peter. "I am absorbing and reflecting some of that prayer energy or, as the group in the Earth calls it, prayer power. Because of what you might call my level of acceptance, I can reflect and even amplify this and still sustain individual consciousness."

"That is fascinating. Sometime, could you ..." Peter's voice trails off as he considers what he is asking.

Zachary interjects, "Yes, yes, Pete. We know. Could she show you." They exchange a murmur of humor, and Zachary resumes. "But not now. Look around you. There is much opportunity here. Let's re-focus on our commission, shall we?"

Peter apologizes, stammering, "Oh, uh, of course, Zack. Thank you for bringing me back to the prime purpose. Goodness, I do have a curiosity about all this, though!"

Softly, Rebecca offers, "Don't worry a bit about that. It's the quality we all know and love about you, perhaps above all else. But Zachary is correct. It is time that we should see if our commission is at all receptive to communication."

Peter becomes visibly excited, and his cloak gains in luminosity though, to his credit, we note that it does not become erratic.

Seeing Peter's control over himself, his colleagues issue silent approval by smiling and nodding to one another.

Then Peter asks, "Well, Rebecca, what do we do and how do we do it?"

She moves close to Peter to the point that he almost becomes uncomfortable. "From here on, much of the work will depend upon you. And before you object, stating your unworthiness, let me anticipate your comments: The qualities that you have in and about you at this moment we have all concluded to be the best for the need before us. What we mean by this, as succinctly as I can convey this to you, is review what you have learned.

"This beautiful soul is here because of an attempt to help another, or perhaps others, to break free of what she considers to be an illusion. Here you are, recently arrived from the Earth, comparatively speaking, having achieved some considerable degree of spiritual … I'll call it, luminosity. You are far less encumbered spiritually than you even realize. Again, before you can comment on that, please bear with me and let me finish. The entity within this sphere now covered by the beautiful prayer energy is very wise and she may perceive things well beyond what you expect. Although I know you have no great expectations … in fact, more questions than expectations."

That last comment warms Peter a bit, putting him at ease, and he notes a smiling nod from Elizabeth and Zachary.

It is Elizabeth who comes close to him now. "Peter, if acceptable to you, I will help you. Together, I believe we can be a complete enough expression of truth that this soul, this fallen angel, will communicate with us. What Rebecca is trying to tell you is that our commission will know us as we are. In other words, we can't hide anything from her."

Peter attempts to assimilate all of this information as rapidly as possible, and his colleagues, though obviously wishing to proceed, are measuring their comments so as to not overload his *internal circuits*, (that being a colloquial expression, of course).

Several more comments are exchanged in this regard, and Peter is given further reassurances.

Rebecca speaks again. "Peter, Zachary and I cannot go with you, but we shall remain right here. What we would like you and Elizabeth to do is to move as close as you feel you can to the commission. We will be immediately behind you, but out of what we'll call the realm of focus of the commission so as not to interfere in any way by our presence. She will be dealing with you two and you two alone. I would like to emphasize to you that you have all of the energy that you see around the surface to use as you see fit. These loving prayers, this healing energy, which is directly from the spirit of God within all of the group in the Earth, called members, is offered to this work and, therefore, to you and Elizabeth. Do you understand this, Peter?"

From within, he remembers the Great Entity in the Hall of Wisdom and the reassurance that he only has to ask, to go within, and his needs will be met. Studying Rebecca, he senses something of that same nature within her now. Turning to Zachary, he sees in his trusted companion that which is simply truth.

Though he understands not why it is that only he and Elizabeth can approach the commission, he accepts without question.

"Very good," Rebecca nods at Peter, "if you will, then, at your own inner guidance, proceed. Zachary and I are ready, as are the others in the Control Center. Others beyond your perception are also ready to assist as is appropriate or as you would discern the need. All of this is available for you and Elizabeth to use as your guidance directs."

As though he has become the center of a spotlight in a huge drama, Peter feels himself familiarly heavy. A fleeting memory of his physical body in the Earth passes through him like a swift breeze, until he feels a flood of warmth come over him and realizes that Elizabeth, at his side, has made contact with him. Peter smiles at this, and turns to face the wonder of the commission now before him.

Many thoughts pass through his consciousness, not the least of which is *Why me?* Somewhere from within him, he hears what he discerns to be the voice of the beautiful Entity from the Hall of Wisdom, *All are equal, Peter. Therefore, the task at hand and thee are equal. Proceed.*

Reassured, he moves, gradually entering the color. The

first veils or rays of its brilliance cascade over him and as they do, he feels wonderful. With this ray, he feels joy, with that one, hope. Now, in this moment, he feels as though he is a flower in the spring, bursting forth. Next, he feels the love and compassion he now knows is coming from someone in the Earth. Peter senses an essence from a male whom he knows and feels a bond with inside this envelopment.

On it goes, again and again, until Peter perceives some resistance. Turning to Elizabeth, he meets her consciousness, as though two pairs of eyes would meet.

Together, they turn to observe what is in front of them.

Peter intuits that this is the former substance that looked so dull, but now it bears a continual steady luminosity, as if millions of wonderful lights are focused upon it. It is glowing so that it is literally vibrating, as though what had earlier seemed like plaster or cement or the silvery-gray web of a butterfly's cocoon is now living light. "What do you think this means, Elizabeth?" he asks quietly.

"I believe she is stirring, Peter. I believe the prayer and all of the loving thought and energy have elicited some degree of awareness from her."

Time passes. Peter and Elizabeth remain hovering immediately before the sphere in which the commission is believed to be.

"We must do something, Elizabeth. I don't know what, but we must do something."

"Go within, and see what you find."

Obediently, trusting, Peter pauses and turns within. As he does, he feels a great flood of reassurance, warmth, and a surprising flow of remarkable energy, which seems to revitalize him, as though he is sparkling with wisdom and joy and life itself. He realizes that what they should do next is to knock.

Without his having verbalized this, Elizabeth nods, and Peter realizes that she knows completely what he has just experienced. A flash of wonder over this goes through him, but he casts it off so that he does not become distracted.

He turns to be face-on to the commission, and with some monotone-like steadiness to his voice, he is startled as he hears himself communicate. "Hel-looo-there. Greet-tings. If-we-may, we-would-like-to-visit-with-you."

Taken aback at the seeming ineptness of his comments, he again feels warmth come from Elizabeth and hears her silently communicate, *Peter, it is not what you say. It is not the words but what is felt behind the message. She will know. If she wants to hear us, she will know what is in your heart. I'm sure of it.*

Peter begins to respond with a comment something like, *Well, that's good because it certainly didn't sound all that good to me,* when he is abruptly interrupted by a flow of musical-like energy which, astoundingly, seems to be coming from within the shimmering sphere immediately before them.

That's her, Peter! That's her! She's answering you. Speak again.

Floundering, Peter quickly brings himself up and hears his own communication with wonder, "We greet you. We would ask, if it's not an intrusion, that we might visit with you. We mean you no harm or seek no interruption of your choices, but we have come to know of your being here, and we would …"

Before his words can continue, Peter feels himself and Elizabeth pulled through the envelopment of light, as if some tremendous magnetic force had snapped up a few bits of iron particles cast before it. He is dazed and struggles to sustain balance and awareness, buoyed all the while by the warmth and steady calm of Elizabeth at his side.

He looks about himself, with thoughts such as, *Where are we? What is this?* and so forth, but before he can have too many such thoughts, he becomes aware of an almost magical glow of a soft pastel blue orb some brief distance before him. It seems to be rotating with small spires of light emanating from its core. As it rotates, the spires reach out to all that is within what Peter now understands to be an immense chamber of light. For an instant, Peter reflects and draws from his Earthly consciousness the image of an egg. He imagines for a moment that this might be what the inside of an empty egg is like, only here in its center is this astonishing robin's-egg blue orb of light simply rotating in front of them.

Spellbound, he looks in wonder and awe.

Then, he sees a focused shaft of incredibly beautiful light reach out to touch Elizabeth, who is at his side.

Startled, he turns, concerned for her, but instantly sees that she is sending her own light to the wondrous bluish sphere. Elizabeth's light, though different somehow, has qualities similar to the magnificent orb of light before them.

Peter stands awe-struck watching the two streams of light flowing between Elizabeth and the radiant, blue sphere, which he knows is be the fallen angel. What is taking place between Elizabeth and the angel is beyond him. Various emotions are coming and going until suddenly he realizes that he must, at all costs, maintain control. Immediately, he goes within himself to recover the orb of light given to him in the Hall of Wisdom. When he reaches it, he thrusts his consciousness into it, remembering the promise given to him, that his every need would be met through this, the wonder of this Great Entity, and that which is his own spirit.

Renewed and in a state of complete ease, Peter thrusts his consciousness back to the expressions before him in time to see the two streams of light being exchanged terminate and slowly draw back – the fallen angel's back to the beautiful blue sphere, and Elizabeth's back to her.

Softly, he calls out, "Elizabeth! Elizabeth!"

"Yes, Peter. I am fine. I am well. Do not be concerned."

"Well, what happened there? Elizabeth?"

"She was communicating with me, Peter, and I returned the communication. She asked if she might know me, and I accepted and granted her that right, of course, for it is we who are the visitors here so that seems only appropriate. Wouldn't you agree?"

Pausing but a moment, Peter, more dutifully than logically, responds, "Yes, I'm sure it is appropriate."

At that point, he is startled to feel something strike him on the side. He turns to see that the same shaft of light he just saw on Elizabeth now seems to be focused on him.

A bit apprehensive, he is calmed by the presence of Elizabeth yet again, "Easy now, Peter. She is simply attempting to communicate with you now. Remember, though, she has not been in physical body like you have."

"Well, what do I do, Elizabeth? I don't understand."

"Simply think with your infiniteness. Don't think with your finiteness. You are as unlimited as you are able to accept. Remember the Entity in the Great Hall."

Peter focuses on the flow of what he sees as a living light. It is wondrous. It has a bluish cast yet, within it, he can perceive whites and silvers, not unlike the Entity in the Great Hall, he recalls.

As he strives to find in his consciousness some level of communication, it is like someone twisting and turning a dial on a radio receiver in the Earth. Shortly, Peter is aware of a communication, which amazes him.

May I know you?

Turning to Elizabeth, he perceives her to nod, smiling. *Go ahead, Peter. There is no problem whatsoever in accepting or agreeing. Remember what this is.*

Slightly taken aback at his own forgetfulness, Peter reminds himself that, after all, this is an angel, not just someone from one of the other realms, like the realm that dissipated or one of Todd's realms.

At the point of that thought of Todd, Peter notes that the shaft of light changes. A pink hue flashes over it, and he sees it radiate back and forth between the angel and himself, and he is fearful that he has committed some error.

Elizabeth is also surprised by this. *Remain calm. Our intent is pure. I do not believe that we could commit an error that would unsettle her because she knows our intent.*

She does?

Yes, but might I remind you that she has asked for your permission to know you?"

"*Gosh, I'm sorry. I forgot that. Things are moving so fast and, here we are in the midst of this huge ball, communicating with this sphere of ... Well, you know, this is very strange and almost beyond my ability to absorb or deal with.*

You're doing fine. But, again, I suggest you answer her, or we may find ourselves on the outside looking in again.

Really?

Really, Peter. It is only by her grace that we are even here. She has chosen of her own free will to be in a state of isolation and she could, in the twinkling of an eye (as they say) set us outside again and strengthen her cloak, and we might not be invited in again.

Peter turns to focus on the shaft of light, which has resumed its brilliant blue purity. *I do not know how to communicate with you, but I would like to invite you to know me, or whatever it is that you are seeking. We have come to you in ...*

Instantly, a sound that is like thousands of choral voices singing all at once with a flood of lights focuses on Peter, each light a different hue and a musical chord that seems unending from its beginning to its crest.

Peter is awestruck by the reaction, and he knows that he is being examined or explored by the angel. Striving to sustain a state of balance, his awe and wonder and admiration grow, moment by moment. It is as though his very being, every fiber, every minute particle of his consciousness is being illuminated and explored, and he feels an incredible sense of peace and wellbeing. Interestingly, his thoughts wander, and he feels somehow detached from the probing consciousness (as he would define it) of this fallen angel.

He is reminded suddenly of himself as a small child, seated upon his mother's lap, and he remembers the feeling of, as an infant, looking up into his mother's loving eyes while she caressed his forehead, his brow, rocking him, singing to him softly. Reveling in this incredible breadth and depth of love, his thoughts dance across his many experiences in the Earth, not just his previous lifetime, but others he had long forgotten. On and on it continues, until finally it is complete. Once again he observes the beautiful spiraling blue orb before him; the finger of light that had previously extended from her to him now has been drawn back into the sphere of blue light.

Some time passes. He cannot discern how much, but he knows there is the passage of time. It matters not to him. He savors the wonder of this experience, the memories flowing over him. He is enveloped by a love so incredibly profound that he cannot even define it to himself.

Only after some length of time that he is incapable of defining does he become cognizant of Elizabeth communicating to him. *You see, Peter, I told you it would be fine.*

What is this that I am experiencing, Elizabeth?

Let me put it as succinctly as I can. You have just been touched by an angel. I know that may sound trite, but it is all I can offer you at this point.

Puzzled, but still radiant in the essence he now presumes is the result of the angel 'knowing him,' Peter focuses his perception once again on the blue rotating orb of light before him. To his amazement, it slows, then stops.

There, in its midst, a form begins to appear.

What's happening, Elizabeth?

It's okay, Peter. Just know that it's always okay.

Reassured and utterly spellbound, he watches.

The form shifts and swirls, like some master craftsperson attempting to make a work of art changes the design, shifting, moving the patterns, until, with incredible suddenness, Peter finds himself looking into the face of one who is now expressed in physical form. Even more incredible, he perceives this form smiling and speaking to him.

"I welcome you, Peter. And you, Elizabeth," to his utter amazement, he hears coming from this form.

From Elizabeth he hears, "It is we who are most grateful for your hospitality and your trust in accepting us. We do thank you, and we wish you the very best."

Peter, still numb with the experience, cannot respond.

The angel seems to understand and, now expressed in this physical-like form, looks at him in a way he cannot describe, simply radiating a flow of loving warmth through him. He is absolutely speechless.

In the periphery of his consciousness, he realizes that Elizabeth has taken form. She now is expressed in her physical form.

Wondering the next obvious question, he looks down at his own being and sees that he, too, is now expressed in an image of his physical form, and quickly looks up.

He hears the angel communicate again. "I thought, Peter, that this would be a bit more comfortable for you, since it seems to be more familiar in your consciousness. Is this acceptable to you?"

Peter hears his own voice answering robotically, "Why-yes. Thank-you. How-considerate. I-am-very-much-at-ease."

An awkward moment, to Peter, at least, of silence passes.

Then he hears the melodious flow of communication from the angel again. "So, Peter, you have passed through the experiences involving finite expression, have you?"

Incredulous, he turns quickly to look at Elizabeth, who gives him the faintest nod, smiling softly.

"Uh-h … in truth, I cannot answer that I have. I only know that I am here and that I have learned much, and I would presume, dear lady, that you would be the better judge of that than I."

His response obviously pleases the angel. Her exploration of Peter had conveyed to her, that, indeed, he has sojourned in the finiteness of the Earth and other such realms, and has emerged in a state of honesty and truth.

Peter can see that this is doing something positive to her, for her luminosity seems to increase a bit. With the angel focused steadily on him, warmly smiling, he realizes that there is little, if anything, that she does not know about him. He considers in his consciousness that perhaps the next best thing to do would be to ask her a question. He feels a flow of warmth from Elizabeth, which he detects as an affirmation.

Again, almost as though someone else is speaking, Peter hears himself ask, "If I might inquire, and I do not wish to intrude, but why have you chosen to be here?"

The flow of warmth that comes to him is awesome. "It is difficult for me to place into thoughts or what you call words, Peter, for I do not fully understand it myself. And it is because I do not understand it that I have chosen to place myself in this particular place and consciousness, that I might not inadvertently do anything that would not be in harmony with my Father and His Will."

Peter reflects for a moment. "You mean to say that your concern for possibly doing something wrong is why you have come to this place and … well, forgive me, but, cemented yourself in … in that spherical whatever?"

Smiling, again radiating warmth, which simply undulates Peter's very being, he hears, quite simply, *Yes*.

Turning to Elizabeth, somewhat puzzled but understanding deep within himself that he must continue, he reverts to all that he knows to do, which is to follow his own inner guidance, to rely upon, quite simply, truth. From Peter it flows as innocent truth, like the innocent curiosity of a child, and this is the quality for which Peter has been identified as *the* one to approach the fallen angel. It is the acceptance of his innocent truthfulness that has gained him and Elizabeth entry into the angel's consciousness and this communication.

"From all that I have learned," begins Peter, "I cannot understand how you would ever be capable of doing anything that would offend God."

"I am knowledgeable of His Law. Therefore, I am completely responsible for my actions."

He pauses only a brief moment. "Well, I think I understand what you are saying, though certainly you must know I cannot grasp it completely. But wouldn't God love you … I mean, wouldn't He have the same regard for you, whether you erred or not?"

Peter detects a shadow of pinkish color passing briefly over the angel's countenance. As swiftly as he perceives it, it vanishes. Nonetheless, he has noted it.

Now he feels and hears at a strange new level within him a communication, and he knows it is Zachary. *Good, Pete. Good. Steady on, now.*

Looking quickly to the angel, Peter is surprised that she does not appear to be aware of that communication. He strives to not dwell on it, for he knows that doing so could create a thought-form, which he is sure this most perceptive angel would note. Yet, on the other hand, he seeks, as he looks within himself, not to deceive her.

In the moment of his decision that he would rather be cast outside than in any way deceive her, he sees the angel increase in radiance. Beautiful spires of silver-white light dance off of her, and he hears softly from her, "Then it is true. You have attained that degree of honesty and truth, haven't you?"

"Uh-h … forgive me, what do you mean?"

"You would rather give up this opportunity than to make any effort of falsehood to attain your goal. Isn't that what you just went through in your consciousness?"

"You mean, you did hear the communication from Zachary? And you heard my thoughts afterwards?"

The angel simply nods as she smiles at Peter.

"Then I guess you know my answer. Yes, I would not deceive you. I would rather fail than gain through falsehood."

[pause]

(Forgive our pause. The entire group ... those in the Control Center, the angel, Elizabeth, our group, and many others... We must have a moment ...)

[pause]

(Very well. We thank you for your indulgence. The experience of observing the Christ quality being demonstrated by Peter is of such a joy to all of us that we requested that moment, that we might be a part of it. It is such demonstrations of the Christ Consciousness within you that make any labor, any effort, by those who serve you in the Earth, humbly, lovingly, in God's Name, easily justifiable and worthwhile. For what we have just observed freely demonstrated by Peter of his own free will is a quality of the very highest. This is the spirit of the Christ awakening in the man called Peter. And all of us and you in the Earth have been granted a wondrous gift to have been allowed to be present, that we should witness the emergence of such beauty. We thank you, and we return now to our commentary from whence we left it.)

The angel is visibly affected by Peter's total truthfulness and willingness to give all for righteousness and truth. So much so, that she is, again, reaching out to Peter. This time, not only does light come from her, but she extends her hand towards him as well.

In wonder, in awe, he moves towards her and extends his own hand.

The angel slowly raises her other arm, and Peter can perceive Elizabeth also moving towards her.

In the next several moments, Peter, Elizabeth and the angel actually embrace.

There is a rapture-like joy, for the angel has discerned that here is a ray of hope because this one, called Peter, and his beautiful companion, called Elizabeth, can pass through the many-layered veils of illusion, delve into the depths of finiteness, and at some point in consciousness and experience emerge beyond these to the other side in what she knows clearly to be the Christ Consciousness.

Within her a song begins anew.

It can be said of the Angelic Host that they have not a heart, for the heart is gained through experience, through testing, through challenges that require giving, long-suffering, patience, hope, and the development of love, trust, and honesty. Yet, in every angel there is a song comparable to the heart of those who have followed these paths of finiteness, who have journeyed through the halls of illusion and temptation and who have wrestled themselves free from the lure of finiteness and habit.

And now, here is a heart that has emerged and bears the essence, the first light, of the Christ Spirit. Her song pours forth over Peter and Elizabeth.

Though not unlike what Peter recalls when his small group rolled about in the Realms of Laughter, he equates this many degrees above that, as though he is reveling in a river of love, enchanted by musical flow and color.

Finally, he reflects to himself, in wonder and awe, *So this is an angel. This is what is meant by the Angelic Host!*

"But one, Peter, just one. And by your own recognition, a fallen one at that."

In the moment of those messages to him, he again hears himself respond, "Oh, no, dear friend. Not fallen. Never. Beauty such as yours belongs only upon the throne of God, not here, not in these realms, and certainly not here where you've chosen to be. I and Elizabeth, and our colleagues beyond, implore you. Let us share with you what little we have learned. Let us give you some insight into that which you have explored in following your comrade. I hope you know that we would never seek to coerce you, trick you, or anything of that sort. We only wish to share with you. There are so many things of beauty in the Earth, not just the dreariness, not only the greed, the avarice, and all of the other qualities that could be thought of as being so far apart from God. Please allow us the opportunity to share with you the beautiful side of the finite realms, for there are many. You yourself, dear lady, have reminded me of one of my fondest memories in the realms of finiteness … a mother's love. Do you know of it? Have you experienced it? Would you let me show you?"

The angel steps back, yet holds onto each of their arms, one hand in each of her own, and looks carefully at Peter. "How could I decline such a sincere and loving expression? Please. Become comfortable, and do remain. I wish to hear what you have to share with me."

So, dear friends, we shall conclude at this point, for we must release the Channel and allow the resources being employed here, of which there are many, to become re-balanced. Know that we shall return and you shall not miss one whit of the beauty and joy that is about to unfold.

Our gratitude to each of you for works thus far well done. We know that you shall continue, and it is our combined prayer that these works shall bear the fruition that is in the hearts of all.

CHAPTER 12

Learning About Angels
DECEMBER 22, 1991

As we come together once again about this joyous and blessed work, we wish to express our thankfulness for your participation as well as your prayers and loving thoughts, and for this opportunity to share with you the magnificence of those works which lie not only before you now, but all throughout eternity in the Earth and also in these and other realms beyond.

When next you might consider for a moment what shall lie beyond, think of it as a joyous hope, as a purpose, and as a wondrous expectation of the opportunity that is awaiting you in accordance with your will and choice.

Before we return to Peter and Elizabeth, we pause before the area of the fallen angel and observe the effects that the activities within the greater sphere are having, viewing this from the perspective of Zachary, Rebecca, and a number of others who are gathered here now, some whom you have come to know in the past and others, as well. In terms of your measure of time in the Earth, only moments have passed since our last meeting.

Zachary, Rebecca, Zeb, David and a number of others who are serving here, are performing works likened unto focusing a certain level of their consciousness to surround the prayer of your group and other resources. All of this is being placed into service and is available to Elizabeth and Peter, serving as an enrichment to the commission and those works which are ahead.

Peter, Elizabeth, and the angel are seated cross-legged in a triangular pattern, Peter to the left, Elizabeth to the right, and facing both of them, directly in front of them, is the angel. That which is beneath them appears to be a billowy white firmament, supple, yielding, yet as though supporting the three of them upon it.

There are, without question, indications of the increase of awakening consciousness on the part of this, our commission. The interior of the somewhat spherical cloak of the angel has taken on a greater luster. A luminosity seems to radiate from it and focuses upon the trio.

Peter is gazing upon the angel with wonder. "It is difficult for me, good lady, to know just how to proceed from this point forward. If I might ask of you to again review my recent experiences, you would know I am only briefly a member of these realms. I have just recently departed the Earth."

The angel responds with a knowing nod and smile, clearly indicating that she has done as he has requested.

Glancing to the side, he perceives Elizabeth studying him compassionately before turning to face the angel. "What Peter is expressing to you, I would also express. We have had no experience to compare to this but we are certain that you can ascertain the genuine intent of our presence. And, as Peter suggested to you, if you would but allow us, we would strive, as best we know, to share with you our understanding of the more finite realms and activities of existence in the Earth.

"We have followed your earlier pathway to the extent that we were capable, and know somewhat of your interaction and the activities which preceded your decision to locate yourself here and to move into a state of inner contemplation. There are many things about the path you followed which we do not, of course, know or understand at this time. Perhaps as we attempt to proceed, you might share your perspective and understanding or reactions to what you perceived with us."

The angel merely grants Elizabeth the same radiant smile

and gentle nod she just gave Peter, and then turns back to focus upon him. "Peter, if you are willing, I would now like to hear about your experiences and the perspective that you have about eternity, your relationship with God, and why you chose to follow the path you did. What did you hope to gain by so doing? And do you feel that you have accomplished that intent?"

This has a significant impact upon him, for he realizes that much of what she is asking he hasn't given much conscious thought to. Indeed, that in order to truly answer her, he would have to reach beyond himself in a manner to which he is unaccustomed. He also realizes that in the recent past, comprising approximately several Earth years, he relied heavily upon his friend Paul in such times as these, then Zachary and Elizabeth, Rebecca, and all the others.

As his thoughts continue to seek out all of these considerations, Peter is again a bit surprised when the angel comments, "I do understand all that, Peter. Please be assured that I would not expect you to give what you do not have, or to state what you do not know."

In this assurance, he is instantly reminded that the angel is astutely aware of all that is within her *domain*, so to say. In other words, these two are, in essence, within her cloak and here, then, all is known to her.

Peter cannot help but wonder if it might not be so that were she outside of this, even beyond, all would be known, as well.

Again, the angel answers, softly, "It is possible for all to be known, but is not always possible for such as I to understand. This is what you have to offer here, Peter, understanding, because you have experienced while I have not."

Peter realizes now what the angel is striving for. Fortified somewhat by this realization, he is reminded of the golden orb of energy that was given to him as a gift, its glow now growing within him as it always does when needed, as though he can see it, as though he can feel it increasing in its energy.

Reassured, he begins, "As you probably know, I have reviewed some of my past experiences to varying degrees of depth. Most significantly, I have reviewed my just-previous incarnation, my life, in the Earth. I have gone over it with several of my friends on numerous occasions. My dear friend Elizabeth, here," and he gestures to her, "is what you would call the Keeper of my Book. Therefore, I am certain that she could answer any questions that I cannot. But I do comprehend that what you are saying is that my experiences relevant to these events are what interests you most at this moment. So, I shall simply just begin and do the best I can."

This commentary again generates a gentle nod and a warm smile for Peter from the angel.

For a flickering instant, almost as though it is a different entity outside of him, as he thinks, "Good grief, Peter! This is an angel we're talking to here. How can this be? Being dead is one thing, but talking to angels? Perhaps I'm not dead at all. Maybe I'm only dreaming. Maybe I'll wake up."

This humors the angel. Her smile broadens and a bit of rosy glow emanates from the upper portion of what she has presented to him as her torso.

(Many are amused here in our group, as well.)

"Well, let's see now … Apparently I had a series of experiences in the Earth, so I've been told, and in other realms, as well, all of which led up to my just-previous incarnation in the Earth. Evidently, it was then that I balanced considerably with what some there called karma, collective thoughts and emotions carried over from one experience to the other."

The angel asks softly, "Did these influences motivate you to continue?"

Pausing to understand her question, Peter slowly answers, "As I see it, yes. It would appear that once one has, in a manner of speaking, committed themselves to a series of finite incarnations involving the Earth and other such realms, it seems to be important, if not maybe mandatory, that one continues on until they've dealt with whatever the results were of the first or first several experiences. Elizabeth, does that fit in with what you know?"

Elizabeth nods. "Yes, that's well put, Peter. We can explore specifics later, but that is quite comprehensive."

Pausing for a moment to study Elizabeth, almost hoping she had continued on, Peter turns back to the angel. "Well, I guess I was in fairly good shape when I entered the last incarnation. My good friend Zachary told me that in fact I was in better shape than most. He even suggested that I wouldn't have even needed the last incarnation but that I had chosen it for a combination of purposes, a number of which were, as he calls it, benevolent."

The angel asks, "Could you expand on the term *benevolent*, please?"

Pausing, thinking, searching as diligently as he can, Peter again turns inward to the sphere of golden consciousness within and is instantly reassured. "Benevolent in the sense that some of my life, a good part of it, I accepted because it would be contributive to other souls, other people. That's what's generally meant by the term *benevolent,* as best I understand it. I guess when one of us, who follows benevolent paths of incarnation, which I have heard some call the Wheel of Life and the Wheel of Karma and things like that (I truly don't understand any of that very well), it is like harvesting some of the last aspects of purposeful works in finite realms, while giving all that we can to others that they might, too, have more opportunities, that should they wish to break free, they can do so."

"So, then, you are free of finiteness, Peter?"

Peter is a bit startled at the question, for he hadn't really thought of it in that sense previously. "I am not utterly certain of that, but from what I have been told, it appears that I have no mandatory need to return, but also that I have a choice in the matter. I think that's normal for most everyone. Is that true, Elizabeth?"

"True to a degree. One must be capable of rising to a very unlimited spiritual awareness, or be a very free spirit."

The angel asks again, like a gentle wind, "Free, like the soul itself?"

Peter is glad that question is directed to Elizabeth and not to him.

"Yes, like the soul itself," she responds, in utter confidence, which causes Peter to admire her all the more.

The angel then turns back to Peter, "This Zachary you speak of … Do I know him?"

He quickly glances to Elizabeth, and she turns to answer for him, "You know him by having known Peter, in the sense that Zachary is in Peter's consciousness and is a part of his spirituality, just as I and several others are as well."

Still looking at Peter, the angel responds to Elizabeth's comment, "Then you are a soul group?"

Also continuing to look at Peter, Elizabeth answers, "Yes, a soul group."

Peter illuminates a bit, realizing that this is something he knows very little of.

The angel detects this in Peter. "This I know about, Peter, and I can share some insight regarding this with you at some point, if you would wish."

"Oh, yes, I would like that. You might already know that the noteworthy characteristic that seems to precede me wherever I go is that I have a great curiosity." He smiles with a bit of embarrassment.

"You have this, and another blessing, as well, Peter, and that is truth and honesty. They go well with your spirit of curiosity. But this is an expression I have practically no experience in."

Peter, looking at the angel, cannot fathom that one would not have curiosity. "You mean you aren't curious about existence? About the different realms? The nature of one's expression? What happens after life in the Earth? Karma? The Akashic records, as they call them. Any of those things?"

The angel continues to smile gently, with her eyes transfixed on Peter. "I know of these things by knowing you, but I have not experienced them. I have come unto this expression of consciousness, which you call a realm, because I followed, what you would call, a brother. This brother was awakened to this *curiosity*, and the curiosity evoked something which I also have little consciousness of in terms of experience. You would call this thing an emotional entanglement or an emotional bond. I speak to you of these things in terminology I have drawn from you by *knowing* you. If they are inappropriate, I hope that you will identify that to me, that I can communicate with you in the best of all ways."

This surprises Peter, for it is the first indication that the angel is interested in learning, that the angel is interested in what he is interested in, such as understanding the seemingly infinite expressions of consciousness. This reassures him even more. "I am flattered by your comments, dear lady, and I would state unequivocally to you that I understand completely what you are communicating to me. In fact, it is amazingly clear, and I now understand why it is so, and I thank you for using these terms and this methodology that obviously must be foreign to you. Is that true?"

Only a smile and a nod are given in response.

"Might I ask, how are you expressed? I mean, normally. I mean where would you normally dwell? Where did you come from, before you began to follow your brother?"

Studying Peter again, the angel responds with gentleness yet clearly audible, "Perhaps in a time I might be privileged to show you, should there be that wish on your part to return."

"Return? To your realm? How could I do that?"

"Where do you think you came from, Peter? Is it your conception that you were created in these realms of finiteness and limitation?"

Peter again goes inward to contemplate the question. Obtaining his best guidance, he returns. "I perceive that this is not so, that I am in these realms because of choices I myself have made. But they are so far distant in my memory, I would need to re-explore them to comment about them clearly."

The angel merely smiles and nods.

Peter pauses, glances at Elizabeth, and then back at the angel. "A thought comes to me. I have many colleagues who are far greater in the breadth and depth of their consciousness or knowledge. If it would please you, or if you find it acceptable, perhaps we might somehow join with them and they could augment some of this and more clearly answer you."

The angel gazes steadily at Peter. "No, thank you. You and Elizabeth are all I care to deal with in the moment."

He is disappointed to hear this, very much so, and apparently this is visible to the angel.

Her gentle smile is unwavering, and she continues in her soft flowing manner, "My response has distressed you in some way, and I note that you generate unique energies as you experience this. Is this an example of what you like to experience in the Earth? When you meet challenges that do not flow with your will, is this how you respond?"

Peter had never considered it in this way. "Yes, I guess so. I am indeed disappointed. I had hoped that you would be willing to join my friends, because I believe they can contribute much more here than can I alone."

"This you feel with certainty?"

Peter must pause and reflect upon this, unsure of his answer. "If you will forgive me for a moment, I will go within myself and find an answer of truth to your question."

"There is no need. I know that you go to visit with the Christ, do you not?"

This energizes Peter greatly. Elizabeth, in her constant vigil, makes contact with him, and he feels the stabilizing warmth and balance of her presence.

"This upsets you?" questions the angel further, unimpeded by Peter's reaction.

"Uh, uh, I guess it would be foolhardy of me to say that it did not," which seems to invoke an even broader smile from the angel than normal. He continues, "You see, I never think of myself as … well, worthy, to be anywhere near the Christ …" and he even states the name with hesitancy.

Before he can continue, the angel asks, "Why?"

"Well, I guess as I consider that, I'm not sure. It just seems to me that somehow or other this is may be sacrilegious or something."

"What would be sacrilegious, as you call it, about being one with the Christ?"

Again, Peter is at a loss for a clear answer, for he, in fact, doesn't know why that would be so. He cannot find any justifiable reason, except that he remembers from his just-previous incarnation that this is what he was taught. Continuing to reflect, he responds, "I guess it's because of conditioning from the Earth."

The angel, gazing steadily at him, queries further, "And this you find to be of value to you? To allow yourself to be *limited,* to use your terms, by such teachings therein?"

"Well, no, not exactly. But, you see, in the consciousness called Earth, not everyone … In fact, most people are unaware of their full potential. Only a few years back I would have probably closed the door on anyone who came to my front door to tell me of such things. I'm not even certain that I can accept it all now. Yet, here I am, obviously no longer in a finite form. So, how do I answer your question?"

"You have. I would next ask you, what is the value of such experiences, then, that carry you further away from God, rather than closer to Him?"

"In all truth, dear lady, I have never thought of it in that light. Actually, I doubt that there are many in the Earth who would even consider what we are discussing at this time. But I do understand that somehow or other, as we repeatedly incarnate in the Earth or have experiences in other realms, we learn about this bit by bit, a little here and a little there. Sometimes we don't learn very well, and other times it seems like we might bungle it very badly and have to repeat some earlier learning experience. But what I can see from what I have learned recently, all of this leads us to continual growth, and finally to some stages, I'm told, that are like my own. In truth I must say that I don't know what I have done to warrant being at these stages, but from what my colleagues tell me and from all that I've seen, there must be something to it." There is a pause as Peter respectfully awaits the angel's comment.

"Then you do not know at this time that you are, and always have been, what you are seeking?"

Peter is truly dumbfounded by this possibility. Not so much so that he cannot keep his balance, for he is completely at ease with her. But his response tells her that he grasps this only in a very limited sense.

"Peter, I perceive that you understand that you are capable of much more than you have even at present allowed yourself to accept. I would submit to you that perhaps you should rise to that highest position now and not, as you would say, *bother* with all the other activities. What do you think of that suggestion?"

Peter reflects to himself, *Goodness! This is the most challenging exchange I have ever had with anyone, anywhere. This angel is so astute. And she has a way of bringing forth questions and possibilities from within me that I hadn't even yet considered, much less thought of acting on.*

Unwavering, the angel continues her steady gaze. "If I have caused you duress in some way, Peter, you need not attempt to answer. But it seems very logical to me."

Peter turns to Elizabeth and she is smiling, warmly, reassuringly. Since he knows it would be futile to attempt to communicate with Elizabeth without the angel knowing it, he speaks openly. "Elizabeth, I feel that I am bungling this. I don't know how to answer these questions. Some of these things I've never considered, and I don't feel I have sufficient awareness to deal with them. Can you help in some way, that we can contribute the most to her and not waste her time?"

Elizabeth nods and turns to the angel.

There is a flash of light between the two of them, and now the angel's focus has turned completely to be transfixed upon Elizabeth.

He hears Elizabeth say to him, "Forgive us for a moment, Peter. I will attempt to communicate with her in other ways, which I hope will be more understandable for her."

Peter is relieved. So relieved that he leans back and becomes at ease. His consciousness is joyful for this opportunity. He feels as though he has been in an intense mental and spiritual exchange, and now, with the focus off him, he feels remarkably relieved.

As he looks from one to the other, he observes the passage of a bright shaft of light between them. He lets his curiosity come to the surface again and sees the flow of varying colors. *These colors*, he thinks to himself, *must be some form similar to word expressions, like thought-forms.* He remembers being in formless states wherein he noted such occurring, but at this moment he has no desire to attempt to tune into that. He is simply thankful for the opportunity of rest.

After a time, the angel and Elizabeth turn to Peter, and Elizabeth speaks. "She understands, Peter, as best I can convey to her, having no experience of her own to draw upon, and she has consented to a broader meeting."

"Truly?" Peter is exuberant at the thought, at the possibility, and turns to the angel. "Are you meaning that you will allow our group to include several of the others?"

She nods slightly, and Peter turns to Elizabeth, absolutely beside himself with joy, so much so that he almost misses the angel's soft comment.

"And this is the opposite of the other expression? When things do go your way or when you accomplish what you had hoped for?"

"Oh, yes, dear lady! This is joy."

The angel smiles and nods, "This I know about, although not in that term nor in such a limited sense. But I can relate to this for, you see, we do know what you call joy."

"How do you experience joy?" Peter's curiosity has gained a foothold again.

"Perhaps you would like to personally experience our expression of joy."

This has a significant impact upon him, as though he feels it might be a one-way trip were he to take it.

Elizabeth assures him that is not so, that no one in her realm of expression would usurp another's free will.

Reassured, Peter turns back to the angel, "Yes, I would like this. As you must know, my curiosity would lead me practically anywhere."

The angel sends him a shaft of warmth, which he equates with laughter.

"How, then, might we facilitate this?"

As she continues to gaze softly at him, he begins to realize that she has been inviting someone to enter. Her gaze unwavering and without any perceptible change as far as he can ascertain, he suddenly recognizes inwardly, though he does not perceive, the presence of Zachary. "Zachary, are you here?"

"Indeed so, Pete, thanks to you and Elizabeth. Greetings, dear lady, as Peter has come to call you. Are you well?"

The angel shifts her focus to a point just behind Peter.

Peter turns, and there is Zachary, behind and to his left. "Come join us, Zachary. Come up here."

Zachary looks to the angel, who nods, and he moves up to the left of Peter.

"Could you help here, Zachary? I am so hopeful that you can respond to her in a more complete sense than I can."

Zachary pauses only for a moment. "We'll see, Pete. But first, I must progress with formalities. If you will excuse us, I would introduce myself to her, and she to me."

The shaft of light now flows between the angel and Zachary. This time, Zachary emulates something Peter had not noted earlier in his own experience or in that which he observed between Elizabeth and the angel. Now there seems to be some greater breadth and depth to the shaft of light. And the angel's countenance seems to be glowing more and more. Peter can even feel it within himself.

After what seems to be only brief seconds, it is concluded.

Zachary turns to Peter. "Well done, Pete … Elizabeth. You have served the commission and the greater very well."

Peter cannot comprehend what it is that he has done, but from Zachary's emanation, he determines that now is not the time to question.

Zachary continues, "She has agreed to depart these realms. And …"

"What?" exclaims Peter.

"Just as I said, Pete. She agrees to leave these realms."

"When? How? I thought we were sliding downhill. I had the distinct feeling that I was getting nowhere, and that …" Suddenly remembering that the angel is right there, he is a bit embarrassed. "Please forgive me, dear lady. It's my nature. I just have to understand these things."

Before he can turn back to Zachary, she comments, again with a softness that is remarkable, which he notes inwardly, "I know this, Peter. I accept it."

This disarms him again, but he turns back to Zachary. "Well, how does she know that? And what is it that we did here that has changed things? I mean, I would like to know, if it's not a trouble to anyone … excuse me, dear lady … what turned things around."

Zachary looks gently at Peter. "Your honesty again."

There is silence as Peter studies Zachary, who is very sincere and not his usual playful self, though still with a sparkle in his eye, so to say. But in this event, he knows Zachary is telling him pure and simple truth.

Peter begins to look from one to the other, nodding as he turns to look again back at Zachary. "Well, then, far be it that my curiosity should usurp any progression. Do proceed, and whatever I am to do, please let me know."

All smile at Peter, and he feels a warmth coming from Elizabeth again and realizes that she is striving to facilitate some higher degree of balance between them.

He glances at Zachary who is aglow.

As swiftly as is his glance to Zachary, he turns to the angel, and sees she is also aglow.

Then, he feels something within himself and realizes that he and Elizabeth have become merged as one, in a sort of spherical form of energy and light, color, and sound. He glances about and realizes that there are three such forms. One is around him and Elizabeth, one around Zachary, and one great sphere around the angel.

He can feel movement, and he quickly glances around, stunned to see that the great egg-like chamber in which they had previously been located is no longer present. Joyfully, he whispers to Elizabeth, "Are we leaving? Is she leaving the egg, the chamber, that cocoon-like thing?"

"Yes, Peter, we're leaving together. All of us."

"How wonderful. Then we have succeeded? Our commission is successful?"

"Yes, Peter, you could say that it is successful. But you could also say that it has begun another commission as a by-product, one so broad and so glorious that I alone cannot convey it to you. But for now, if you will, just absorb the joy, absorb the experience. You will be glad that you did."

Trusting in Elizabeth implicitly, Peter turns his awareness outward. He can sense, but he does not know, that they are moving past the Control Center. As they do, he notes brilliant flashes of light. These flashes of light seem to be reflected back to their source from within their group now, which seems to be enveloped in a very bright, luminescent sphere of incredibly brilliant light.

As he struggles to perceive the source of the returned light, he can see that the angel is returning these flashes of light outward. There is a brilliant bluish-green light over there, and the angel emulates that and sends it back several-fold over to its source, and again, and again. Over and over Peter marvels at the seemingly infinite combinations of color and sound and light that the angel replicates and amplifies and returns.

Unexpectedly to Peter, for he had assumed they would travel up the tunnel of light, suddenly their group stops.

The angel appears to have taken on a different glow. A shaft of multi-colored light reaches out from her, out to the outer sphere of the now luminescent orb around her. Peter reflects that this must have been the cocoon, the almost cement-like egg he had previously perceived. But it is radiantly luminous now, and he can see through it, as though it is translucent. He sees the light pour from the angel towards something … no, someone … outside.

With a flash of recognition, Peter perceives Rebecca.

The light increases between the angel and Rebecca. More color, more brilliance, and then there is a series of occurrences that are indescribable in his mind. Flashes, sounds, whirring noises, colors, cascade all about.

Shortly thereafter, it all subsides. But now Peter can perceive that Rebecca is within the luminous sphere, very close to the angel herself.

Before he can inquire, the movement begins again, just as abruptly as it had moments ago stopped. The movement continues, and he can perceive something like what he would detect as upward movement.

This continues on and on, and he notes that Zachary has moved over to be adjacent to him and Elizabeth, both of whom are seemingly surrounded in a smaller orb of light within the much, much greater, immense sphere in which the angel is now enveloped.

There is a subtle feeling of change, a transition or something, and the next thing Peter knows is Zachary's voice.

"Well, Pete. How are you doing? This is quite a different trip for you, isn't it?"

"Oh, Zachary! It is! I am glad to see you. But are we disturbing anyone or anything by communicating?"

"No, Pete, not at all. No one's focused on us at the moment, except to insure that we are in good stead. They are maintaining our well-being, but they are engrossed in their own communication. Certainly they could know of our communication if they wanted to, but at the moment it appears to be of no purpose for them. They are in their own exchange."

"They?" questions Peter. "Are you talking about the angel and Rebecca? How did she get in here? What was it that took place between them? And why does it look like the angel appears to know her? Is Rebecca one of them?"

Zachary smiles with a tinkling note of melodious laughter. "You haven't changed a bit. And you are well. I don't need to ask about that. I can tell by your questions and your curiosity. And yes, very astute of you … She is one of them."

"Well, how can that be, Zack? They're as different as night and day. Look at them over there. They look the same now, pretty much. But, I've been traveling around with Rebecca and she knows about things. Why doesn't the angel?"

"Rebecca has followed and worked in realms of finiteness for a long time. And the dear lady, as you have named her, has obviously not. But I can assure you, Rebecca is a member in good standing of the angels' realm."

"Remarkable! What distinguishes them, one from the other? Is it simply the longevity that Rebecca has had experiences here? What kind of experiences did she have that enabled her to appear no different than any of the rest of you?"

"The *rest* of us? Uh, Pete, does that mean that you perceive the rest of us less than she?"

"Hey, wait a minute, Zack! You aren't going to tell me next that you're *all* from her realm."

"Well, actually, Peter, I'm not going to tell you anything about that. You're going to experience it yourself. Fair?"

"What do you mean by experience it myself?"

"Well, the angel invited you, and you accepted, and ..."

"Wait a minute! Wait just a minute, Zachary! I said, if I recall correctly, that I would like to know about her realm, or whatever it's called, and indeed I would. But ... now?"

"Would you rather wait until tomorrow, Pete?" asks Zachary with obvious humor and a tinkling to his response.

After a brief pause, Peter glances from Elizabeth to Zachary, and back to Elizabeth, and back to Zachary. Then to the angel and Rebecca, who are simply great spheres of light within the greater sphere, and then back to Zachary, who is expressed more finitely within the smaller sphere containing the trio.

"Well, Zack, if it's all the same to you, I think tomorrow would be just fine."

Laughter pours forth from Elizabeth and Zachary, and Peter finally joins them.

Their laughter fills the sphere in which they are expressed, and they begin to roll about, and Peter finds himself engrossed in the laughter, as though it is a means of balancing himself as the result of the intensity of his earlier experience.

After a time, they come to a restful state, and Peter senses that they have some "time and space." He turns to Zachary

Zachary and Elizabeth, who, obviously very well-balanced, are glowing softly, yet projecting themselves to Peter in the finite forms that are comfortable and familiar to him.

"Zachary, Elizabeth, it's just amazing to me to consider that we were successful in convincing the angel to leave that dismal realm! And that we are, in fact, if I understand you correctly, en route to her realm?"

Zachary nods gently, and Elizabeth simply smiles an affirming smile.

"Well, what is going to take place in her realm? Would that be the realm of the angels?"

Zachary smiles very broadly now, looking down to somewhat shield his amusement. "That would seem logical. Wouldn't it to you?"

"Well, yes. But I mean … goodness! You know what I'm driving at. You mean to say we are going to visit the angels?"

"Why not? Is there some reason that you would not wish to visit them?"

"I'm not ready to meet the angels. I mean, I have a lot to learn. I don't even know that I'm comfortable with everything that all of you have shown and taught me up to this point, much less, now, a visit to the angels."

"Hold on a minute, Pete. Not too quickly, or you'll short-circuit yourself, as you have a habit of doing."

That softens things, and they all smile at one another.

"Think about it from this perspective, Peter. Now you know that Rebecca is an 'angel' and perhaps you could assume, and accurately so, that some of the others you have met are also, 'angels' …"

"Like who, Zack? Like who?"

"Well, I'm not going to bother with all that now, if you don't mind, but just to give you one example, Zeb. He's an angel."

"No kidding! Zeb? Why, he's just like you, Zack. I mean, he's humorous … he's … he's almost human."

Zachary cannot contain himself any longer, and laughter echoes, reverberates, off their smaller sphere, and Elizabeth, too, responds with musical laughter.

Peter very slowly joins with them. But as swiftly as it subsides, he continues on with his questioning. "Okay. I'll accept the fact that you don't want to reveal any other angels I've met," which elicits a broad smile from Zachary again, "and I assume you have, as always, very good reasons," to which Zachary exaggeratedly nods an affirmation. "So, what you're asking me to do is to just sit still and be carried inside the cloak of an angel," with which he glances over to the angel, "to the Angelic Host? Good grief, Zachary! That's more than I am able to accept. I'm just not sure I can handle that."

"Why not?" Zachary inquires softly. "What is that you anticipate?"

"Well, you know. Angels … well … Aren't they at the right hand of God and all that sort of thing?"

"What if they are, Pete? Do you have a problem with that? Is there something you'd like to tell us now that you haven't told us before?" and, again, the impish, humorous look appears on Zachary's countenance.

Elizabeth smiles very broadly, looking from one to the other, and Zachary nods at her, indicating for her to speak. "Peter, let me help here a bit. Zachary is not intending humor at your expense, but is, in a style you know only too well, working to draw out some realizations within you. The more he can do this in the manner for which you've come to know him, the sooner you'll be able to be unlimited. That's what this is all about now, and that's what Zachary is doing. So, think about what he's asking you from the broadest possible perspective."

Before Peter can comment, suddenly they are all together.

Peter, Zachary, Elizabeth, Rebecca, and the angel are all in a form that Peter is comfortable with, and he hears the angel speaking to him.

"Rebecca, my sister, has shared much with me of you, Peter. I feel honored and privileged to be with you."

———————————

With which, dear friends, we shall now conclude at this time.

CHAPTER 13

Home
DECEMBER 24, 1991

Not one step, one action, one accomplishment herein has been made without the involvement of each of you, dear friends. Through your loving thoughts, your prayers, your attitude of hopefulness, this work has been accomplished. And thereof we wish you to know and to remember: This is a light that shall follow you throughout all of eternity... a good deed, a good work, a mark (as it were) of brilliance upon the skein of time called by some the Akasha. Unto that as already written, we add, as well, our blessings to continue with you for that which you have freely given.

It would be well for us to add a bit more commentary here before we attempt to re-join Peter and his colleagues:

The works as have just been completed in our earlier meeting could not be complete because they required that we communicate with you by your language, through words and thought-forms. Certainly much more transpired during the course of those events which elude descriptive words, but we trust that in your spirit you have heard everything, witnessed every event, and have, as well, gained the knowledge thereof.

It shall be, during this meeting, somewhat similar because of the nature of those levels of consciousness that are involved. We shall attempt as best we can to translate and communicate to you the events, the commentary, and such. But we know in advance this will fall considerably short of delivering to you an understanding of the immensity of communication available to all therein and of the woefully inade-

*quate terms we have with which to convey to you the beauty
and magnitude of what you are about to witness.*

*To this, then, we suggest that you open your spirits, your
hearts, your minds, that you might not only receive our communication through the recording device or the transcribed
word, but that you might receive in spirit, as we shall communicate there to you, as well. See?*

*We wish to express a brief note of gratitude to those
dedicated souls who have continued to make the way passable that this communication might be made.*

---

*We are now before Peter and his colleagues, the angel in
our commission, and Rebecca. Once again, only several moments have passed in your Earth-time measure.*

Peter is speaking. "Here? You welcome me here? Does
that mean we're there? You know, where you live? I
mean ... Goodness! Are we where the angels are?"

Warmth comes from those gathered, along with a bit of
tinkling emanating from Zachary, once again coming to the
aid of his companion. "What Peter is attempting to ask is, are
we in the realm of the Heavenly Host, as he calls it?"

The commission, the fallen angel (which is a misnomer
at this point, with a note of joyous humor), answers Peter
with directness, as is her manner. "Yes, Peter. We are here."

Swiftly glancing about, Peter perceives nothing extraordinary, but he recognizes that the angel's "cloak" is still very
large and seems to be surrounding them completely.

He ascertains that it is still translucent to an extent, but
he can't discern anything beyond it very clearly, with the exception of some luminosity. He turns back to the angel. "This
is where you came from? This is ... Well, what do you call it,
anyway?"

The angel smiles and responds, "Home. Like in your

previous incarnation, I call it home. It is where I have existed throughout time, as you measure it. It is where I am from, and where I belong, it would seem."

The last comment raises some questions in Peter's mind.

The angel astutely notes this, studying Peter. "If you have questions, I invite you to convey them openly, for it is appropriate that I return your acts of kindness, equally so."

It is now Peter who is studying the angel, and she seems to take delight in this shifting of roles. In her delight, Peter again detects the rosy color radiating out from her a few feet and then enveloping her. "Well, I might as well start by asking, what's the rosy color around you at this moment?"

"Love."

"Love? I don't understand. That's an emotion. I thought you didn't really experience emotions."

"Love is a state of being, Peter. At least, it is here. It is not an emotion. It does not rise and fall. It is consistent. Always present."

Peter, surprised at his own astuteness, responds, "Well, then, why is it that I see it some times and not at others?"

The angel does not hesitate a moment. "It is not I, Peter, but you who perceive. It is always present. It is your changing *receptivity*, I think is your word for this, that affects whether or not you see or don't see it."

"This is constant and consistent, always there, never changing? Same volume? Same energy level?"

She merely nods, still smiling.

"That's difficult for me to grasp. I didn't detect any difference in myself when I saw the glow come into being, and now it is subsided again. Let me see if I understand. You said that I changed, not you?"

Again, she simply nods an affirmation.

"Can you show me?"

Glancing quickly towards Zachary, the angel looks back to Peter. "Yes. Ask me a question. Any question."

Peter searches within himself for a moment and then asks, "What is your name?"

Instantly, the rosy glow springs forth from her.

"Look, there it is! I did nothing, I only asked a question."

The angel is still smiling, unwavering, never changing, always the same loving smile, the same understanding. "Oh, but you did change, Peter. You went from thinking and searching inward to a state of receptivity."

Peter can grasp the essence of her comment but, true to his nature, continues on in order to grasp it totally. "So you are saying that while I was thinking about the question, I was not receptive; after I asked the question, I was receptive?"

"Yes. Care to try it again?"

"That seems a very subtle change, if you'll forgive me. And I fail to see how that could increase or decrease, to any measurable degree, my ability to see or not see that beautiful rosy pink color around you."

The angel simply looks at Peter.

Realizing that she is asking him to try again, he turns inward and then comes forth with another question.

As he is about to speak, she stops him with a gesture. "Do you see the color now, Peter?"

Caught with a word in mid-air, Peter looks carefully, and he does not.

"Very well. Now, state your question."

"Well, uh … let's see … How long have you been here?"

Instantly, the glow reappears. Brilliant, vibrant. "You see it now, correct, Peter?"

"Yes, I do. So, after asking the question, I am attuned differently in order to receive or perceive your answer?"

The angel again nods. "Yes. You would call that *listening*, in your finite realms, but you could also call it focusing or being attentive, couldn't you?"

"Yes, I suppose so."

"Well, if you would care to focus and then look around,

you'll see what I am attempting to share with you."

"How would I do that?" turning to Zachary and then glancing over to Elizabeth.

It is Elizabeth who offers Peter assistance this time. "Peter, recall when Zachary encouraged you to go within and to become, what he called, creative, and to look for a need? Then, remember when we first took you to one of the realms of expression that I told you was one of my favorites?"

Swiftly, Peter draws those memories to his consciousness, "Yes, I believe so."

"Well, repeat the process. Not necessarily looking for that as the end result, but try to recapture the state of being, the feeling."

Peter shuts himself down a bit, similar to closing his eyes, and to his surprise, he is quickly in a state in which he feels only a gentle, undulating peace.

"Now, focus again, Peter."

Turning to the angel, he sees her in a beautiful, much larger, soft pink orb. When he looks toward Rebecca, who has been silently nearby, he sees this around her, as well. A thought comes to him, and he shifts his attention to Elizabeth and sees a subtlety of this same hue around her. With a quick glance over to Zachary, who is knowingly smiling at him, he is astounded to perceive a brilliant pink hue.

"Hello, Peter."

Startled, he turns about, and there is his dear friend Paul, also surrounded in a beautiful pink hue.

"Oh, how wonderful to see you, Paul!"

In that instant, the rosy hue dissipates.

"Oh, my!" Peter states. "I hope I didn't do something wrong."

"Not at all," Paul comments.

"It is so good to see you! How are you? How have things been?"

"Well, I ..."

"Is it true that this your realm, too?"

"Well, in a manner of speaking, it is. But it's not my home, in the sense that I have chosen to continuously reside here or express myself here."

"Why is that?"

"Well, it's a question of choices."

Peter turns to observe all the group. "There is so much, so very much, to all this that it seems I can't absorb it all. One thing leads to another, and on and on and on. I believe that if I were expressed physically at this point, I would be extremely tired. I don't seem to have that reaction here, but at some level of my being I am in a state of uncertainty. And forgive me, Paul, for not spending a courteous amount of time in discussion with you. It certainly is no indication of my lack of joy to see you and my interest in how you have been and what you have been doing."

"Not at all, Peter. I have been and am well, and I have been with you in one way or another all along."

"Truly?"

"Yes, truly."

"Somehow I think I have known that." He turns back to the angel and glances at each one of the group. "I believe I need some assistance now. Is our commission complete, concluded?"

Turning to Zachary, he receives a smiling nod, and a less exaggerated wink.

"Oh, good. And we were successful?"

"Utterly so, Peter. Well done."

"Well, then, is it okay for me to ask some questions to try to understand a few things? Or do you all have other work or things you need to be about? I wouldn't want to disrupt or take away from anything important that you have to do."

In a continually calm, gentle, loving voice, the angel answers, "There is nothing that I am aware of, Peter, that is of greater value than being here and answering your questions."

"Oh, how lovely. What a blessing that is."

A tinkling bit of humor comes from Zachary and a soft comment, "Indeed so, Peter, a blessing, indeed."

Smiling, Peter casts a glance at Zachary and, obviously not wanting to lose a moment of his opportunity to question, he begins. "Dear lady, do you have a name?"

The angel, again, incredibly consistent in her manner, in her countenance, and in the radiance that pours to Peter from her being, answers, "I have that which is God's name for me, as do all. But in terms of what you call a name, I have had none. I am without what you would call a reference, a name."

"God's name, or the name that God calls you? God speaks to you?"

The angel softly nods.

"When? How does He call you? Where do you meet Him? What does He look like? Does He do this often?"

Smiling, the angel simply answers, "All of these things could be known to you, Peter, if you so wished."

Puzzled, Peter reflects a moment, then asks, "What does it mean when you say 'if I so wished'? I am … Forgive me, but I am asking the question, so therefore you must know that I am wishing to receive the answers."

A bit of melodious humor comes from his colleagues.

"What I mean, Peter, is that you have come from here."

"*I?* I have come from here?"

The angel merely nods.

At that moment, Peter hears a strange sound, feels a strange energy, and the angel, still looking at Peter warmly, lovingly, raises a hand in a gesture for him to pause. And she turns to glance off to Peter's left.

Peter follows her gaze and sees in the outer shimmering essence of the angel's cloak a beautiful light approaching. He can see others, too, as though a stream of them is moving towards where they are. One seems to be well in the forefront, and it is heading towards them at what Peter discerns must be a remarkable speed.

Peter inadvertently braces himself for what he anticipates to be a collision of the sphere of light against the greater orb of light surrounding the group.

The light continues with remarkable velocity until it abruptly halts what looks to be mere millimeters from the outer periphery of the angel's cloak.

Peter can hear some delightful little sound and sees dancing rivulets of color emanating from his dear lady towards the light.

In that instant, the light moves swiftly in to position itself immediately before his (previously) "fallen angel."

Again, shafts of light emanate between the angel and this new orb of light, and then, in the passage of two or three moments, a form appears.

The angel turns back to Peter. "I have suggested, in honor of your presence, that this, one of my dear brethren, also adopt the form understandable to you, in order that communication with you could be with the greatest possible ease."

Nodding and a bit speechless, Peter studies this new entity, who is every bit as beautiful as his dear lady, and notes remarkable similarity in their essence. They seem very much alike in many ways, and yet there are distinct differences that seem to be emanating from within this new entity. To Peter, they both appear to be, by Earth measure, to be very young, which he hadn't particularly noticed earlier about his dear lady. Both are of radiant beauty, and the warmth emanating from their eyes is utterly magnificent.

"May I extend my greetings and welcome to you, Peter, and express our loving gratitude for your efforts on behalf of our associate here," glancing slowly and deliberately at Peter's dear lady.

Peter seems to detect a bit of flare-up on the outer periphery of his dear lady and therefore he knows that he must have, according to her teachings, been a bit more receptive in that moment. Realizing this, Peter makes what you would call a mental note to learn to do this in a more controlled and instantaneous way.

The angel nods to Peter who recognizes that she has just given him approval for that mental note. He smiles just a bit.

He remembers his manners, albeit a bit tardily, and turns to the new arrival. "Oh! I greet you, as well. And thank you for welcoming me here, though I must admit I'm not truly sure where I am," which again spurs a bit of humor from his colleagues. "But wherever this is, it is certainly remarkable, as are you … all of you, for that matter," nodding at all three now standing before him just a short distance away. "And whatever was accomplished on her behalf was not accomplished by me, but by all of us and so many others that I couldn't begin to tell you about them all."

The newly arrived angel turns to the dear lady and gives her a nod. "He is as you have described."

She returns his nod.

Peter looks to Zachary, Paul, and Elizabeth and sees them all smiling broadly and, he thinks, with a bit of joyful pride. He looks down for a moment and then glances back up. "May I be permitted to continue my questions?" He turns to the angel he has come to call the dear lady (in truth, it is difficult to discern whether she is a lady or not, but Peter had her essence defined to him from the earlier stages of the commission as feminine, so he continues with that presumption).

The newly arrived angel answers, "You may certainly inquire as you have a wish to do so. We welcome your questions, and we hope that you will choose to remain."

Peter is startled by this. "Remain? You mean stay here?"

The angel nods, smiling, his gaze equally as warm, if not moreso, than the dear lady's, and he notes a hint of blue in his countenance. *His*, Peter thinks. *I am detecting a 'he' here.*

"That is acceptable to me, Peter, because for the purposes

of your definition you would perhaps define my uniqueness as having more of what you consider the masculine energy balance. While it has no relevance to the gender expression in finite realms, it does have relevance in terms of energy balance and those types of expressions."

"You know about these things?"

The newly arrived angel nods ever so gently.

"Do you have a name, sir? And for that matter, do you, dear lady, have some way you can convey to me what it is that you said God calls you?"

(Peter's Earthly memory is still having a significant impact upon him, so, as translators and interpreters, our communication to you is somewhat awkward here because of his continual curiosity to ascertain differences. Here and in other realms, the uniqueness of the individual is not measured in accordance with male-female criteria, but by the soul essence. In truth, there are many other levels of perception and techniques of perception beyond the colors, sounds, and those sorts of sensory definitives that are available to you in the Earth, which, even if we had terms with which to describe them to you, would escape your understanding. At any rate, we are finding considerable humor in his line of questioning.)

"If I might for a moment, Peter," states the newly arrived angel, "perhaps I can offer some assistance."

"Oh, please do, sir … or, uh … however I call you."

"We'll tend to that, Peter." Turning to the fallen angel, he asks with remarkable gentleness, "What caused you to move into finiteness?"

Peter becomes a bit alarmed, momentarily wondering if she is to be chastised or criticized for perhaps failing or falling. Perhaps she wasn't supposed to wander out there, or whatever or wherever it is that angels consider the Earth and other realms to be. His senses intensified, he focuses all of his consciousness on his dear lady.

The fallen angel explains her activity of following a fellow angel. To Peter's amazement, she explains that she had followed him for hundreds of thousands of Earth years; observed him as he moved into more and more finite expressions and continually made efforts to convince him to return to the realm of their nature, their home, each time failing, each time gaining less and less attention from her brother, until finally, she could not communicate with him at all.

She goes on to explain that, at that point, she lost what she calls (turning to Peter) hope.

Peter detects the slightest change in the newly arrived angel, and the dear lady turns back to him.

He (and we'll use the reference of *male*, since Peter views him this way) is nodding, indicating that he wishes her to continue.

The dear lady then explains how she realized that, without hope, she could not return and take a rightful position with her brethren. She felt that, in that state, she was too imbalanced to attempt to move into such a beautiful, pure realm as their home. Therefore, she searched until she found a realm that was so basal and so inactive that she would not disturb any other entity or consciousness, wherein she strengthened her spiritual cloak, her countenance, to the point where it became impenetrable.

There, she sought to reflect and to speak to God in order to understand what to do next. "I was, at this time, utterly without hope. I was certain that once one entered into finiteness, based upon my experiences, that one would be lost."

The heaviness of the angel's statement impacts Peter dramatically, and he sparkles and illuminates here and there, until Elizabeth gently touches him, her warmth and stability settling him down again.

"What were you experiencing, Peter, if I might ask?"

"Oh, I'm sorry, sir. My friends here will tell you, I don't

have the greatest control yet. Haven't got the hang of this. But I'm getting better. What I was experiencing was … well, empathy … a tremendous sadness for what I could visualize and experience remembering her large cocoon-like, almost concrete-hard cloak. That hit me pretty hard, you know? If I had a solar plexus, that's where it would have hit me."

Peter sees the newly arrived angel studying him carefully. "I beg your pardon, sir. It dawns on me that it is possible you don't comprehend all that I have said."

"Some of your thought-forms or terminology is unusual to me. I have some knowledge of finiteness, but not to the degree that you are communicating." He looks at Peter warmly for a moment or two and turns back to the fallen angel, "So, then, Peter and his companions gave you hope."

The fallen angel smiles (Peter interprets it so, at least) and nods to her companion. They stand for a moment, their eyes transfixed on one another.

Then the newly arrived angel turns back to Peter. "Well, then, Peter, it would appear that you have defined an appropriate name for her. If it is acceptable to you," and turning to the angel, "and to you, *Hope* is a beautiful name."

The angel turns to Peter (and again, Peter believes, smiles very radiantly) and he nods, excited, even thrilled at the concept of his possibly having named an angel! He can discern a tinkling sound from Zachary, knowing that his dear friend is again humored. "Well, then, uh … Hope … May I continue with my questions?"

She nods.

The male angel interrupts, ever so gently, "If you will forgive me, Peter. I know how important your questions are, but I wish you to know of several other opportunities available to you. Then, with that knowledge, if you wish to continue with your questions, it will be quite acceptable to all of us. But we wish you to have the knowledge, in order that you can make a decision completely informed."

Puzzled, Peter simply nods an affirmation.

"My colleagues have come to greet you. Many of them know you, and they are joyful to hear that you are in our midst again. They would like to escort you to where you are from. That is what I wanted to convey to you. Now you may choose whichever you prefer."

Peter is astounded, for all the while the male angel is conveying these concepts which are revolutionary to Peter's thinking, his countenance hasn't changed one bit. It would be analogous to telling about the outcome of the World Series and in the next breath asking about the weather. Peter's mind races over these comparisons to his Earth incarnation.

As the male angel nods and smiles Peter realizes that his thoughts have been observed.

Again, the tinkling of Zachary's laughter flows over Peter as a ribbon of luminous light and sound. "Well, Pete, now they've got you. It's a question of whether or not your curiosity is greater in hindsight or foresight, isn't it?" chuckling to himself, pleased to observe how Peter is going to handle this.

"You always seem to delight in my predicaments, Zack!"

"Not at all. I just love the nature of your being. It's such a wonder to all of us," with a sweeping gesture, he notes the other members of the group gathered, and they smile in return, "that I can't help but point it out to you. And, hey! Suppose I were to do that in what you call heavy-duty style? You know, point it out with some attitude of moroseness and that sort of thing. That wouldn't be any fun, and you'd start taking yourself too seriously, and then what? See what I mean?"

As always, Peter cannot ever experience Zachary's logic, his humor, his good cheer, and the sincerity of his intent, without agreeing wholeheartedly.

"Okay, Zack. Well, how about giving me a hand here with this *heavy-duty* decision?"

Zachary, nodding, steps forward. "Certainly. What are friends for, anyway? Let's see now. On the one hand, we could ask questions here for a year or two, and you'd still have a few more to go at the end of that time. On the other hand, you don't know what our friend here is talking about, or at least you don't remember it at the moment. And look. There's a goodly number who apparently are here to welcome you with, you know, a bit of nostalgia. They want to show you your roots." Chuckling as he states this invokes humor in Paul and Elizabeth. Even the angels, Peter thinks, smile a bit more broadly.

For the first time, Rebecca comes forward, positioning herself immediately before Peter. "If I may, I would like to offer further comment."

"Oh, Rebecca, yes. How wonderful that you're here. I always knew there was something special about you, but I never thought you were an angel."

Zachary bursts out with laughter, the music cascading all about the chamber in which they are now positioned. Peter perceives some sort of light fast-moving rainbow of colors projected from the angels, and Elizabeth is looking down, laughing.

Paul comes forward to rest his hand on Peter's shoulder. "Never mind, Peter. Go ahead, Rebecca. I know Peter would welcome your comments."

"Oh, yes, me too," laughs Zachary. "Let's get on with it. We're wasting what Pete calls *time*."

Peter glances over his shoulder at Zachary and winks at him. "Thanks, Zack."

Rebecca begins, "I highly recommend that you accept the invitation. The reason is that this is an opportunity for you to come before some significant decisions. These decisions would be better made if you have the most knowledge possible and the background for understanding that you can have."

"Decisions?"

Rebecca simply nods, softly smiling at him.

"Uh, these aren't ..." glancing back and forth at his companions, "you know, like real serious decisions, are they?"

"Could be, Pete. But then, on the other hand, everything is relative, isn't it?"

Peter reflects on Zachary's comment, and recognizes that it has a ring of truth within him.

Then Paul adds, "It is so, Peter. Everything is relevant … heavy-duty, if you believe it so."

"I think I understand. Of course, I can't grasp what the decisions might be. But they do feel like they're significant, I'll tell you that."

"Good, Peter. That's a very astute perception."

The angel Peter has, inadvertently, come to name Hope, comes forward to stand beside Rebecca. "Rebecca and I both would be honored to accompany you, Peter. You may bring your companions, certainly." Turning to Elizabeth, "And, of course, we wouldn't think of taking this journey without you, Elizabeth. Come stand by Peter where you belong."

Puzzled at the last part of that comment, Peter looks at her and sees her smiling back at him. "Yes, Elizabeth. Do come here. I may need you before this is over."

There is tinkling humor from Zachary again, and a reassuring touch from his dear friend Paul.

Hope turns to the male angel. "We would like to accept the offer from our brethren, and to do so now."

Nodding and smiling, he turns. A light flows swiftly from him, and all the orbs (there must be twenty of them, in Peter's estimation) more or less fashion themselves together. The greater sphere that is formed by this larger number seems to move over Hope's cloak, or outer spherical periphery.

Peter feels a marvelous new sensation. He looks, and Hope's earlier sphere or cloak is drawing itself inward toward her. As it does, he has a moment of apprehension, wondering what will become of them. In that same moment, he hears a melodious sound, incredibly brilliant. First it seems to come from over here; and then, as though it's an aria, it comes from over there. Then a harmonic begins here, and another one there. Again and again and again comes this wondrous collage of symphonic melody.

Peter cannot comprehend how such beautiful tones could be so continually flowing from all directions, without one note in conflict or discord, like an immense orchestral arrangement, each instrument with its own unique melody, but together composing one grand movement.

Hope speaks softly. "They are greeting you, Peter, identifying themselves to you."

"They are?" he asks in wonder.

"Yes. Each has given you their name, welcoming you."

"I hear no names."

"This is their uniqueness by which they are called by God. Just as I explained to you earlier that I, too, have such a name. You do, as well, Peter."

He reflects on that thought and listens intently, singling out first the sound coming from one brilliant sphere, then the next, and the next.

Lost in the wonder, the incredible unlimited depth and breadth of the brilliance of this music, he feels them moving. The motion is swifter than any he can ever recall. As quickly as one might snap their fingers, that is the span of the motion and they have moved from one place to what Peter knows intuitively is an infinitesimal distance from point A to point B.

"This is where you are from, Peter," states Hope softly.

"Here? But I see nothing. I mean, I see all of you and all of the brethren there. But I see nothing beyond."

"Would you like to experience what is beyond?"

With a bit of reservation, Peter turns to look at Paul, remembering that he was the first to greet and guide him.

Paul is smiling, and the depth and genuine nature of his love is clearly felt by Peter. "It is all right, Peter. You have free will. You may easily return. And there are none, I assure you, who mean you any harm. To the contrary, their only desire is to give to you, and that is all."

Peter thinks about this. "Their only desire is to give. Is that what they do, Paul?"

Paul nods gently, smiling.

Peter reflects further. "Giving …"

He turns back to look at Hope, and realizes that this does indeed fit her. She is a giver. She can give and give and give. Peter intuits that she has an inexhaustible resource from which she can draw.

As he studies at great length, absorbing, feeling each of the gently revolving lights radiating colors and sound, each one seems strangely familiar to him. Somehow each one creates an awakening within him. Another light, and another corner in his being that was dark is now illuminated.

Finally, Peter comes out of this altered consciousness, literally glowing. He looks at Hope "I gladly accept your generous offer. Do show me. I wish to know from whence I have come."

Feel the exuberance coming from all the spheres, Peter realizes that they all hear and know and understand all of what he is experiencing.

Hope moves to one side of him, and Rebecca moves to the other. Immediately behind him is Elizabeth. To their right are Paul and the male angel. To the left is Zachary and a newly arrived entity whom Peter cannot discern, for this one is in an orb of light.

Their movement is easy and gentle. As Peter feels as though they are approaching the periphery of the greater sphere created by the brethren, it slowly dissipates. Similar to sucking in one's breath, Peter holds himself in anticipation. *What,* he reflects, *will happen now? What is next?*

He feels marvelous. It is as though he has moved out into a very softly moving, gentle wind. The wind has the essence he saw come forth from Hope now and then, and he thinks back to her comment. Yes, this must be that continuous flow of love she spoke of. *Oh-h, it is so wonderful,* he thinks, turning to glance from Rebecca to Hope and then to his companions. He turns to cast a glance at Elizabeth, and she smiles and nods to encourage him.

All manner of experiences occur for Peter, each one more beautiful, more brilliant, and more profound.

(These are such as we mentioned earlier that escape definition.)

Finally, he realizes they have come to pause. Here, he sees another group of spheres of light moving, dancing, and vibrating towards him. He feels a remarkable sense of joy in the midst of his being, and hears and feels a radiance of energy coming from each one.

In a split second, he realizes that he knows them! He remembers them vaguely, dream-like. As he does, he can perceive their being. Where there was first one light, he now perceives something that is not form, and yet it is. It is not simply color and light, yet it is both. It is neither music nor sound, yet it is this and more.

He can feel with every sense imaginable from the Earth and a myriad of others that is unimaginable.

The overpowering desire to race forward and collide with each of these spheres reaches such intensity that Peter glows with a vibrancy he has heretofore never, ever, experienced that he can remember. As he does, he perceives that Rebecca has moved off slightly and released him, as have Hope and all of his companions.

He hears Hope softly speak. "These are what you might think of, Peter, in the Earth as a family, while different in the sense that they are not temporary or passing."

Peter is moved beyond measure. He is straining to sustain his consciousness as Peter.

"You have nothing to fear, Peter," comments Hope

softly. "I assure you that I shall withdraw you if *you* cannot do so yourself."

Peter, with great effort, turns to acknowledge a nod from Zachary and one from Paul. Elizabeth, to his astonishment, is glowing with a radiance that is beyond his ability to express. "You, too, Elizabeth?"

"Yes, Peter."

"Come by me, Elizabeth. Let us visit."

Instantly, Elizabeth and Peter are side by side. They rush to become one with the group, and the group unites in a massive display of color, sound, and light, which is echoed back to the group from distant positions in what you would think of as the universe. The echo, the resonance, begins here and there, and it comes from over here and again over there, and another and another, until the entirety of this expression is filled with this resonance: Joy, exuberance!

(We cannot tell you the amount of time that passes. Comparatively speaking, there is no measure. But we can tell you that during this time many entities could be born again and again in the Earth,)

Now we move to that point in consciousness in which Hope calls Peter by his name and retrieves him, and calls out Elizabeth and retrieves her, as well.

Peter is still Peter, and Elizabeth herself, as well. But their radiance is utterly different.

Hope, softly, looking at Peter, asks, "Are you well?"

"I am well and joyful. And I thank you."

Elizabeth responds in like kind.

Another prolonged period of discussion ensues between Hope, Peter, Elizabeth, and the male angel (whom Peter now knows by his spiritual name).

There is another prolonged period of exchange between them.

(Dear friends, you must know that we are at a point of some marked decision.

It shall be given or presented to Peter soon whether or not, as his friend Zachary had forearmed him, he would choose to stay or to return. For Peter has freed himself from what you could call the bonds of finiteness. The offer that is being made to him is whether or not he would wish to remain here.

At this point, we can move to what we would gauge to be the decisive point of the conversation in which you would be most interested. Zachary has moved to join the group, as has Paul. Paul and Zachary are reviewing with Peter and Elizabeth, Rebecca, Hope, the male angel, and others.)

"Your choice, Pete. You certainly have earned the right to remain here. After all, it would seem that's what it's all about, wouldn't it?"

Peter slows his vibrations down a bit as he is drawn back into a memory of his relationship with Zachary and with Paul and their many experiences together. He looks at Elizabeth, who is mirroring Peter's level of energy or vibration. "This is so wonderful, Zachary. It is like nothing I could ever imagine. I feel complete, balanced, harmonious, joyful. Any joyful word I could come up with from my Earth memory would apply here, and all of them together would fall woefully short of adequately defining what I am experiencing."

"Understood, Pete. Completely understood. No problem. But, hey! Paul and I would just like to present a thought to you. You realize now that we are capable of remaining here, too, or somewhere like this," chuckling a bit to himself. "But the question is whether you wish to stay here, and just *be*, and all that sort. Well, you know what I mean now. You've had enough of it to understand. Or whether, perhaps, you might like to join us, or others like us, who are attempting to do …

well, let's say, some rescue work. Some service. You know, a bit of help to those who haven't found the Light yet."

As he looks from Zachary to Paul, Peter is touched by the light that is emanating from Paul and also from Zachary. He considers that Zachary could have stayed here, but he didn't. Turning to Paul, he realizes Paul, too, certainly could have stayed here, without question, and Paul gives him a gentle nod. *What if they hadn't,* he considers within himself. *What if they weren't there for me? Would I have made it here?*

Before he can answer his own question, Zachary states, "Oh, I'm quite sure you would have, Pete. You've got what it takes. I don't think you'd have had that much trouble. But it was our joy, our pleasure, to help and to share with you. You know, that's half the fun of it, don't you think? Sharing?"

Fun? Peter considers. *What's fun about being limited?* His mind races over all these things. He reflects upon the hardships, the challenges, the heart-wrenching struggles. They are all too familiar within his being.

"Well, I'll tell you what, Pete. You think about it. And we'll come back here … oh, say, in a week or so. You know, Earth time, and all that. We'll discuss it again. And perhaps we can go somewhere where we can get a bit more perspective on it all, and you can meet some of the others we work with that you haven't had much opportunity to interact with on a personal level."

"Others?"

"Well, yes. You know, we didn't do all this alone, Pete. We had help, after all."

A tingling begins within Peter … soft, gentle, melodious. *The golden orb,* Peter remembers. *Of course!*

We will conclude here.

But the question is not only presented to Peter, but to each of you. We would like you to ask of yourselves what your choice would be. Would you stay in this position of infinite joy, indescribable wonder? Or would you return?

Reflect on this.

CHAPTER 14

The Decision

MARCH 7, 1992

We have gathered together here in this meeting a number of additional souls (our brethren, to be precise) who are to be involved in those works, that commentary, of which you are soon to be a part.

As we prepare to re-join our colleagues in their quest for knowledge and understanding, we would like to express here again that much of the commentary that will be given to you will be interpreted or translated into verbal expressions as best we can. We ask your understanding that much of what is to be experienced and expressed is beyond known terminology, as we have it relevant to the Earth. Therefore, we shall adapt and modify and attempt to interpret using those terms, those thought-forms, as we can find best suited to convey to you the experiences that shall transpire.

We are joyful in the anticipation that you will find a considerable expansion of your awareness yet before you in those works that are to come.

We would remind you that at the point of our last commentary Peter was evaluating his choice whether to remain in the realm which he considers very clearly at this point his home or whether to re-join Zachary, Paul, and the many others in whatsoever works they might have yet ahead unbeknownst to him.

We would also remind you that Zachary had stated to Peter that he would return and perhaps they could join together in the discussion, and also that Peter might be intro-

duced or in the presence of others who had assisted in his progress and in the accomplishment of the last commission, as it has now been completed to your knowledge.

We would also remind you that the beautiful soul, the object of the earlier commission, whom Peter came to name, albeit inadvertently, Hope has given her will, her choice, to join Zachary and the others in whatsoever works lie before them.

So, with that bit of recapitulation, we now turn to the Realm of Angels, and find before us Zachary, Paul, Rebecca, Hope, the "male angel," and, of course, Peter and Elizabeth. Just a bit to the rear, off to the left as we would view the group, where Peter and Elizabeth are now positioned, is also a goodly number of others, positioned there unobtrusively but very evident in their radiance. We identify those to you as Peter and Elizabeth's friends or brethren, with whom Peter and Elizabeth have been sojourning.

Again, we shall attempt to speak as we hear spoken, reminding you again that speech is not by the vocal chords or by the uttering of words, but in the more direct sense of the communication of what we might call thought-forms.

Zachary is speaking. "Peter, so good to see you again. You look well, and in fact, if you will forgive me, the best I have ever seen you."

Peter is an utterly radiant being, as is Elizabeth immediately to Peter's right. They are like looking at a reflection in a mirror and then at the real image. In other words, so similar are they in their vibrations, their coloration, and their essence, that it is difficult to distinguish them, as though there has been a sort of merging between them that almost makes them as one.

"Zachary," Peter replies, "Paul, all of you, so wonderful to see you again. Elizabeth and I ... well, our experiences have been beyond expression. I find it curious even now, my good friends, to come together with you and to attempt to communicate in this way, which I now am aware is somewhat limited, somewhat narrowed in its scope."

Zachary, studying Peter perhaps with a more serious countenance than is usual for him, just nods softly, studying, probing.

It is Paul who speaks next. "That is wonderful, Peter. You certainly have grown a great deal and, if you will forgive me for saying it, no one deserves such joy more than you. Your path has been exemplary, and your actions and service equally so. I speak for all of my companions here in saying that we all rejoice in your accomplishment and have a great sense of well-being for the privilege of having served with you and walked along those pathways of choice at your side."

The sincerity and utter love of Paul's comments, as always, strike the core of Peter, and we can see a glow begin within him difficult to define. Yet, at this core of his being, a differentiation in the essence, the color, the vibration, can be perceived.

Peter is surrounded with the wondrous pink luminosity that he had so admired around Hope before, and Elizabeth is so ensconced, as well.

"Peter, have you found joy in your journey and in your experiences?" questions Hope, sending beams of light to him as she does so.

We perceive a smile from Peter, for he knows that Hope knows the answer to her question already. But dutifully, he answers, "Indescribably so, Hope. I never envisioned in our first meeting together (you and I along with the others) that it would come to such a conclusion. In so many ways, I have such gratitude and so much to thank you for, Hope, for having had the opportunity to, as Zachary and Paul called it, serve you. I have gained all this. It is incredible as I strive to regain my finite consciousness in order to express and to experience my communication to you from that vantage point."

As is her nature, Hope merely nods, communicates a

glowing warmth to Peter, and then, with a lingering look at him, turns back to Zachary and states softly, "As you will recall, Zachary, I made it known to you that I shall follow you."

This comment creates a reaction in Peter and is echoed in Elizabeth. "Hope, what are you saying? Do you mean to say that you will return to limitation? No offense, Zachary, but, Hope, remember the dreary realm in which we found you, the state of your being? You had lost ... well, hope."

Gently, Hope turns back to Peter "I remember only too well. I remember the searching and the questioning between God and me. I remember the first glimmer of understanding, the feelings of finiteness, if ever so subtle, and the joy as I beheld you and Elizabeth, and then our friend Zachary here, and then the others. I remember how much it meant to me, and I remember how it resonated and how I thought to myself, *What is it that brings these souls into this realm to seek out me? How can these souls give so freely, at the same time giving up (what you would call) all of this wonder and joy and completeness?'*

"So, yes, Peter, I have reflected on this at great length. I have asked of God if this is permissible, and I have received an affirmation, a blessing. I choose now to journey under the guidance of Zachary and Paul. And my sister Rebecca shall journey with me, since she has knowledge of these things. I will learn from her that I might better serve whatever works would bring joy to God and the reunion of all souls."

As we look over the group to tell you what is transpiring, Zachary is positioned as though he has his chin in his hand, studying, thinking, and reflecting. Studying Peter again, then looking at Hope with a trace of a smile emanating from him, but with more seriousness than he is usually noted for.

Paul is, in essence, unchanged. His personality, if you would call it such, his being, his individuality, is ever so consistent--always loving, always gentle, patient, and ever present to support and encourage.

Rebecca stands aglow, the coloration of her being clearly showing the series of experiences she has already had in the Earth. As she looks at Hope, she clearly admires with all of her love the decision of her sister.

Peter is obviously at a loss for words. He considers what it is that Hope is choosing. He is remembering by way of retrieving his finite consciousness. (As we view him it is like someone in the Earth striving to put on a suit of clothing that was worn twenty or thirty years earlier. It doesn't fit him well at the moment, but he struggles, nonetheless. We can see him remembering Hope's initial mission-- the quest for her brother, lost in the depth of finiteness. He turns to look at Elizabeth and then at all of his family, the other souls he has found again after all those hundreds of centuries, tens of thousands of Earth years or more, during which he explored finiteness.

Breaking the state of reflection, Zachary speaks softly, somewhat out of character for his being, "Peter, I mentioned to you earlier that perhaps you would like to meet, in the individual sense, some of those who have assisted us. Maybe in so doing, you might have a clearer perspective of your choices, of the alternatives. Certainly not to coerce you, for I would be the last to do so."

Paul nods, clearly, to affirm to Peter that he is utterly free.

Zachary goes on, "If it would be acceptable to all of you, I would like to join our group with another group that is a part of what I will call *the Way*."

Hope, Peter, Elizabeth, and the male angel shift a bit in their vibration, their essence. The male angel comments, "You are saying, then, that we should move to finiteness. As I understand it, this is a part of the Way."

"That is not necessary. Remember we have not lost our awareness or our ability to be one with you simply because we have journeyed in finiteness. I offer this to you only as a loving reminder, and to prove this, you have Peter now in the midst of your group, in utter harmony and bliss."

Immediately nodding, the male entity affirms Zachary's comment and Peter's presence. "Accepted," he states, with no hint, not one whit, of any emotion, doubt, or hesitancy.

Half into and half out of his *suit* of finite consciousness (as we might call it, with a bit of loving humor) Peter notes this and marvels at it just a bit. *Utter faith, utter trust ... beautiful*, he thinks.

What transpires next is a combination of changing expression, accompanied by color and light, but almost instantaneous. The largest single occurrence that would depict the change would be a brilliant instance of a clear bluish, silvery-white presence of light lingering for a millisecond, through which it seems that the entire group passes.

As we look at the group now, although still the same, their appearance is somewhat transformed, as though they have been placed within their cloaks looking utterly radiant and beautiful, emanating color, light, and sound profusely, just wondrously beautiful to behold.

From the right, we can perceive activity, and we note that a number of entities are moving to join the group.

"If you do not mind," offers Zachary, "could I ask all of you to adopt a form? Since we have others, as you might know, who are participating but are unseen, who are expressed in other realms and are our co-workers, it simplifies things if we can refer to you in understandable terms for them, as they come from a variety of realms."

Immediate approval and acceptance are given by the male angel, Hope, and the others, and the change is instantaneous, somewhat to the surprise of Peter.

As though they are floating, the lower portion of their being obscured, expressed only in a sort of muted assembly of color and light, Peter studies them as they come forward. Each of them raises a hand to gesture a greeting, and he can clearly see the radiance and warmth coming from them.

(We'll have to pause just a moment here because we are a part of that group and, therefore, in order to continue to comment to you, we need to make a certain adjustment here. [Pause] *Very well.)*

Now, as we perceive the group before us as we approach them, we note some degree of recognition on Peter's countenance, which is splendidly radiant. We greet and exchange comments with each of the group, while Zachary and Paul move to stand by Peter's side, one on either side of him and Elizabeth, who stand close together almost as one.

"Peter, we are most pleased and honored to be with you here, and we wish to thank you for allowing us to participate with you in your commission. And we greet you, Hope, and wish to express to you how much we feel that the name given you does, indeed, suit you. You have given to our group, both present and those in other realms, a most joyful understanding and illumination of many things that otherwise would be difficult to have expressed and learned."

Hope responds to our comments, again, with a soft smile of warmth that seems to radiate over everyone's being. As she does, we hear her. "It is I who wish to thank you, all of you, those seen and unseen, for your prayers and the joy of your spirit in the form of your love, which I felt always present around me from the moment of our contact. And my gratitude to Peter, of course, who was the spokesperson of your combined works on my behalf. I shall ever hold a special love and warmth for him in the center of my being."

Peter is obviously touched by this, and Zachary seems to be loosening up just a bit.

One of our group comes forward and extends a greeting to Peter. Peter looks to be somewhat in a state of surprise, as his memory comes back to him. "Oh, sir, it is so wondrous to behold you again. I am joyful to be before you and thank you for your gifts earlier, which sustained me as I sought, with my colleagues, to fulfill the commission you gave to us. There is no means for me to express to you the gratitude and the honor that I feel within my being for having been able to serve in that commission."

Recognized now as the Golden Entity from the Hall of Wisdom, the entity's luminosity fills our group and transforms it into an indescribable radiance. Rivers of light pour forth. There are essences, sounds, sensations, utter emanations at the core of one's capacity to experience joy and well-being, whose vibrancy scintillate the very core molecule of our uniqueness, until there is absolutely no portion of our being that is not warmed and loved by the immense, utter magnitude and glory of this soul.

"Peter, you have served so well and rightfully have attained the position of your spirit's acceptance. Know in your core of being that I wish for you, as does my Father, whatsoever is in accord with your personal joy.

"I have come forward with this group for this gathering at the request of your colleagues that I might present certain information. Having that knowledge, thereafter it is your choice, in accordance with my Father's Law of Free Will, that you may do with this as you wish. As you choose, I and all here shall honor and uphold that decision to the uttermost of our being.

"What you are experiencing, Peter, is a position of rightful heritage which is in accordance with the creation of my Father for existence. You can and do have every right to remain here, as you will, throughout as much of eternity as is your choice.

"What Zachary, Paul, Rebecca and Hope, as you have come to know them, now plan to do is to continue to illuminate what is called *the Way*. It is a path that has been created which leads ultimately to oneness with God. While you are now in this state of being and awareness, one with God, the path that we call the Way contains an essence that you may recognize as not predominantly present in your current consciousness. This is the gain, through experience, of that which is called wisdom. As wisdom is used upon a pathway of truth and righteousness, it is an elevation, an increase in the potential of your individuality, so as to ultimately merge into oneness with all of existence.

"So it is now that I shall depart, leaving you to discuss this with your colleagues. As I do, I bless you in the Name of the Father and pray of Him for your continued joy and glory in evidence of His wonder. For now I leave, Peter, and I thank you."

Before Peter can speak, the golden spherical orb takes form, pulsates, spews forth luminosity, expands briefly, and closes in upon itself, and is gone.

"We, too, Peter, shall depart from your presence. But we shall maintain contact with you. Those of our colleagues in other realms shall, because of that contact, be able to sustain some degree of communication and participation in these works and other works that lie just ahead. Zachary, we shall be at hand and continue the commentary, as agreed. Paul, we shall continue to support your activities in the other realms and shall be (as it were) on call, should you need us."

Paul responds with an affirmation to our group. Blessings are exchanged. Zachary nods knowingly and comments, "I will sustain the communication and ensure that the continued work will unfold in accordance with the choices of your group in other realms. Of course, I am deeply grateful for your assistance in that which lies ahead."

At this, we confirm and affirm what Zachary has stated and exchange blessings. We now depart from the group.

(We pause a moment here to resume our previous position. [Pause] *We are re-positioned so as to be able to con-*

tinue to observe and comment to you, just as in the past.)

Zachary turns to Peter and says, "Well, Peter, that's about it. I believe we'll be moving along now. We have works to attend to. And so, I wish you, my dear friend, continued joy in your expression and in those things which are before you."

As Zachary turns to reply to the male angel and to the other members of the group, Peter interrupts. "Just a minute, Zachary. Was that who I think it was?"

"*That*, meaning the entity in the golden sphere, Peter?"

"Yes. He was from the Hall of Wisdom. True?"

"Yes, Peter, indeed."

"And this *Way* that he mentions, is that *the* Way … the Way of the Cross, the Way of the Christ?"

"It is often thought of in that sense," replies Zachary softly.

"And the completeness that he spoke of … the Golden One … this oneness with God … am I not one with God now, Zachary?"

"It is so, Peter. You are one with God. You can communicate with God. You are in the presence of His pure blessings. You are unlimited in terms of finiteness. While it is true you do not have the command of creativity that perhaps you did earlier, in other respects you have immense creativity but only in different ways."

"What do you mean by that, Zachary, that I don't have the same degree of creativity?"

"Oh, I meant no insult, Peter, no lessening of the beauty or joy. Just different. You know, like two beautiful colors. One's this color and one's that color. They're both beautiful. Neither one is, as such, better than the other. At least not from the perspective that we are speaking."

"Why do I get the feeling, Zachary, that same old feeling I used to get when we were … well, wandering about in finiteness, when you were about to cause me to discover something?"

A hint of Zachary's normal nature flashes forth as he feigns looking down and shuffling his foot a bit. He cocks his head, then looks up at Peter. "Well, you know, Peter, old mannerisms and habits. They're hard to shake. And as Paul here would tell you quickly, I'm sure, that's my nature."

With a beaming smile, Paul nods.

Peter, Paul, and Zachary all smile at each other for a few moments as they mutually remember their many experiences and adventures together.

"Goodness," sighs Peter, "that does strike a familiar chord. I did find great joy in all that, though it did often seem like a great deal of effort and pressure. Well, not pressure … uh, anticipation I guess, excitement even, during each of your little sorties, Zachary."

Standing more erect and now nodding vigorously, with a broad smile, Zachary states, "Yes, yes. Yes, they were fun, weren't they?"

Memories fly towards Peter from Zachary and Paul, and even from Rebecca a bit, as Peter exchanges those thought-forms with them, noticing that Elizabeth at his side is doing the same.

"Well, look, Pete, this has been swell," Zachary comments. "Just wonderful. To you, good sir, our profound gratitude for your kindness. You have, as always, been an outstanding host and a dear brother."

Smiling warmly and nodding to Peter and to Zachary and then to Paul, the male angel communicates something that could be translated simply as, "You are welcome. Farewell and fare joyously," and the entity fades completely away.

Peter knows that he has not really faded, but has simply re-joined the larger group elsewhere. He knows this because he has created a bond of oneness with all of these angels, and what is known by one is known by the others.

Zachary begins to move and extends an arm to Paul who raises his hand to gesture to Peter, whereupon Peter asks, "Wait a minute, fellows. Wait. What is it that you're going to do now?"

"Well, look, Pete," comments Zachary, "you know, you could come along. You can come back here any time you want for old times' sake. But if you want to come along, we're going to go to the Hall of Wisdom. Remember? There's going to be a gathering, and some works are about to be done, and we really do need to be present. You remember how wonderful it is and how important it is."

Nodding vigorously, Peter does remember, and responds swiftly, "If, you know, if Elizabeth and I were to join you, we could always come back here?"

"Certainly, Peter. This is your home now, and you certainly would always be welcome here."

"Yes, yes, I'm sure of that. "But would I be able to do that easily?"

"In the twinkling of an eye. But, look, we really do need to be going along here. Not to rush you, but if you're undecided, simply stay here. We can always stop back by and chat with you, if you'd like. Or you can tune in to us in the way that we taught you before. Remember?"

"Oh, yes. Yes, I remember. I could do that, couldn't I?"

"Certainly. As easily as falling off a log."

The comment invokes humor in Peter and a sense of warmth. Suddenly, a thought comes to him. "Will you be seeing Wilbur?"

"Of course," responds Zachary.

"Oh, yes," comments Paul. "In fact, just after the gathering, I intend to visit him. I have, indeed, been away too long, even though I've visited briefly here and there. There are several things I would like to do there, and the top of the list is to be in the presence of Wilbur again. He's such a wonderful being."

"Oh, yes, he is," comments Peter, as memories come back to him of their journeys into the Garden, and beyond the Garden through all of the green. A collage of memory floods Peter, at which point Hope speaks, "Peter, those thoughts you're having there, they're very finite."

"Oh, yes, I know."

"Are you bound to them?"

"What do you mean, by *bound*?"

"Well, it looks like they are elevating your spirituality as you are reflecting on them."

"How is that? What do you mean, elevating my spirituality?"

Hope, in her continually soft, loving, and gentle countenance, continues, "Well, look at your being. Your being is transformed. You are far more radiant."

"Far more radiant? How could I be far more radiant than the radiance of an angel? *Your* radiance, in fact. Can there be greater than this?"

"I am only repeating to you, Peter, what I am perceiving. I did not intend to cause you any loss of your joy or what you would call duress."

"Oh, forgive me, Hope. I didn't mean it in that way. But…"

In that moment, Zachary interjects, "Look, friends, we're departing now. If you are coming, you'll have to do so. Otherwise, if you'd like, I'll stop by here after the gathering and rejoin you. But for now we must be on our way."

"Well, wait, then, Zachary … wait. Hope, you're going too, correct?"

"Yes, Peter, indeed I am. I have given, as you would call it I think, my word."

Peter smiles broadly and nods. "Excellent, Hope. That's it. That's the expression. Pretty good, don't you think, Elizabeth?"

Elizabeth, who has been markedly silent, looks at him,

utterly bathing him in warmth, compassion, love, and what could be called an essence of God. "Yes, Peter, it is; and I think you're right. I think we should join them. I can perceive that within you there is the wish to so do. Agreed, Peter?"

"Well, why not, Elizabeth? We can come back here. Let us just tell our friends."

"There is no need," comments Hope. "They know all that is transpiring here. If you'll turn about and perceive them, they are all greeting you and sending you what you would call love."

"Now is the time, folks." Zachary turns, and there is a transformation. Peter and the entire group are enveloped in some sort of essence, and as we move to follow them, the movement is a matter of, in Peter's terms, a snap of a finger.

We are now upon the lush expanse of Peter's favorite spot, the green knoll in his Garden.

"This is lovely."

"Yes, I love it here, Hope," comments Peter.

"And I, too," echoes Elizabeth.

"Is this a creation of yours, Peter?" inquires Hope.

Zachary can be heard muffling some laughter off to the side, and Paul is radiating a warm smile, obviously on the verge of laughter himself.

Rebecca, standing to the side of Hope, explains, "Well, in part. But others have been involved, too."

"I see," responds Hope, with a nod of some obvious appreciation and respect as she peers at Peter.

Peter is a bit uncomfortable with that. "Wait a minute, Hope. Don't get the idea … I didn't create this."

"Peter, this isn't time for modesty or any of the other," Zachary interrupts. "We must enter the Temple."

"Oh, yes, certainly, Zack. Forgive me."

At this point, the group moves to the front portion of the Temple.

As they do, Hope comments, again and again, on the

beauty. The essence of thought that is permeating the structure is a source of wonder to her.

As Paul moves over to her side to answer her questions, they move to the entry of the Great Hall.

A familiar sight befalls Peter's consciousness as he perceives the beautiful, immense, sweeping table at which he can perceive gathered many entities, some of whom are now quite familiar to him. Turning about and gesturing vigorously, he can see Zeb. "Oh, look. Zachary, Paul, there is Zeb."

"Why, indeed so," agrees Zachary and echoes a greeting to Zeb.

"And David. Over there! There's David."

And so it goes, until our group seat themselves before the wondrously beautiful table.

Entities come and go to greet them, and Peter is particularly joyous to introduce Hope to them as they pass by.

Hope, in her consistently warm, loving radiance, is admired and welcomed generously by each entity.

Finally, there is a sound, which Peter recognizes as the pending entry of the Entity in the Golden Light.

A sphere commences, small, pulsating, rotating in its wonder and beauty. Soft white and blue radiating spires of light emerge from it … now golden … now blue-white … now utterly pure in its essence. It grows rapidly, and in its center of being is the one Peter has come to know and love-- the Golden One, as he calls Him.

Peter can again perceive the greeting or greetings flowing from this wondrous entity to all who are gathered. Again he can perceive, in an incredibly brief bit of time, that the entity not only greets each of these present, but communicates to them with breadth and depth, acknowledging each; yet all this, in the twinkling of an eye (as it might be called).

Finally, the entity's gaze falls on Peter. "Well, Peter, I see that you have decided to join us for this gathering. We are most pleased and joyful to have you with us here, and of course, you dear friends and colleagues of Peter. And, Hope, we thank you for the gift you have given us of your pledge of service to the works which are offered to us by our Father."

Consistent to her nature, Hope expresses herself eloquently and with an aria of rose-like sound and color that reaches out to embrace the Golden figure before Peter.

Peter is awe-struck that Hope would be so bold as to venture forth and to make such contact.

To an even greater level of his wonder, he perceives clearly that this wondrous figure before him transforms into an orb identical to Hope's and adds to it many times over other radiant colors and essences, and these cascade back to Hope with accompanying sound and utterly magnificent essences. Whereupon Hope nods her head downward a bit and extends what Peter can perceive as this comment, "It is I who am humbled before you, O Lord, and am, at your Word, thy servant."

(So powerful is this, so utterly moving, that we have all that we can do to sustain the communication here through this Channel in order to communicate those words, woefully short of the magnificence of the communication between Hope and the One of Wisdom before her.)

Peter is spellbound, transfixed, riveted in awe of the exchange. He can see, sense, and know the most magnificent exchange of love and understanding, of hopefulness, and of strength. What pours from the glorious entity standing before them Peter recognizes as non-existent in the Realm of the Angels. It is complete magnificence in wisdom, in sacrifice, and in a state of joyous ecstasy that is boundless in its magnitude.

It is, as he recalls from the Earth, like standing at the edge of a great sea to observe the sun merging into its horizon, while the finiteness of his being attempts to comprehend the vastness that follows as the rays of the sun's last light dance upon the heavens. And here, then there, and over here and more and again, the stars burst forth, as though they are flowers of light upon a velvety earth or soil upon which they draw their sustenance. He remembers the immensity of the evening sky, the magical transfixing power of twilight. The transformation that would occur within his being as he would lean back to peer upwards in wonder at the possibility of many other planets or worlds as his own Earth. And watching in awe and humility the infinite nature of that before him, he might see a trail of light here and there, as some stellar body would be making its way across this immense void. Then here and there, one of the lights would send him a blink of this or that color, as though it were signaling him, calling him, beckoning him. All of this and much more, Peter experiences as an exchange between Hope and this One he now knows.

[Pause]

(The events which have now transpired must be told in retrospect, for we were unable to sustain sufficient communication through this Channel in physical body to communicate that to you as it was taking place.)

Finally Peter realized that the One before him was and is the Lord who lights the Way. It was at this point that Peter's spirituality moved into a new dimension. What occurred in a moment's passing was a discovery of magnitude sufficient in light to illuminate your planet for a decade or more.

As he looks upon this magnificent soul, in the glory and radiance of His humility, of His capacity for long-suffering and understanding, of the immensity of His forgiveness, and of His love, Peter compares this now to what has been called his new home. As he does, he realizes what Zachary was saying to him in his own uniquely individual way, gently but with a bit of mirth, a touch of humor.

As he makes this realization, he turns to Zachary and sees that he is looking directly at him, straight in the eye. It is his Zachary again, smiling, the twinkle in his eyes back again. And then, a wink.

Peter throws himself upon his friend with utter abandon. Zachary embraces him beyond that of the embrace of the Earth, and Peter can hear joy and expressions of encouragement and blessing from the entire group.

Finally, Peter and Zachary stand.

Zachary extends his arms to Paul and to Hope, to Rebecca and Elizabeth. And then come Zeb, David and many others.

Then, to Peter's utter awe, this wondrous One, who moves in the golden light, comes to Peter and embraces him mightily.

Peter is … *(and we ask your understanding)* … Peter is weeping.

The Master speaks to him. "Why weepest thou, Peter? Rejoice. For the kingdom of the Father is before you. Rejoice, Peter."

"I cannot, Lord, for I am not worthy. Neither have I that which gives me the right to stand before Thee. I had, as you well know, nearly decided to abandon you."

"You are here, Peter, and you have chosen. And I am joyful for your presence. You can be a light to the others who have lost their way. You can carry the healing balm of our Father's grace unto those whose wounds run deep. You can nourish those who hunger for His love. You can slake the thirst of those who call out from the eternal river of God's love and forgiveness. All these things, and greater, can you do, Peter. And I give unto thee my Spirit as that eternal staff upon which you might lean when weary."

Peter falls before the feet of Our Lord, and the Master

grasps him and lifts him up. "Do not do so, Peter, before me or any, for thou art a Child of God! What you do, do in honor to His presence within you. You, I accept as my brother, and I ask in humbleness that you would, in return, grant me the same. Together, with all of our brethren here who are dedicated in our Father's Name, we are as one. Not one greater or lesser in the sight of my Father, lest they in and of themselves inadvertently position themselves so.

"I must now depart from you in this form, Peter, and my colleagues and brethren. But I am ever with thee in all things. You and I and the Father are one. It shall come to pass that one day, in the measure of the Earth, all shall know thereof, and the rejoicing shall fill all of existence to its utmost. My Spirit will be with thee, the Glory of my Father known ever in your thoughts. I bid thee adieu for the moment, my friends."

The sphere gathers, intensifies, around the Master's form, and the light pulsates and grows and then draws unto itself.

And the Master is not before them.

There is great joy and jubilance among the group gathered in the Hall of Wisdom.

Peter, in a state of wonder, perhaps you might call it shock, or incredulity, is led, as though numbed by the experience, dazed by the brilliance and wonder and awe of it all, borne by his friends comfortably, until they are upon his wondrous knoll again.

They seat themselves silently, all somewhat focused upon him.

No one speaks.

Finally, Peter can hear a small, tinkling sound. He remembers the sound, upon which he would turn to look, whereupon he would see friend Zachary coming up over the hill off in the distance.

Looking up slowly to fix his perception on Zachary, he sees that Zachary is seated, looking down at the earth, his fingers caressing the lush greenery, rocking to and fro ever so slightly. Peter then hears a beautiful, crystal, single note, and another, and he realizes that Zachary is singing. He then hears from Rebecca and Paul, and soon they are all, save himself, in joyous song.

Peter is uplifted, and he finds himself expressing a note, then two and suddenly, they are all in joyous song. They raise their arms and lock them unto oneness, and stand. In joyous song, they move this way and that, and Peter hears in the words of their song rejoicing, blessing, and thanksgiving.

With this, we must conclude for the present. As we do, we are joyful for Peter's choice, and for the revelation of the presence of the Master, and for the work that is along the Way, the Master's Way, the Path.

When next we meet, we know there will be many activities and many works that will be considered. It is our prayer that you all will choose to join with us as we discover the immensity of that which lies ahead in terms of opportunity, in terms of works, in which we might all joyously participate.

We thank you for your indulgence in these works. Know that our prayers are ever with thee.

May the grace and blessings of our Father's wisdom ever be that lamp to guide your footsteps.

Fare thee well, then, for the present, dear friends.

A Note from Al and Susan Miner…

The complete works of the Peter Project include more than 200 readings, and take place over a period of 10+ years.

The Project includes two components:
- The Peter Chronicles. Book Two spans the second year.
- Questions about the chronicles submitted to Lama Sing by members participating in the project at that time.

Many people have told us that the great wealth of information, beyond the excitement of Peter's story itself, lies within the Q&A readings, which actually make up more than two-thirds of the Peter Project.

We are very pleased that these Q&A readings are currently being made available as companion workbooks, a research tool, to each of the Chronicle books.

ABOUT LAMA SING

More than thirty years ago for our convenience, the one through whom this information flows accepted the name Lama Sing, though it was stated they, themselves, have no need for names or titles.

"We identify ourselves only as servants of God, dedicated to you, our brothers and sisters in the Earth."

–Lama Sing

೫

ABOUT THIS CHANNEL

"Channel is that term given generally to those who enable themselves to be, as much as possible, open and passable in terms of information that can pass through them from the Universal Consciousness, or other such which are not associated in the direct sense with their finite consciousness of the current incarnation."

–Lama Sing

Books by Al Miner & Lama Sing

The Chosen
The Promise: *Book I of The Essene Legacy*
The Awakening: *Book II of The Essene Legacy*
The Path: *Book III of The Essene Legacy*

In Realms Beyond: *Book I of The Peter Chronicles*
Awakening Hope: *Book II of The Peter Chronicles*

Death, Dying, and Beyond: *How to Prepare for The Journey* Vol I
The Sea of Faces: *How to Prepare for The Journey* Vol II

Jesus: *Book I*
Jesus: *Book II*

The Course in Mastery

Watch for ...

Sacred City

The complete books of The Peter Chronicles

The Peter Chronicles Study Guides:
    Companion Guides to the Peter Chronicles
    consisting of questions from study groups
    about the Peter Chronicles
    with answers from Lama Sing

The movie based on The Peter Project

For a comprehensive list of readings transcripts available, visit the Lama Sing library at www.lamasing.net

ABOUT AL MINER

A chance hypnosis session in 1973 began Al's tenure as the channel for Lama Sing. Since then, nearly 10,000 readings have been given in a trance state answering technical and personal questions on such topics as science, health and disease, history, geophysics, spirituality, philosophy, metaphysics, past and future times, and much more. The validity of the information has been substantiated and documented by research institutions and individuals, and those receiving personal readings continue to refer others to Al's work based on the accuracy and integrity of the information in their readings. In 1984, St. Johns University awarded Al an honorary doctoral degree in parapsychology.

Al conducts a variety of field research projects, as well as occasional workshops and lectures. He accepts requests for personal readings, but is mostly devoting his time to works intended for the good of all. Much of his current research is dedicated to the concept that the best guidance of all is that which comes from within.

Al lives with his family in the mountains of Western North Carolina.

www.ingramcontent.com/pod-product-compliance
Lightning Source LLC
LaVergne TN
LVHW051727080426
835511LV00018B/2915